Alfred Smith

Up to Now

AN AUTOBIOGRAPHY

by

Alfred E. Smith

New York · THE VIKING PRESS · *Mcmxxix*

To

MY COMPANION ON THE JOURNEY

My Wife

Table of Contents

Table of Contents

List of Illustrations

List of Illustrations

Up to Now

AN AUTOBIOGRAPHY

CHAPTER I

When I Was a Boy

MY mother's father and mother, Thomas and Maria Mulvehill, were born in Westmeath, in Ireland. I remember my mother telling me that her mother's father was a barrister. My mother's parents came to this country in 1841 with one son who was then an infant. My recollection of what my mother told me is that they came on a clipper ship belonging to the Black Ball Line of sailing vessels. The ship docked at the foot of Beekman Street.

They walked three blocks from the place where they had landed, to the corner of Dover and Water Streets, and saw a sign out: *Rooms to Let.* They took up their abode on the second floor of a building, the ground and first floors of which were occupied by one of the old-fashioned grocery stores, owned by a German family named Dammerman. My mother was born in that house and so was the daughter of the Dammerman family. The girls were about the same age and their friendship lasted through the years. Last summer, in the middle of the campaign, this old-time neighbor and friend of my mother traveled to Albany with some of her children, about my own age, to visit me at the Executive Chamber and congratulate me on my nomination.

While living in this house, my mother became acquainted with my father. He was a boss truckman and

3

the barn in which he kept his horses adjoined the grocery store. After their marriage in September, 1872, they moved to 174 South Street. I was born in this house on December 30th, 1873.

My father was born in Oliver Street between South and Water Streets. He was fifteen years older than my mother and she was his second wife. He was a widower and had one daughter who died only a few years ago. She lived practically all her life in Brooklyn. I do not remember ever hearing him tell where his parents came from. He was a tall, heavily built man, standing more than six feet, and weighing upwards of two hundred and twenty-five pounds. He spent practically his entire time in the open air, as he drove one of the trucks himself. He was well known and very well liked in the old neighborhood. He worked all week, and Sunday was his only free day. Every Sunday in the summertime he took the whole family either to Coney Island or to Staten Island, where a friend of his was the owner of a road house. I remember my mother telling of an incident that happened in the summer of 1871 while they were keeping company. He found fault with her because she was not ready on time to catch a given boat on schedule for Staten Island. That boat was the *Westfield*, the boilers of which blew up that day while she was in her slip before starting to Staten Island.

My father was a good swimmer and a good oarsman. My mother often told me the story that while they were keeping company he had brought her down one Sunday

4

ALFRED E. SMITH'S BIRTHPLACE
174 South Street, with Brooklyn Bridge overhead.

THE EARLIEST PICTURE OF ALFRED E. SMITH

to visit his friend Daly on Staten Island, and they missed the last boat on the Staten Island ferry. He scared her to death by insisting that he row her across the bay to South Brooklyn.

With a selected group of his friends he maintained bath houses at the end of the bridge dock built up against the easterly side of the New York tower of the Brooklyn Bridge. On warm nights in the summertime after work they put on their bathing suits and swam in the East River. You had to be a powerful swimmer to keep going against the tides and currents at that spot.

In 1875—strange to say, in the same month and on the same date as I—my sister was born, so we have always celebrated our birthdays together.

My father was then trucking for a machinery house. The senior member of the firm displayed a personal and friendly interest in my father and inquired of him one day whether he intended to bring up a family on the water front of New York. He offered my father a farm, giving him the chance to pay for it and own it at the monthly rental that he was then paying for his rooms in South Street. That was about fifteen dollars a month. My father declined the offer, saying that it was too far from New York and that he himself would not be contented in the country. He wanted to be near his business. He gave various other reasons, none of which, in the light of later events, proved to be important. The farm spoken of occupied what is now two city blocks on Fifth Avenue, South Brooklyn, in the vicinity of Fifty-Fifth Street, now covered from one end to the other with apartment houses.

In the latter part of 1884 the house in South Street changed ownership and the floor upon which we lived was required as part of a boarding house for the employees of a café one door above us; we moved to 316 Pearl Street, where my mother's mother died in 1885. I have but slight recollection of her.

I saw very little of my father. In those days there were no union hours and no eight hours a day for a truckman. His day's work was done when he delivered all the freight for that day, and not before, no matter what the hour. Trucking was then a very hard job. A man engaged in that line of business had little chance to be with his family except on Sunday, and even on that day my father went to the stable in the morning to see that the men taking care of the horses were on the job.

A favorite resort of the folks downtown was the Atlantic Garden, where musical performances were given. It was patronized largely by the German population which then inhabited Christie, Forsythe and Eldridge, Broome, Delancey, Rivington and Houston Streets, north of Canal.

Professor Esher had a band of lady musicians. Light lunches were served at tables and the universal drink at Atlantic Garden was lager beer. I remember as a small boy going with my father to the Atlantic Garden and listening to the popular airs played by the lady musicians and to the songs and jokes of the vaudeville performers in vogue at that time. Their acts usually consisted of songs and clog dancing. My sister and I were given chocolate to drink, and huge slices of cake, while the elders drank their beer, gossiped and listened to the entertainment.

In 1885 my father's health began to fail and he was unable to stand the hardship of the trucking business any longer. From that point on until his death he worked when he could as a watchman. He was so well known and so well liked in the neighborhood that he had no trouble at all securing easier work.

In the spring of 1886 we moved again. This time we went to 12 Dover Street, right alongside the anchorage tower of Brooklyn Bridge. In November of that year my father died. His long illness and almost complete disability for months before he died left us in very straitened circumstances. The bill for his funeral was paid by his many friends. I was just one month short of thirteen years old.

The trucking business requires personal attention, and after my father's prolonged absence from it because of his illness, there was nothing left of his business at the time of his death and we were entirely without resources of any kind. He had gradually disposed of the horses and trucks in order to meet the financial requirements of keeping the family and getting what medical assistance he could for himself.

Before her marriage, my mother had learned the trade of umbrella making. The evening of my father's funeral, my aunt—my mother's sister, who lived with us—my sister, my mother and myself returned to the little flat. It was cold and cheerless. I made the fire in the kitchen stove and we ate a hurriedly prepared dinner, and then my mother and I went to the residence of the forelady of the umbrella factory in which she had been employed before her marriage. She lived at 107 Madison Street, a short walk from Dover Street, and my mother made arrangements to resume her occupation as an umbrella maker. What she was able to earn working by day at the factory, supplemented by what was then called homework or nightwork, brought home for manufacture in the evening, provided us with enough to keep the family going until 1887, when early hours and hard work were beginning to tell upon her health.

Assisted by the landlady of the premises in which we lived, we purchased the stock and fixtures of a small combination candy and grocery store in the basement of 12 Dover Street. The earnings of the store were sufficient to keep me at school during 1887 and the winter of '88. After school hours my sister helped in the store while I sold newspapers between four and six and waited on the counter after dinner until bedtime.

I had established for myself a definite newspaper route which comprehended Beekman Street, South Street between Beekman and Dover, the lower part of Fulton Street and the lower part of Peck Slip. The newspapers then in demand in that neighborhood were the *Daily News, Sun, World, Post, Commercial, Telegram,* and *Mail and Express.* Henry George, then the leading advocate of the single-tax theory, owned a paper known as the *Leader*, published on the corner of Spruce and William Streets. This publication office afterward became the headquarters of the *New Yorker Staats-Zeitung*. Newsboys were given two copies of Henry George's paper for one cent. In the event of the sale of both, there was 100 per cent profit. I had only one customer for the *Leader*. He was a shoemaker in Dover Street. His trade would have been of no use to me were it not for the fact that the rest of his family bought a copy of practically every other paper I sold. So with an eye to business I bought two copies of the Henry George paper and brought the other back home for my mother to read, though I do not think she understood Henry George's tax theory any more than I did myself at that time.

In 1883 when I was ten years old, I had joined the Altar Boys' Association of St. James' Church and served constantly on the altar until I went to work. The altar boys drew lots to see who would serve the early masses in the winter. A boy named Johnny Keating, who lived in the double alley in Cherry Street, and myself drew six o'clock mass in the month of January. My mother insisted that I have a cup of coffee and a roll before I left in the morning, and her sacrifice during that month was even greater than mine.

In 1888, on March twelfth, New York witnessed a phenomenal snowstorm referred to ever since as "the blizzard." On the Sunday night before the blizzard, carrying out my part of the work of management of our

9

little store, I put up the shutters, at the suggestion of my mother, at ten o'clock. It was then misting rain. No high wind was apparent and no warning of the impending storm. When we awoke on the morning of March twelfth the candy store was buried under snow, and there being no way of reaching it from the inside, we lost all track of it until midday on the following Tuesday. I distinctly remember that I was not very much concerned with the inconvenience of our customers or the fear for the perishable quality of the merchandise, but I was very deeply concerned about the welfare of a Scotch terrier dog with four puppies to which I wanted to get food. The terrier dog was down in the back room of the store.

On Tuesday, the thirteenth of March, the day after the blizzard, for the first time within the knowledge of anybody alive at that period, the East River froze over. Some very busy fellows, with an eye to private profit, erected a ladder at Pier 28 on the East River, charging five cents to go down the ladder so that you could walk across to Brooklyn. In company with a number of small boys, I beat the ladder game, slid down the side of the pier, got down on the ice and walked over to Martin's Stores, just opposite in Brooklyn, and back. There is always one individual around who wants to outdo everybody else. He wants to be able to say that he did something nobody else did. Together with the same crowd, I saw a harnessed horse swung onto the ice, and a man ride across on horseback.

Toward three o'clock that afternoon, a large piece

of ice broke away and went down the river with the tide with some twenty or thirty people on it. The tow-boats on the river went alongside the cake of ice and picked the people off safely. The cake broke up before it reached Governor's Island.

The schools were closed and there was not much for the school boys and girls to do, so I became a volunteer member of No. 32 Engine Company located on John Street. The engine company had borrowed four sleighs from a leather concern, manned them with firemen and hose, and used the horses of the Fire Department to make their way as best they could through lower New York.

I can distinctly remember the predictions made by experienced fire fighters that had a fire of any consequence broken out on the lower end of Manhattan Island on the Monday morning of the blizzard, nothing could have stopped it from sweeping Manhattan right off the earth.

Volunteer work of that nature was agreeable to me because I had always had a strong desire to be a fireman and performed my probationary duties under what was then called the Buffaloes. The Buffaloes was an order of young boys interested in fire fighting and in the glamour and excitement of the engine house who were willing to give volunteer service. In my after-school hours, for recreation, I practically lived in the engine house of Engine Company No. 32 on John Street. I rode on the hose cart and performed the various duties around the engine house required of the boys belonging to the Buffalo corps.

John Binns, afterward deputy chief of the Fire Department, was then the foreman of 32 Engine, and I had the great satisfaction, in later years, when I was sheriff of New York, of assisting him in securing the admission of his son to the West Point Military Academy. During this period the father of my intimate friend, W.F. Kenny, was the foreman of Engine Company No. 7, situated in City Hall Park. When the National Horse Show Association gave their annual show at Madison Square Garden great rivalry grew up between the engine companies for a prize offered by the Association to the engine company that hitched the horses and moved the apparatus in the shortest time. Bill Kenny's father had so trained his horses that they were able to hook the collars on themselves. The collars were drawn close to the floor, and the horses were trained to throw their heads into the air so that the collars snapped on without assistance from the fireman. Engine 7 won the prize, much to the discomfiture of the Buffaloes and men of Engine 32, who had to be content with second prize.

Great interest was manifested in engine companies and firemen by all the residents of the old-time downtown districts. Today, with the motor-driven apparatus, the fire department has lost much of its glamour for me. The old sentiment attached to it is gone. Its spectacular features are lost and we have only the satisfaction of knowing that the old horses, known by name to everybody in the neighborhood and beloved and admired by the small boy, have given way to the efficiency of the motor.

I probably inherited my interest in the fire department.

In the days of the volunteer department, both my father and my uncle, Peter Mulvehill—my mother's brother—were members of Liberty Hose No. 10, which was then quartered on the site of the present *Police Gazette* Building at the corner of Pearl and Dover Streets. Immediately after the Civil War the volunteer department was abolished by law and the paid department was organized. In the process of organization my uncle became a member of the paid fire department, although in weight and stature he would not be able to meet the requirements of today. Nevertheless, he served well and faithfully, and for more than thirty-five years was the driver of No. 10 truck in Fulton Street, and in all kinds of weather responded to every alarm of fire that occurred south of Canal Street from the North to the East Rivers.

Years ago it was customary for the Volunteer Firemen to parade on certain holidays. But the ranks of the old Volunteers have so thinned out that parading has been abandoned in Manhattan. In Brooklyn the old custom still continues and the Volunteer Firemen have their annual parade on Washington's Birthday. The original Volunteer Firemen of the old city of Brooklyn parade each year with the existing paid departments of the villages of Long Island. Annually Mr. William H. Todd, president of the Todd Shipbuilding Corporation, being a former volunteer of the city of Wilmington, charters a train and brings all the members of the Volunteer Fire Department of Wilmington and their wives and families to Brooklyn for this event. The Wilmington volunteers participate in the Brooklyn parade. After the parade they have dinner at the Hotel Bossert in Brooklyn with Mr. Todd and exchange greetings and stories about the days of the early fire fighters. I reviewed this parade every year of my governorship, and then usually addressed the visiting firemen and Brooklyn Volunteers at the annual dinner.

In the summer of '88, when I was not quite fifteen years old, the pressure upon the family treasury was so great that it was necessary for me to branch out and find greater earning capacity. I left school before graduation and engaged in the trucking business with a man by the name of William J. Redmond. I held the position known in those days as truck chaser. There were no telephones or other means of easy communication and the truck chaser was a young man or boy who could run along the water front, pick up the trucks of his employer and deliver orders to them before they came back to the base of operation.

As a truck chaser, I earned three dollars a week. In an effort to better myself I went to work as an assistant shipping clerk and general all-round handy boy in the oil establishment known as Clarkson & Ford, in Front Street near Peck Slip, for eight dollars a week. I took advantage of opportunities in the nighttime to earn a little more for the promotion of the welfare of the family.

I remember one night's work very distinctly. Gifted with a good loud voice, I was paid to read off the ticker tape on the night of the Sullivan-Corbett fight. Like most of the young fellows of my time, I was a strong rooter for

John L. Sullivan. A few months ago I told this story to James J. Corbett, the victor on that occasion, who has since that time become a warm personal friend.

In 1892 the pressure of necessity again made itself apparent, and as the ordinary clerical position of that day did not pay sufficient for the needs that I was compelled to meet, I found employment, at what at that time was regarded as a very good salary, in the Fulton Fish Market. I received twelve dollars a week. Salaries were large because the work was very hard. I reported for duty at four o'clock in the morning and worked until four o'clock in the afternoon, five days of the week, and reported at three o'clock in the morning on Friday.

I was employed by the wholesale commission house of John Feeney & Co. My position had the lofty title of assistant bookkeeper, and consisted of doing about everything there was to be done around the market. In addition to the salary, all employees were permitted to take home for their own use and the use of their families as much fish as they wanted. I think I may well say that for a long time we had such a complete fish diet that the entire family developed a fear of them. A live one might at some time or other wreak his vengeance for the devoured members of his finny family.

The great science about the wholesale fish business in my time was a knowledge ahead of time of the catch. Fish had to be sold when caught, as the only known means of preservation was packing in loose ice. Economy suggested that the market be cleaned every day, and the shrewd commission merchant was the man who had a knowledge in advance of either a glut or a scarcity. Part of my job was the use of a pair of strong marine glasses from the roof of the fish market in order to pick out the fishing smacks of the fleet operated by my employers as they turned out of Buttermilk Channel into the lower East River. A low draft was a big catch. Riding high on the crest of the wave meant a failure, and as it was known to the owners of the business where each particular smack was operating, so also was the cargo known. In September, the smack that was operating off Seabright, New Jersey, was in quest of bluefish. The well-laden smack, turning out of the Channel, indicated a plentiful supply of blue, and that regulated the price. Cold-storage warehouses had not been invented to circumvent the economic law of supply and demand.

From the fish market I naturally sought promotion and went to work in Brooklyn as shipping clerk for the Davison Steam Pump Works. It was while I was in their employ, in January, 1895, that I received my first political appointment as a clerk in the office of the commissioner of jurors.

During my governorship I have been interested in the setting-up of playgrounds and places of recreation for the children of New York. Naturally, my mind drifts back to the lack of playground facilities and of ordered and properly directed recreation when I was a small boy. But somehow or other, everybody is cared for and we were not without means of amusement and opportunities for exercise and recreation, even though they may have been very crude. No gymnasium that was ever built, no athletic club in the country, could offer to anybody the opportunities given to the small boy along the water front, using the bowsprit and the rigging of ships as a gymnasium. When the ship came to port laden to the water line, trapezes, parallel bars, everything that would take the place of the modern gymnasium was available. As the ship was unloaded over a period of weeks—all by man and horse power—she rose with the tide, and when one bowsprit was no longer available, there was a new arrival every day; so that, while the gymnasium might move a block or a block and a half, there was always one at hand well stocked and ready for use.

The East River was the place for swimming, and as early as April and as late as October the refreshing waters of the East River, free entirely at that time from pollution, offered the small boy all the joys that now come to the winter or summer bather on the shores of the Atlantic Ocean. The dressing rooms were under the dock. Bathing suits were not heard of. In fact, it would have been dangerous to suggest them, for fear you might be accused of setting a fashion that everybody else could not follow.

The popular swimming place was the dock at the foot of Pike Street, built well out into the river, and there was a rather good-natured caretaker who paid no attention to small boys seeking the pleasure and recreation of swimming in the East River.

In the warm summer days it was great fun sliding

under the dock while the men were unloading the boat-loads of bananas from Central America. An occasional overripe banana would drop from the green bunch being handed from one dock laborer to another, and the short space between the dock and the boat contained room enough for at least a dozen of us to dive after the banana.

Beginners learned to swim in the fish cars. These were directly back of the fish market. The water in them was about three feet deep and the cars were six feet wide and about twelve feet long. They were used for preserving fish caught alive, and particularly for green turtles. When empty, the covers were lifted from them and they pro-vided a kind of swimming pool for the amateur who was not quite ready to trust himself in the East River.

Roller skating in City Hall Park was something of a luxury, and a trip to Central Park, with a ride in the goat wagon, was something that came to you on your birthday if you were lucky. Our favorite way of reaching Central Park was on the open cars of the Second Avenue horse-car line in the summertime. They started from Fulton Ferry and gathered in all the downtown children lucky enough to get a trip to Central Park.

Coney Island was entirely out of the world. The favorite way of reaching it was by boat from Jewell's Wharf, which lay alongside the foot of Fulton Street, Brooklyn. We went by boat from the wharf to the foot of Sixty-Fifth Street, South Brooklyn, there transferring to the old Sea Beach route through which the subway trains are now running. We transferred to cars pulled by a steam locomotive and landed at Vanderveer's Hotel at the extreme westerly end of the busy section of Coney Island as we know it today.

Less than a mile of the Atlantic Ocean water front was then Coney Island. The largely built-up residential section now known as Sea Gate was then called Norton's Point, because it was the property of a man named Norton, and was entirely undeveloped, there being no way of getting to it. In 1889, Norton offered the property to Richard Croker and Phil Dwyer as a possible site for a race track. Croker and Dwyer conferred with Austin Corbin, of the Long Island Railroad, in an effort to have a railroad station established there. Failing to secure this, they were obliged to decline Norton's offer. Norton had offered them the entire property for $80,000, and in 1922, when I spent the summer in Sea Gate with my family, a single house with three lots attached thereto was appraised at $75,000.

The playthings for boys in my neighborhood were the animals brought to the port of New York from the West Indian islands and Central and South America. Goats, parrots and monkeys were the favorites. They were brought to port by sailors as pets, and when a sailor was short of funds and ready to ship again, it was easy to drive a sharp bargain with him for his pet monkey.

For a time I had a West Indian goat, four dogs, a parrot and a monkey, all living in peace and harmony in the garret of the South Street house. Sailors' boarding houses located on the streets adjacent to the water front were small menageries, and many of the stories about talking parrots were invented in sailors' boarding houses.

There were no dog catchers. Dogs of all kinds and varieties were allowed the absolute freedom of the city, and one of the hobbies of the small boy was collecting dogs. At one time, in company with half a dozen companions, I had gathered together as many as seven dogs. Being unable to take them home at night, we left them in the shed of a warehouse in Front Street near Dover, and each member of the firm was charged with bringing his share of food from home to take care of the dogs. My familiarity, in later years, with various breeds of dogs makes me realize that this early collection in which I had an interest was probably just dogs.

My early relations with animals and my recollections of them probably account in at least some degree for the private zoological garden at the Albany Executive Mansion that has since been so frequently commented upon.

The New York tower of the Brooklyn Bridge was completed the year that I was born, and I often heard my mother say—she having knowledge of what was going on, because we lived directly under that tower—that if the people of New York City had had any idea of the number of human lives sacrificed in the sinking of the caissons for the towers of the Brooklyn Bridge in all probability they would have halted its progress.

The Brooklyn Bridge was built by hand. Pneumatic tools and compressed air were unknown. All the riveting of the steel in the structure of that great bridge was done

20

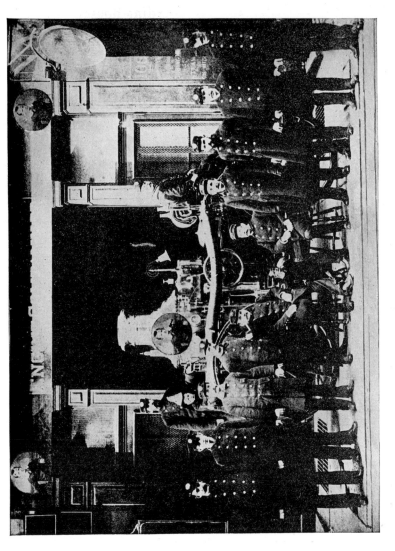

"AL SMITH THE 'FIRE BUFF'" WITH ENGINE COMPANY 32 ON EAST BROADWAY

A composite made in later years by the neighborhood photographer.

FROM THE SMITH FAMILY ALBUM

In the tin-type Alfred, aged 6, is shown with his father, his uncle Peter Mulvehill, and his cousin Tommy Mulvehill. 1880.

by hand, and it was the pride of New York and Brooklyn when, on Queen Victoria's birthday, on the twenty-fourth of May, 1883, it was opened to the public. Newspapers of the time contained a great many stories about the character of its construction, its strength, the load it could carry, and the other details of its construction. Militia crossing it in step or too many elephants crossing it at one time, because they are known to keep in step, were mentioned as dangerous because of the rhythmic vibration they would cause.

It must have been these newspaper stories stirring in the minds of some of the pedestrians on Decoration Day, 1883, six days after the opening of the bridge, which caused the cry that the bridge was falling. Regiments of the national guard, in celebration of the opening of the bridge as well as in celebration of Decoration Day, were crossing it. The cry of alarm started a stampede for the New York end and twelve people were killed and thirty-five injured in the mad scramble to get to the masonry work and away from the suspended steel.

I was a boy of ten, and with other boys was standing under the bridge in South Street. We were unable to discover what was the matter when we saw hats, coats, parasols, umbrellas and pocketbooks dropping from the bridge into the street, until we later found that there was an emergency call to all the hospitals of the city to send ambulances to the New York end of the bridge. We learned then that it was due to what was called the "crush," in the

21

effort of the people to get to what they considered to be a place of safety.

In its early days the bridge served as more than a utility for transportation between the two cities. It soon became a place of recreation and of pleasure. So much so that it was referred to in songs and popularized on the variety stage. I can still sing "Danny by my side."

The Brooklyn Bridge on Sunday is known as lover's lane,
I stroll there with my sweetheart, oh, time and time again;
Oh, how I love to ramble, oh, yes, it is my pride,
Dressed in my best, each day of rest, with Danny by my side.

CHORUS:

Then, oh my, do try, on the bridge on a Sunday,
Laughing, chaffing, happy the lovers go by;
Moonlight, starlight, watching the silvery tide,
Dressed in my best, each day of rest, with Danny by my side.

In the early forties, when immigration was at its height, no ships from foreign ports landed north of Corlears Hook on the East River. Before the days of railroads or entry in any other way than by boats, the old section of nearly every city was close to the water, and though Manhattan Island is surrounded by water, it is, nevertheless, true that no parts of it except the lower section were then accessible for ships.

The lower end of New York might well be called the cradle of the city. It is where the city was born. Aside from the sparsely settled sections in villages on the northern end of the island, the real population of New York was south of Fourteenth Street.

Since all of the celebration of Evacuation Day, November 25, 1883, occurred south of Fourteenth Street, it indicates the size of New York at that time. The major celebration was a nighttime display of fireworks on Brooklyn Bridge, when Pain's fireworks reproduced Niagara Falls in fire over the side of the bridge into the East River. Seats were rented at a quarter apiece on the rooftops of the houses on South and Front Streets, for a good view of the fireworks demonstration. I saw the display from the roof of John T. Smith's house on South Street, one door from the corner of Dover.

When I was a boy, South Street from Market Street Slip to the Battery was the busiest part of New York. It was there all the trucking was done. Produce of all kinds from foreign countries was received there. The North River was mostly given over to boats plying between New York and New England cities and to railroad freight terminals. But the big clipper ships that sailed the seven seas came across the Pacific Ocean, around Cape Horn, up the Atlantic, and landed at South Street.

The foot of Market Street was where the tea ships landed. There, day and night—by candlelight at night—the men would be leading horses up and down the dock and pulling up chests of tea from China and India out of the holds of the ships. Farther down, and south of Brooklyn Bridge, were the docks of the Port Line, whose ships sailed between New York and the ports of Europe. South of that, and below Fulton Street, were the ships trading with the West Indies that brought fruit and the products of Central and South America. Coffee was unloaded at the foot of Burling Slip.

The passenger ships landed, some in New Jersey at Hoboken and some on the North River water front in the vicinity of the Chelsea district.

Practically all the warehousing was done along the East River, whole blocks being devoted to the storage of coffee, tea, cocoa, and spices· of all kinds.

The residential sections of New York during my boyhood resembled, it seems to me, the small cities of today in other parts of the state. Henry Street, East Broadway, Monroe Street and Madison Street, running north and south, and the cross-streets between East Broadway and to within a block of the water front were given over to residences and were lined with trees. I remember climbing up into a tree in Pike Street to witness the burning of Hecker's flour mill.

Only recently, at the laying of the cornerstone of the Museum of the City of New York, which is intended to portray old New York in figure as well as in story, one of the orators of the occasion referred to the fact that, were it not for Central Park, Washington Square, Gramercy Park, City Hall Park, and the Battery, nobody today would ever know that trees once grew on Manhattan Island.

CHAPTER II

Growing Up with the Neighbors

ONE of the very striking differences between the New York of my boyhood and the New York of today is what I might call the absolute disappearance of neighborhood spirit. When I was growing up everybody downtown knew his neighbors—not only people who were immediate neighbors but everybody in the neighborhood. Every new arrival in the family was hailed not by the family alone but by the whole neighborhood. Every funeral and every wake was attended by the whole neighborhood. Neighborly feelings extended to the exchange of silverware for events in the family that required some extraordinary celebration. Today on Manhattan Island, people live in large apartment houses and do not know the family living right on the same floor with them.

The old-time neighborhoods as we knew them had their meeting places where they would exchange opinions as to what was best for their particular regions. Every man, woman and child knew the alderman. Today, a large percentage of the people do not even know the number of the assembly district in which they live, and when called upon to forward some civic movement and to write to their alderman or their assemblyman, they are unable to do so. Several years ago, two women called upon me to complain of the nuisance of an ash dump in their district, and I referred them to the alderman. One of the women said, "Oh, have we an alderman?"

In my boyhood all men, young and old, leaned quite naturally toward politics. They might never hold a political position of any kind, but they nevertheless took an interest in what was going on. My father, for instance, never held any political office but was always deeply interested in politics. Young men were prompted to be active for the purpose of securing political preferment, which then and in those neighborhoods really meant something. Men often sought public office because of the salary. Few bank clerks forty years ago received as much salary as a policeman or a fireman did. Thirty-five or forty years ago the members of the police and fire departments were well known in their neighborhoods. Political appointment gave them an income greater than they could earn for similar work in private occupations, and it also gave them prestige among their neighbors. The clerk of the district court was well known and was looked up to by the people of the neighborhood. Today the average man or woman in New York does not know the name of the clerk of the district court, or even where the court is.

Policemen were known to all the neighbors, and the police captain of the precinct was as important as a United States senator. When Alec Williams was captain of the Oak Street precinct, everybody in the Fourth Ward knew him when he walked down the street in civilian clothes. In the old Fourth Ward, the families

26

spent their summer evenings on the sidewalks, sitting on chairs and camp stools, and the policeman, as he came along on the beat, formed a friendly and social relationship with most of the families. In Henry Street and Madison Street, where the private houses were, people were seated on the stoop, and the policeman stopped at each stoop to bid everyone "Good-evening."

In the tenement districts they sat on boxes or benches. Trucks were left on the street during the night and they formed a place for the children to play and for the old folks to sit down and talk. All the slips leading down to the East River, like Pike Slip, Market Slip, James Slip, Peck Slip, Coenties Slip, and Rutgers Slip, were favorite places for storing trucks at night, and when, in 1894, an ordinance was enacted against leaving trucks on the street at night, the whole town wondered what would become of the trucks. Forced to it, the truckmen found places for them along the marginal way or against the stringpieces of the docks.

In the late eighties and early nineties, it was customary for each alderman to nominate one fireman and one policeman from his district; of course, provided he could pass the examination for physical and mental fitness. The aldermen generally presented these appointments to large social organizations in their districts, and the man selected was usually the most popular one, because the position was one very much desired. That, of course, was all changed by the amendment to the constitution in 1894, placing all police and firemen under civil service and

27

providing for competitive examinations for these posts.

The neighborhood political club was always the center of all activity. It provided the excitement of the election every year. It took part in all the charitable and social endeavors of the district throughout the year. The people of the neighborhood could go to the political club for advice and information on any subject.

In fact the Tammany Clubs are noted for their interest in the personal affairs of their members and neighbors. They perform every function from charitable relief— a ton of coal, food and clothing for a family newly orphaned, hospital or medical care, jobs for the growing boys and girls—to Christmas parties with gifts for everybody. The young men aspiring to political advancement spent their evenings there, and the elected official reported to his constituency and tried to minister to its needs from the same headquarters.

I have heard, in my time, stories calling attention to the phenomenal growth of New York City in the lifetime of a single individual. My father as a young man drove a team of horses for a grindstone yard in Front Street, and my mother told me that for recreation on Sunday he went in a stagecoach with a number of his friends to play ball in the vacant lots back of the Bull Head Tavern at Twenty-Fourth Street and Third Avenue. General E. A. Merritt, once collector of the port and the father of my friend Ed Merritt with whom I served in the assembly, told me the story of a young friend of his in the tobacco importing business who resided on Park Place between Broadway and Church Street, and talked over with his wife the desirability of buying a place in the country where they could go on Friday and return home from on Sunday night. She expressed a preference for the Orange Mountains in New Jersey. He spoke to her of a possible location of a farm nearer the city that could be purchased reasonably. She took exception to the location on the ground that it would be nothing but a Sunday road house where his friends could play cards. At any rate, they moved to the Orange Mountains in New Jersey, and the place there is probably worth today what he purchased it for. The site he had in mind was afterward occupied by Hammerstein's Theater at Forty-Second Street and Seventh Avenue.

As late as 1895 a cow was grazing on a plot of land now worth two and a half million dollars at the corner of Nineteenth Street and Fifth Avenue, the original residence of the Goelet family. A few months ago, after visiting a friend in a hospital on the upper West Side, I rode in an automobile through Central Park West, and I saw block after block, in a solid row, of substantial apartment houses averaging fifteen stories in height, and my mind went back to the day when I walked up Central Park West with an armful of jury notices, and there was nothing there but rocks, with squatters living in little shanties on top of them, surrounded by goats and dogs.

Unknown to the youth of today are the old-time parades. In the lower end of the city, on both the East and West Sides, on Washington's Birthday, there would

29

be a turnout of target corps, rifle corps and musketeers, who assembled at a given point in the morning and paraded in hired uniforms to a park where, in the afternoon, after luncheon and refreshments, they would shoot for prizes. The prizes were donated by the business men of the locality and presented to the captains of the companies during the parade. Silver castors made out of lead, and remaining bright and brilliant for a day, were the favorite trophies; although, in some instances, orders for hats, boxes of cigars or even suits of clothes were handed out to the paraders.

Thanksgiving Day on the lower East and West Sides provided amusement for the people by a parade of what are still called ragamuffins. Nowadays only the children dress up. In those days the men paraded under the name of Rangers. We had the James Slip Rangers, who usually formed the line of parade in James Slip. The Rutgers Rangers had their headquarters on Madison Street; and the Hudson Rangers came from Hudson Street on the West Side. They were arrayed in all kinds of fancy costumes. One man would be dressed up as Uncle Sam, another in the costume of a prince, and there one could see all the various costumes that might be expected at a masquerade ball. Several nights after the parade, at Arlington, Standard or Pythagoras Hall, there would be a fancy-dress ball.

Political chowders, which were quite an institution in old New York, have entirely died out. Nearly every assembly district leader, it seemed, at one time or another during July and August, gave an annual outing. These were for men only, with the exception of a few districts which, instead, gave a picnic to which the children were invited in the afternoon and the men and women at night. As a small boy I remember attending the district ox roast when the big ox was roasted in public, carved and huge slices passed around. This took place at Sulzer's Harlem River Park.

Tom Foley's annual picnic held at Sulzer's Harlem River Park at East 127th Street on the East River was an event every newspaper in New York wrote about and of which cartoonists made pictures. At night, people came from every part of New York, Brooklyn and the Bronx to attend the Foley banquet. In the afternoon children would receive free rides on the carrousels and the swings, and all the ice cream, cake and candy they could eat. It required a volunteer committee of as many as fifty men to keep order and distribute the refreshments. I know, because I was often one of them. The children were brought uptown from the lower end of the city in special street cars and, in later years, in buses gayly decorated with bunting and large signs announcing the name of the Downtown Tammany Club. The last political picnic of the district was held at Steeplechase Park, Coney Island, in 1926, where the children were allowed to have free all the amusements which that enterprise afforded.

The biggest chowder of the year was given by the Timothy D. Sullivan Association with headquarters in the

Bowery. Big Tim Sullivan led the parade, and after passing through the district, the parade would head toward the dock, where the boats would be ready to take the picnickers to the picnic grounds. As many as seven thousand men have attended one of these outings. The old steamer *Grand Republic* could carry only about thirty-five hundred. It was impossible for the steamboat inspectors to keep track of the guests, as they were jumping on the boat along its length and many times it pulled out from the dock with as many as six thousand men aboard.

When it arrived at Donnelly's Pavilion on College Point, Long Island, the parade would form again and march from the boat to the pavilion, where breakfast was immediately served. Six or seven thousand people could be seated at a single time. When the head waiter rang a large bell, waiters would appear on all sides with clam fritters, ham and eggs, fried potatoes, rolls and coffee.

After breakfast there would be games. There would be a fat man's race, a hurdle race, an obstacle race, and three or four different games of baseball. Kegs of beer would be on tap around the entire place. Strange to say, in those days, out of a gathering of six thousand men, there would not be a dozen who drank anything stronger than beer. When evening came along, dinner would be served, which consisted usually of clam chowder, roast beef, lamb chops, ice cream and coffee.

Returning home at night, the picnickers would again parade through the district, and there was great rivalry in the various parts of the district as to which would give them the greatest reception. Fireworks were so freely used that on the morning after one of the chowders I found my best suit and my straw hat covered with burns from stray sparks.

In those days political leaders had very little spare time to themselves in the summer. They were expected to attend one another's outings, and leaders of the prominence of Tom Foley, Tom McAvoy, John F. Ahearn, Timothy D. Sullivan, and The McManus spent a large part of their summers sailing from Manhattan to Donnelly's or Witzell's Point View Island, eating clam fritters and parading through a shower of fireworks at night.

The line of march of the various set parades indicates the northward growth on the island of New York's population. The St. Patrick's Day parade, which now forms above Fourteenth Street and parades up Fifth Avenue to 110th Street, when I was a boy, paraded up the Bowery and Fourth Avenue to about Twenty-Third Street. As some indication of the growth of New York since the days of Ned Harrigan, the lines from his popular song, "The Mulligan Guards"—which reflected the custom of the day—speak of the guards' parade:

We shouldered guns, and march'd and march'd away,
From Baxter Street we marched to Avenue A.

A lost sport to the children of today is sleigh riding. It is next to impossible now in New York City, except in Central Park, or here and there on the west side of the

33

city. Prior to 1894, no appropriation was ever made by the city for the removal of snow. It remained on the streets, just as it does now in the country sections of the state, until the warming suns of spring melted it away. When Colonel Waring was appointed street-cleaning commissioner by Mayor Strong in 1895, he shocked the whole community by appearing before the Board of Estimate and Apportionment and asking for two million dollars to remove the snow after a snowstorm. Nobody had ever heard of such a thing and it created much discussion. Tobogganing and sleighing on hills was a popular sport. Dover Street was probably the center of it, because there is a sharp incline from Franklin Square to Water Street. I remember one side of Dover Street where there were no buildings and which abutted upon the masonry work of the Brooklyn Bridge, and which, after a night's sleighing, would be left as smooth as glass. People then were not required by ordinance to remove snow from the sidewalk.

In 1894, in company with Henry Campbell, I attended a meeting of the executive committee of the so-called O'Brien Democracy, then lined up against Tammany Hall. The meeting was held at the St. Cloud Hotel at the corner of Forty-Second Street and Broadway, where later stood the Knickerbocker Hotel, which has become an office building. After the meeting, Henry Campbell and I stood on the corner of Forty-Second Street and Broadway and waited for a Seventh Avenue horse car to take us across Forty-Second Street to the Third Avenue Elevated. At half-past eleven at night there was not a soul in sight. It was quieter than the road between Albany and Saratoga. The bells on the collars of the old horses could be heard before the car turned the corner. New York was lighted by gas, and very poorly lighted at that.

The center of activity of the city was between Fourteenth and Twenty-Third Streets. The old Morton House at Fourteenth Street and Broadway, facing Union Square, and the Hoffman House, were the meeting places for Democratic rallies. Richard Croker, then the leader of Tammany Hall, was often to be found at the Hoffman House. Thomas C. Platt, the Republican state leader, and his men used to hold forth at the Fifth Avenue Hotel at the corner of Twenty-Third Street and Fifth Avenue, where the Amen Corner was established. The group of leaders and politicians who gathered there was said never to differ with Tom Platt. They just said "Amen" to whatever he proposed. Hence the "Amen Corner."

All the hotel life was south of Twenty-Third Street, and when the Windsor Hotel was built at Forty-Sixth Street and Fifth Avenue, it was predicted that it would be a failure because it was too far uptown. The popular hotels were the Sinclair, at Eighth Street and Broadway; the Morton House, at Fourteenth Street and Broadway; and the Holland House, at Thirtieth Street and Fifth Avenue. The Grand Union, at Forty-Second Street and Park Avenue, was considered well uptown, and it was said that it succeeded only because it was opposite the Grand Central Depot. Commercial travelers stopped at the Broadway Central, on Broadway opposite Astor Place.

Old downtown was not without its fashionable hotels. The Astor House and the Continental on Park Row, where the Syndicate Building now stands, were among the best known. Away downtown at the corner of Fulton and Water Streets was the old United States Hotel. Many of New York's leading business men ate luncheon there, and two fashionable dining places were at Water and Fulton Streets—Dolan & Schaefer's and A. & P. Dolan's in Fulton Market. The fashionable residents of Brooklyn Heights came to the Academy of Music on Fourteenth Street and to the old Grand Opera House at Twenty-Third Street and Eighth Avenue in New York, and, before going back over the Fulton Ferry, stopped at Dolan & Schaefer's for a midnight repast. The popular after-theater supper was an oyster fry and a bottle of ale. The old Astor House was a popular midday dining place up to only a few years ago, when it gave way to a business building, just as the Waldorf-Astoria is now doing at Thirty-Fourth Street and Fifth Avenue. When my mother was a girl, all the fashionable balls were held at the Astor House. As a young boy I only knew where these hotels were. I never had occasion to get into them.

Bicycle riding was the popular pastime of the late eighties and nineties. The bicycle was within easy reach of everybody. Throughout New York renting agencies sprang up, and a bicycle could be hired by the hour or by the day, or it could be bought on the installment plan.

Downtown people learned to ride the bicycle on Wall Street, Nassau Street, and William Street, where there was asphalt pavement, and on a summer's night, when the hum and bustle of the daytime business of Wall Street had quieted down, thousands of people could be seen in front of the Sub-Treasury, learning to ride.

It was at this place that I learned, and I paid as dearly as anybody else in the way of accidents. I lost control of the wheel the first night I came through Nassau Street. It bounced up onto the sidewalk and down three steps into a telegraph office that was open at night.

Bicycle clubs were formed all over the city, and you acquired full membership when you belonged to what was called the Century Club. That meant you had ridden a hundred miles in a single day. With a number of young men from my neighborhood, I left Oliver and Madison Streets at nine o'clock on Sunday morning and wheeled to Far Rockaway. We went in swimming, had our dinner there, and wheeled back.

When Lieutenant Governor Woodruff was park commissioner of Brooklyn he received the full three cheers of all the bicycle riders for constructing two bicycle paths along the boulevard to Coney Island. On a warm night in summer the cyclists were so numerous that they rode elbow to elbow on the Parkway. The lights on the wheels at night, and the bells which riders were required to carry made a fascinating picture of flashing lights accompanied by tinkling bells of all sorts and descriptions.

I started my schooling at St. James' Parochial School in the fall of 1880, when I was seven years old. The old schoolhouse still stands on the corner of James Street and New Bowery. My mother attended the same school when it was located in Roosevelt Street opposite Batavia. The Roosevelt Street school was afterward sold to the city for a public primary school, and St. James' Church, in turn, purchased the plot on New Bowery directly opposite the church.

I was taught by the Christian Brothers, and all of them who were there in my time have passed away with the exception of Brother Baldwin, who is now at the novitiate in the Pocantico Hills, practically retired. Although a man of advanced years, he travels between Pocantico Hills and New York and Albany for every prominent happening in which I have, in any way, a part. He attended all of my inaugurations and was in the Assembly Chamber at Albany on the night that I made my speech of acceptance of the presidential nomination. He was even at Manhattan College this year when my second son Arthur was graduated.

While I was serving as an altar boy in St. James' Church in 1883 and 1884, it was the leading Catholic parish in New York, not excepting the cathedral itself. In that year a parish census showed 16,000 Catholic communicants in this single church. Its school was the largest in the city and was in the front rank of all our Catholic parochial schools.

I might, with justice, say that the old downtown was even more than "the cradle of New York," because boys who were taught in St. James' School can be found in every part of the United States. I never realized that such was the fact until my nomination for the governorship of New York and later for the presidency. On those occasions I received hundreds of letters from all over the country identifying former pupils of old St. James' School.

In the competitive examinations for appointments to West Point and Annapolis given by the district congressman St. James' School stood in the very forefront. It sent to West Point General Paul B. Malone who achieved nation-wide distinction in the recent World War. Among the other well known men who have attended St. James' School were Senator Thomas F. Grady; Judge Joseph M. Mulqueen; Judge Thomas W. Churchill, William L. Ettinger, afterwards Superintendent of Schools; Judge Thomas F. Nolan; Congressman Daniel J. Riordan; John F. Gilchrist, and a long list of men who entered every known business and profession in the city. Cardinal Hayes was born in City Hall Place a few blocks away but his family moved to St. Stephen's parish in East Twenty-Eighth Street when he was very young.

There was keen rivalry among the parochial schools for medals for elocution. There was a gold one for seniors and one of silver for the juniors. The elocution contest, when I was eleven years old, took place in the old De La Salle Institute, Second Street near Second

Avenue. I remember being dressed in my Sunday suit and with my sister being taken to the Hall by my mother who would not let me go so far uptown alone. St. James' School won both medals that night. The senior medal was won by Daniel Donovan and the junior medal by myself. I have been presented with other medals since but none has meant more than this one which I received in my mother's presence. My wife still has the medal. I made her a present of it before we were married.

No small part of the credit for the great success of the old parish of St. James' must be given to the forceful and intelligent direction given it by the Reverend Felix Farrelly, Monsignor John Kean and Monsignor James B. Curry. Father Kean was pastor during all of my boyhood and shortly before my first nomination for the assembly he was transferred to the Church of the Holy Name at Ninety-Sixth Street and Amsterdam Avenue, now presided over by his successor in St. James', Monsignor Curry. Father Kean had a powerful and magnetic personality. He had a strong influence on the young people of the parish. He watched over them constantly and I felt his teaching and example as an influence in my own life such as only a well-beloved and respected teacher rouses in a growing boy.

The church was the scene of many activities. The school for boys and girls was maintained by the Free School Society, a contribution of ten cents a week rendering a parishioner eligible for membership. Then there were such organizations as St. James' Total Abstinence Benevolent

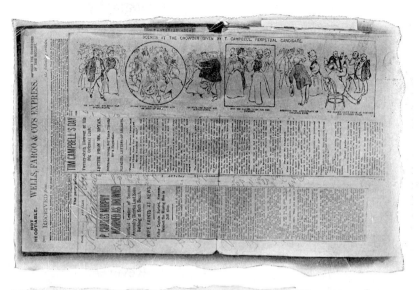

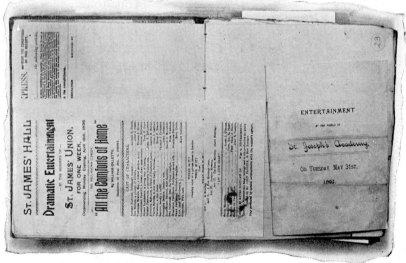

PAGES FROM AN EARLY SCRAP-BOOK

*The Wells-Fargo Express receipt book in which young Alfred Smith
kept his first clippings.*

A FAMOUS CAST IN "THE SHAUGHRAUN" AT ST. JAMES' UNION

Left to right, the players are now Judge Thomas J. Nolan, Governor Smith, Henry McCaddin, an undertaker, Mayor James J. Walker of New York, and Michael Daly. Seated is Sol G. Frost, the dramatic coach.

Society, St. James' Rifle Corps, which took part in all public celebrations, and St. James' Dramatic Society. The poor of the parish were cared for by the active and vigorous membership of the Society of St. Vincent de Paul.

As a charge against the parish, a home for orphan girls was established which housed as many as two hundred and fifty orphans at one time. For the maintenance and operation of this home, St. James' Dramatic Society gave two performances a year. Because of the large number of parishioners and the lively interest of adjoining parishes, the basement of the church was crowded to the doors every night for two weeks at a time while a play was being presented. There were a number of other dramatic societies attached to the Catholic churches in New York and in Brooklyn, but it was freely conceded that none of them approached St. James' in ability.

Theatrical managers and producers generally, in view of the charity for which these performances were given, were extremely liberal in waiving copyrights and royalties. St. James' Union reproduced some of New York's well-known current dramatic productions of the day, in all of which I played a variety of rôles.

I was interested in amateur theatricals before I was old enough to play before a grown-up audience, and to give vent to my desire to produce plays the garret of the South Street house was often turned into a miniature theater. With the boys of the neighborhood for a cast and my sister and her girl friends to act the feminine parts, many a

41

reproduction of current drama and many a home-made play were enacted there.

My first performance as a real amateur was in the Madison Square Theater success, *May Blossom*. I afterward appeared in a war play called *The Confederate Spy*, in which I played the leading rôle. After that we produced William J. Florence's celebrated success, *The Mighty Dollar*, which had played in Washington for a whole season. In this I played Florence's part, Bardwell Slote, the country congressman. As a matter of fact, the manuscript we used was handwritten and loaned to us by Mrs. Florence herself. We played *The Lost Paradise*. Augustin Daly gave us permission to play, under the name, *A Kettle of Fish*, his celebrated comedy, *7-28*. We also gave a comedy called *Incog* written by Charles Dickson. *Hazel Kirke* was one of our productions. We played with great success William Gillette's comedy, *All the Comforts of Home*, and we also performed *The Russian Honeymoon*.

So successful was St. James' as an amateur dramatic society that our services were sought in the interest of other churches in different parts of New York and New Jersey. We produced *Incog* and *The Mighty Dollar* at the Catholic summer school at Cliff Haven in the summer of 1899.

The one amateur production for which we were most famous was Boucicault's *The Shaughraun*. This played three different runs two weeks at a time in the basement of the church. We afterward produced it for two nights

42

in the London Theater on the Bowery, and as late as 1916, when the parish needed funds, it was again produced for a one-week run in the basement of the church. I was sheriff of New York at the time and I played Corry Kinchela, the villain. Harvey Duff, his henchman, was played by Thomas J. Nolan, now a justice of the Court of Special Sessions. Robert F. Folliott, the hero, was played by James J. Walker, now mayor of the city of New York.

Sol G. Frost, theatrical instructor and manager, played the rôle of Father Dolan. One night when we presented this production the audience was almost entirely composed of city officials and judges. After the performance that evening there was as much speechmaking as there had been acting. Frost was the coach for all these plays.

The female rôles were essayed largely by young women of the parish, with considerable help from other parishes, and particularly from Brooklyn. Jennie Lace played Mrs. Gilflory in *The Mighty Dollar*, and it was said that she played the part with the skill of a professional.

For innocent pastime, for recreation, for knowledge, for training the memory, and for giving a person a certain degree of confidence, there is no better amusement than amateur theatricals. I have often said that my prominence in them played no small part in bringing me to the attention of the people of my neighborhood, which, unquestionably, in time to come, had something to do with my elections.

Amateur theatricals are not, of course, without their amusing side, no matter what may be the character of the part played. The greatest fun comes from attempts made to fill in the minor parts during the absence of some of the actors.

There was a fellow named Dinny McMahon, and in an old play called *Eileen Ogue* he was the captain of the English soldiers who came in to collect the rent from the Irish farmer. The farmer's daughter was the leading lady and the country boys came in to fight the English soldiers. Dinny McMahon had on a brand-new bright red uniform, and every soldier would be down on the floor when the boys were finished, except Dinny. Dinny was a little bit bigger than the rest and they were unable to knock him down. It spoiled the end of the scrimmage to see one soldier left standing and the rest on the ground. I played the part of the villain, an English lord, and my secretary was played by a man named Shields, now a lawyer in New York. So one night we made a quick change and got off the fancy costumes indicating English nobility and put on old overalls and joined the hay gatherers who were to repel the soldiers. When the time came for the farmers to set upon the English soldiers, Shields and I took McMahon on, and for one night, at least, the show ended properly. I sat on McMahon's chest. Some of the young lads in the audience who had seen the play the first few nights had noticed that there was one successful English soldier every night until this particular night, and when he was squelched, it met with very popular approval from the audience.

The assistant stage manager once tried the rôle of one

of the henchmen of the villain in a play called *The Colleen Bawn*. He had only a few words to say, but he failed to differentiate between the speech part and the italicized stage directions which indicated the action, so he rushed on the stage and shouted: "Ha-ha! My time has come! Grabs knife and cuts rope!" Needless to say that there was a pleasant surprise awaiting him when he came behind the scenes.

One night I was playing the rôle of Jem Dalton, the villain of the production, in *The Ticket-of-Leave Man*. The last act is staged in a graveyard behind the office of Mr. Gibson. Jem Dalton, after robbing the safe, attempts to effect his escape across the graveyard, and is met by Hawkshaw, the detective, played by a young man about my own size named James Bourke. It was on a Wednesday night and a number of small boys had worked their way down the aisles until they reached the very footlights of the stage. During the struggle, as part of the play, Hawkshaw, the detective, knocks the pistol from the hands of Jem Dalton. Jem is on his knees, helpless. A small boy reached over on the stage, picked up the pistol, put it back in my hand, and said, "Here you are, Al." The audience roared and I had all I could do to keep myself from laughing as I realized that I could change the whole ending of the play.

At one time, when I was living on the corner of Madison and Market Streets, I was rehearsing one of the parts I was going to play, and an old lady living downstairs on the first floor, overhearing me on several occasions, remarked to one of her neighbors, "The young man on the top floor appears to be a nice young man, but I am afraid there is something the matter with him. He talks to himself so much."

All the important professional dramatic productions occurred downtown, and it afforded young men an opportunity to earn a little money at night acting as supernumeraries. A friend of mine in the immediate neighborhood had charge of securing the necessary peasants, soldiers and various other people required to fill the scenes. I appeared as a supernumerary—commonly called "supe" —in the old Windsor Theater on the Bowery. The names of supes did not appear on the program. Their popularity with the audience, if they were discovered, was not helpful to them.

A number of young fellows were supes one night while Blanche Walsh and Melbourne McDowell were playing the leading rôles in a play called *In Siberia*. One of the supes was recognized by the size of his feet and was given three cheers by his friends in the gallery. The curtain was rung down and the leading man came into the supes' dressing room. He lined us all up and then asked, "Is there any young man here known as Blank?" Thinking he was about to be specially commended, the supe stepped cheerfully forward. Turning to the stage manager, the star wrapped his mantle about himself and said with great dignity, "Discharge that young man. He has too many friends in the audience." Unfortunately for him, the cheer had come at a serious moment in the play.

Kiralfy Brothers staged and managed the spectacular

extravaganzas of the day, such as *The Last Days of Pompeii* and *The Fall of Rome.* I had much pleasure and gained no little profit from appearing as a Roman soldier in the latter production. Youth had very little to do with it, because when the make-up man got finished with you nobody could tell your age.

Having, as I did, such a lively interest in theatricals, when I could afford it I took pleasure in going to professional performances. At the Windsor and the People's Theater in the Bowery, I saw all the prominent productions of the late eighties and the early nineties. *In Siberia, The Galley Slave, The Lights o' London, The Power of the Press* were the dramas of the day.

The popular comedians in the eighties and early nineties were Harrigan and Hart. They made their plays, as nearly as possible, conform to downtown neighborhood customs of that period. The youth of today would be unable to recognize New York from the Harrigan songs. In the eighties, the colored population of New York lived on Thompson Street, and Johnnie Wild, a black-face comedian, made a great hit with his popular song, "The Sunny Side of Thompson Street, Away Downtown."

Harrigan left Hart and started out by himself about 1889 or 1890. Harrigan himself had always played the rôle of the neighborhood Irishman of affluence. In his production of *Pete,* the first of his independent plays, he took the part of a colored man, and his friends were apprehensive as to how successful he would be in that character. That was just about twenty-five or thirty years after the Civil War and members of the Grand Army of the Republic were reaping the fullest measure of their attention to the cause of the Union. Harrigan saved the play with a single song entitled "The Cruel Slavery Days Have Passed Away," which he delivered with a great deal of pathos, with a little colored boy seated on one knee and a little colored girl on the other:

> *"Child, come to me and sit upon my knee,*
> *I'll tell the same old story just once more*
> *Of dark and clouded years*
> *Oh, so full of bitter tears*
> *In the cruel slavery days before the War.*

CHORUS:

> *"Shout hallelujah for sweet freedom rules the land,*
> *Bend down low, black people, for to pray,*
> *For the shackle and the band*
> *Have fallen from the bondsman's hand*
> *And the cruel slavery days have passed away."*

Although never able to sing myself—my gift being limited to my ability to talk—I was always amused by singing and always interested in the popular songs to so great an extent that even today I remember not only the choruses but the verses of the popular songs of the late eighties and early nineties.

Of all the plays I ever played in and of all that I ever saw played, I enjoyed most John Golden's *Turn to the Right*. It was well written and well acted, and though I saw it only once, it made so deep an impression on me that,

Thespian and Fish-Market Clerk.

Young Man about Town.

An Early Family Group.

With Miss Katie Dunn (left)

FAMILY TIN-TYPES

THE GOVERNOR'S MOTHER
Snapped by himself in her Brooklyn back yard.

years afterward, sitting in Golden's office, I was sufficiently familiar with it to recite some of the lines of the leading parts. This impressed Golden so much that he presented me with a .handsome copy of the manuscript, beautifully bound, and it had its place in later years in the library of the Executive Mansion in Albany.

Very popular were the museums now quite gone from New York. Huber's Museum in Fourteenth Street and the Dime Museum on the Bowery were the leading ones. Museums of this kind today are found only in the Ringling and Barnum and Bailey circus side shows, and can be seen only once a year.

I remember very well listening to the announcer explaining the various curiosities. I went to the Dime Museum so often that, at a moment's notice, I could have taken the place of the announcer as he described the mysteries of the India-rubber man; Jojo, the dog-faced boy; Professor Coffey, the skeleton dude, the sword-swallower, the tattooed man and the snake charmer.

After visiting the curiosities for a single price of admission—ten cents—you could see a one or two-act drama. It was in the basement of the old Globe Museum on the Bowery that I saw Fanny Herring playing in one-act dramas. They had plenty of thunder, plenty of Indians were shot, there was much fire, and they ended with the usual scenes of victory for the pale-faces.

CHAPTER III

Growing Up with Politics

DURING the recent national campaign I noticed a lively interest in it on the part of small boys, and my mind went back naturally to my early experiences with national campaigns. Although only eleven years old when Cleveland and Blaine were in the national contest, I can remember viewing from the top of a lamp-post at the corner of Broome Street and Broadway, both the Democratic and the Republican parades.

The torchlight procession was an important feature in those days of political campaigning. The men carried kerosene-oil torches on the end of long sticks and wore oil-cloth capes to protect their coats from the drip. Instead of music they had a marching slogan. I remember long lines of men in the Democratic party keeping step with the words: "Blaine! Blaine! James G. Blaine! A continental liar from the state of Maine."

A few nights afterward, in the Republican parade, the Republican marchers kept time with "Ma-ma, where's my pa? Gone to the White House—ha—ha—ha!"

Four years later they marched to song; the Republicans singing:

> *The train is coming around the bend,*
> *Good-bye old Grover, good-bye.*
> *It's loaded down with Harrison men,*
> *Good-bye old Grover, good-bye.*

The Democrats marched to the words: "Four—four—four years more!"

Strange to say, I do not remember any political parades in 1892. From my earliest recollection up to comparatively recent years, most of the campaigning was outdoors and was conducted from trucks or temporary platforms built in the streets.

In 1896, William Jennings Bryan, in his first campaign, not only addressed an assemblage inside of Tammany Hall but spoke at three different outdoor meetings in and around Fourteenth Street and Irving Place.

As a young man I always took a great interest in campaign orators. I liked to listen to Bourke Cockran and also to State Senator Grady. I believed, and I still believe, that Grady was the greatest campaign orator I ever heard. He was certainly the best political debater. I had a more intimate friendship with Senator Grady than I did with Congressman Cockran, because Cockran was out of Tammany Hall for a long time on account of a disagreement he had with Croker. I first became intimate with him during the convention of 1920 at San Francisco, and saw and heard a great deal of him during the years that intervened until his death.

Grady started as a temperance lecturer in the basement of St. James' School about 1870. He had a faculty for making himself understood. He could talk from the platform of a university in the afternoon and to an audience in Miner's Theater in the evening. When you listened to Grady, you had something to remember and something

51

to think about. He had a sense of humor and an ability to belittle his opponent without offense. The man who came nearest to him was Edgar T. Brackett, the Republican senator from Saratoga.

I did not get very well acquainted with Grady until after I had been in the Assembly four or five years, although, strange to say, he knew all about me. He had gone to school with my mother in the old Roosevelt Street school and was assemblyman from my district the year I was born. He himself was born on Madison Street near James.

Grady's speeches and debates in the Senate brought people to hear him from all over Albany. He was a great student, had a wonderful memory, understood government and had such a likable personality that no matter how critical or caustic he might be in debate, he did not have an enemy in the senate chamber. He spoke frankly and freely about the things in which he believed.

During my early years in the assembly, by association with Senator Grady, I found out more about the state of New York and its inner workings in a few years than I could have learned from books in eighteen. I served with him on the committee for the Reorganization and Reform of the Procedure in the Courts of Inferior Criminal Jurisdiction. His advice to that commission was invaluable because he brought with it practical experience, having at one time been a judge of one of our police courts.

The whole conduct of elections in New York City has

been completely revolutionized in the last thirty-five years. In my earliest recollection, Election Day was a universal holiday. Great crowds of men were gathered around the polling places all day. Fist-fighting took place in a great many voting precincts. About midday the small boys began to erect open fires for which they had been gathering fuel for weeks ahead of time. My companions and I stored ours under the piers of the Brooklyn Bridge. We had no asphalt pavements, and inasmuch as fire did no damage to cobblestone pavements, no attempt was made by either the police or the fire department to stop the fires. Downtown, they were usually built in the middle of the big slips running to the East River, where there was no attendant danger to property.

Prior to the adoption of the present form of ballot, each political party printed its own ballots, and I remember as a boy folding election ballots at so much a thousand. This was a form of patronage passed around in the various districts. For years my father had the contract for trucking the ballot boxes. The various political parties set up wooden huts on the street near the voting place and then distributed their own ballots to the electors. To capture one of the huts for an election-night fire was to win a real prize.

Nowadays many of the retail stores do not close on Election Day. Many men, after they cast their ballot in the morning, go out to the country, and the city prides itself on the peace and quiet around the polling places during the day. Yet I cannot help but feel that there was greater interest in elections in my early days than there is now. On election night nowadays places of amusement are packed to the doors. Moving-picture houses and theaters have their gala night of the year. Years ago, every body, it seems to me, was in Park Row looking at the newspaper bulletin boards. It was the only means of securing early information on the results.

When I speak about interest in elections, I do not mean interest in the issues or candidates alone. I mean interest in the election itself. Were I to be asked if there is a greater interest in the issues today than there was years ago, I would be compelled to say yes, because in 1927 one hundred thousand people gathered in Times Square to watch the returns on the vote on amendments to our state constitution.

I attended my first political meeting at the Oriental Club in Grand Street. It was held in the interest of the Hon. Timothy J. Campbell, then member of Congress from what he termed the Oriental district. The meeting was in the nature of a protest against the nomination by Tammany Hall of the owner of Miner's Bowery Theater. His actual residence was on Madison Avenue and it was said at the time that after he married Annie O'Neil, an actress, he desired a place in Washington society and thought it could be secured by his election to Congress.

We were told at the meeting that Mr. Croker, leader of Tammany Hall, had sent word to Timothy D. Sullivan, leader of the district and known as Big Tim, that

54

Mr. Miner was to supplant Tim Campbell as the representative from that district. Tim's friends were incensed over what they called carpet-bagging and the violation of home rule by the attempt to impose a resident of Madison Avenue on the people of Grand Street and East Broadway.

Miner was successful in securing the nomination. Tim Campbell forthwith declared himself a candidate on an independent ticket and joined with the anti-Tammany forces in the election of 1894 which resulted in the election to the mayoralty of the Hon. William L. Strong.

As I was supporting Tim Campbell—although at this point I may as well say that I was unable to vote, as I did not reach my twenty-first birthday until December, 1894—I made speeches for him and for the anti-Tammany ticket, beginning my political career as an opponent of Tammany Hall and as violently opposed to carpet-bagging and the importation into our neighborhood of candidates for office not known to the people they were supposed to represent.

Henry Campbell, a wholesale and retail grocer with a large place of business on Vesey Street, was my personal and particular friend, and prior to that time had displayed a rather fatherly interest in me. I went to his house with him for dinner practically every Sunday. He was a bachelor and lived by himself on Madison Street between Market and Catherine. Immediately after the Strong administration was inducted into office, he secured for me an appointment, on the fifteenth of January,

1895, as a process server in the office of the commissioner of jurors.

I had a choice of hard labor at a small wage of ten dollars a week, or twelve at the most, in the kind of jobs that were open to me, or easier work at a greater wage. I had a fondness for politics and I liked the excitement of public life. I always had plenty of friends and I always took much satisfaction in being able to help them.

The work of serving processes gave me an opportunity to meet all kinds of people, from the small storekeeper in Fordham to the broker and banker on Wall Street. It brought me face to face with all the important men in the county of New York. I probably thought nothing of it at the time, but in my more mature years I came to the conclusion that serving summonses to men requiring them to do jury duty was not a very agreeable occupation. The subpœna server in the offices of a busy business man was about as welcome as a safety-razor manufacturer would be at a barbers' convention, and for sixty dollars a month you were required, day after day, to take a shower of abuse.

By hard work and application to my duties, I was promoted to the point where I became an investigator. As such it was my duty to check up all applications for exemption from jury duty. It was good training for private detective work. Some men who claimed exemption because of deafness, when approached away from the office of the commissioner of jurors, seemed to be entirely cured.

One interesting experience I had was in following up a person who had persistently refused to answer all subpœnas. Upon inquiry, I found it was a woman, and she must have been an early convert to the ranks of equal suffrage. She invited me into her home and read a lecture to me. She told me to take the subpœna back and tell the Supreme Court, the commissioner of jurors or anybody else who, in my opinion, should hear it, that she had frankly said she would not serve on the jury until she was admitted to her full rights of citizenship.

During this period New York County included what is now Bronx County, and during 1896 and 1897 Bronx County was so sparsely settled that there was no means of transportation. The only car lines operating in the Bronx ran on Third Avenue, where there was an elevated and horse-car line, and on the Boston Post Road, where the old green cars ran from the Harlem Bridge to the old village of West Farms. The present Bronx Park and Zoological Garden was a wilderness. However, we thought we had, in those days, the most modern means of transportation, and I conquered the difficulties of serving subpœnas in this district by riding my bicycle.

In 1895, my uncle—my mother's brother—a member of the fire department, was stationed with Engine Company No. 45 on Tremont Avenue, and I made his home my Bronx headquarters. It was considered well up in the country. He lived on a small farm that he leased for fifteen dollars a month on Southern Boulevard. Upon the site today there is a ten-story elevator apartment house, but I can remember the grapevine and the old well at the rear of the farmhouse.

It was the habit of the firemen to drive the engine horses up and down Southern Boulevard for exercise. As a young man, nothing gave me greater pleasure than to drive a team of horses attached to a fire engine.

Between 1895—the time of my appointment in the office of the Commissioner of Jurors—and 1901, I took practically no interest in organization politics. My opposition to Tammany Hall in 1894 was held against me by Patrick Divver, then leader of my district, and it was not until the famous Foley-Divver fight for the leadership of the district, in 1901, that I became an active member of Tammany Hall. That was a memorable primary battle. Thomas F. Foley was successful and I became an active election-district leader.

In the course of the Divver primary fight, Mr. Foley stated that if he was selected as leader of the party he would give young men a chance. Prior to that time, nominations to the Board of Aldermen or to the assembly were made largely on the ability of the candidate to control votes, and in most instances he was a saloonkeeper. Foley began his leadership by nominating Joseph P. Bourke, in the fall of 1901, as a member of the assembly from the old Second Assembly District. Bourke was a young man of my own age, a schoolmate of mine.

My acquaintance with Mr. Foley dates back to when I was a small boy. He was the proprietor of a café on the corner of James Slip and South Street, one block from the house in which I was born. My earliest recollection of him is of an enormous big man with a jet-black mustache, known to all the children of the neighborhood for his extreme generosity. In those days a penny looked big, but when you got a nickel you thought it was Sunday. The friendship formed, practically in childhood, between Tom Foley and myself lasted up to the minute of his death at the Rockefeller Institute in January, 1925.

Because of my very limited income, I got my amusements and recreation during this period from nightly visits to the district clubhouse, and a lively interest in the politics of the neighborhood.

We carried on all the usual social obligations of young men. The mention of New Year's calls will awaken memories in some of the old-timers in New York of the custom of calling on friends on New Year's Day. The business of preparing and printing New Year's calling cards was an industry all in itself, and a man's affluence and standing were judged by the elaborate card he was able to leave with his friends when he called to pay his respects on the first day of the new year. The custom was so universal in lower New York thirty-five or forty years ago that people who, as the result of sickness or death in the family, did not keep what was called "open house" on New Year's Day left a basket hanging on the door knob to receive cards of would-be callers.

White's Bakery, in Catherine Street near East Broadway, was the busiest institution in New York for a month before New Year's, baking New Year's cakes.

Once when I was making New Year's calls I met Jimmie Walker for the first time. He is younger than I am by about eight or nine years, and when I was a young fellow I made a New Year's call on his family in St. Luke's Place. I was introduced by a man named Donnelly, who was the walking delegate of the bricklayers' union. We were calling on Jimmie's sister. Jimmie was a little bit young for that party and was sent to bed early. I afterward met him again when he came to the Assembly in 1910.

At that time the street running from Catherine Street down to Chambers Street was called Chatham and was one of the leading business thoroughfares. Jordan Moriarty and Cowperthwait's large furniture store were located there. Afterward, by resolution of the Board of Aldermen, Chatham Street became Park Row.

Nicholas J. Hays, afterwards Tammany leader of the Harlem district, was a grocery clerk in Catherine Street. Brooks Brothers, which during the Civil War had been on Catherine Street, later moved to Astor Place. From Astor Place they moved to Twenty-Second Street and from Twenty-Second Street to Forty-Fourth Street and Madison Avenue.

When my mother was young Lord & Taylor began business on Catherine Street. They moved from Catherine Street to Grand Street and from Grand Street to Twentieth Street and Broadway. It was in comparatively recent years that they moved to Thirty-Eighth Street and Fifth Avenue.

Growing Up with Politics

We moved from Dover Street to No. 1 Madison Street, at the corner of Pearl. While I was living there with my sister, my mother and my aunt, my sister was married to John Glynn, who was policeman on that beat. After her marriage she moved to the Bronx, while my mother and aunt and myself continued to live together. A short period of separation created a lonesomeness in both families and my sister came back to the old neighborhood. We all lived together then on the corner of Madison and Oliver Streets, where her first son, John, was born. The house was demolished to make room for a new building and we moved to Catherine Street.

In 1898 my sister's family was growing so that no available apartments in the old neighborhood were large enough, and she, with her husband and children and my aunt, moved to Brooklyn. My mother and I continued to live on Catherine Street up to the time of my marriage, when my mother joined the rest of them in the house on Middagh Street on Brooklyn Heights.

We always attended the Emerald Ball, the charity ball of Brooklyn. A lot of the old-timers from downtown had moved to Brooklyn, particularly after the opening of the Brooklyn Bridge. My mother's oldest sister had moved to the Navy Yard section of Brooklyn back in 1888. These old friends settled on the edge of Brooklyn Heights and in the Navy Yard district. These family and social interests caused me, as far back as I am able to remember, to take a deep interest in and maintain a knowledge of Brooklyn and its phenomenal growth.

CHAPTER IV

Growing Up with the Family

I FIRST made the acquaintance of my wife through her first cousin. He was the son of a policeman attached to the Oak Street precinct, and lived in Catherine Street. He had some papers to be signed by his aunt in relation to the family plot in Calvary Cemetery, and he asked me to accompany him up to her house. She lived on Third Avenue, one door from the corner of 170th Street. That was in 1894. I went with him and there I met for the first time Katie Dunn, the future Mrs. Smith. I did not see her for some months after that, but my constant inquiry of her cousin as to whether or not there were some more papers to be signed caused the suspicion to arise in his mind that I wanted to see his cousin again, and we made a friendly visit to the Bronx without papers. I met her occasionally then when she visited the family of her uncle on Catherine Street. As time went on I found myself attracted to the little house on Third Avenue, and a year or two later I became a constant visitor.

In those days it was necessary to change cars at the Harlem Bridge from the Manhattan elevated system to the Bronx system with its old steam-driven locomotives. Returning home and tired from my long day, I occasionally fell asleep from the rocking motion of the rackety old elevated cars. One night while I was dozing off some fellows took my umbrella. The following Christmas my mother gave me an umbrella for a present, and remembering my previous experience, I took a piece of twine and after that tied it to my suspender before I went to sleep. One night at Fifty-Ninth Street, Father Matthew C. Gleason, afterward chaplain of the U.S.S. *Missouri* by appointment of President Roosevelt, came on the train with a number of boys from the old district who had been attending a fair at the Catholic Club on Fifty-Ninth Street. When one of the crowd saw me dozing at the front end of the car, he said, "Let's take his umbrella." Father Gleason had a good laugh when the umbrella wouldn't come off and always spoke of the incident as a good joke on the would-be joker, Jim O'Brien.

In 1900, on the sixth of May, I was married in the Church of St. Augustine on the corner of 167th Street between Franklin and Fulton avenues, the Bronx. At that time Bath Beach, in Brooklyn, was a fairly fashionable seaside resort. In 1898, only two years before, Mayor Van Wyck, while mayor of the city, lived at the old Hotel Bensonhurst there. The Fort Lowry Hotel, right on the water front, was a very stylish place.

We moved into a flat one block back from the water front and lived there during the summer of 1900. We went directly down to Bath Beach after our wedding. There was no other wedding trip.

In the fall of that year we moved back to the old neighborhood, to 83 Madison Street, where my first son, Alfred, was born in 1901. His arrival made the apartment

inadequate for a family of three, and we moved to 79
Madison Street, where we occupied the top floor of an
old-fashioned, three-story-and-basement dwelling. My
oldest daughter, Emily, was born there. I always liked
large rooms and, therefore, always seemed to choose old
houses soon to be marked for destruction. As a result, no
two of my children were born in the same house. A short
time after Emily's birth the landlord sold the house at 79
Madison Street for development into apartment property
and we were compelled to move again. This time we
moved farther downtown to 9 Peck Slip, around the corner from where I lived in 1885. While in this house I was
nominated for the assembly and my second daughter,
Catherine, was born.

I little dreamed of the happiness that was to come into
my life when I made that accidental visit to the Bronx. No
one could have been more unselfish or more devoted than
my wife in all the years of our married life. In the early
years she took care of the children herself and did all her
own washing and ironing, and all her own cooking. She
never uttered a word of complaint of her long hours and
hard work, and her greeting to me on my return from
Albany on week-ends clearly indicated that, notwithstanding the company of the children, she missed me, even
if I had been away for only a few days. When I was
nominated for sheriff she expressed satisfaction by the
simple words: "Now you'll be home to dinner every
night."

Her devotion to me and our children was a great incentive to me for hard work, and I felt that I had been more than rewarded for it when I was able to take her to Albany as the first lady of the state and the hostess of the Executive Mansion. She has always been the head of the household and was christened by one of the children Chairman of the House Committee. During her recent illness at St. Vincent's Hospital, the surgeon who attended her, when he called me on the phone at frequent intervals during the day, invariably said: "The Chairman is doing well."

She made it a point to attend every public meeting at which I spoke in New York City or Albany, and went with me to many public meetings in other parts of the state. When I arose to speak, after I had her located, I felt I was all right.

She has never failed to indicate, by her attitude to me and to her more intimate friends, and she has openly proclaimed that she thinks I am the greatest man in the world; and I have no hesitancy in saying to the world that my life would have been empty without her. My greatest pleasure is sharing with her the honor, joy and satisfaction that have come to me from political success.

In the fall of 1903 I received my first nomination as a member of the assembly, and it came to me as a great surprise. At three o'clock on the afternoon of the night that the convention was held, my old friend, Henry Campbell, came into the office of the commissioner of jurors to see me, and imparted to me that he had just left Mr. Foley and that it was Mr. Foley's intention to recommend to the delegates of the assembly convention that I be nominated.

Peck Slip where I was living was just around the corner from the Fulton Fish Market. My mother and sister were already living on Brooklyn Heights. We had no telephones, so I hurried a pal of mine over to Brooklyn to tell the news to my mother and I hurried home to tell it to my wife.

The practice in the old-time conventions was to appoint a committee of two to find the candidate and notify him of the action of the convention and invite him to express his appreciation to the delegates for their vote of confidence in him. It was accordingly arranged that I should be found to be notified at St. James' Union, the parish club on Oliver Street, around the corner from the convention hall, which was at 48 Madison Street. The demands on the family purse of those days did not permit of a very extensive wardrobe, and my winter suit was in camphor, so that while contemplating my coming nomination, I was in the kitchen of the Peck Slip house wearing my wife's apron while I pressed my summer blue serge in order to be presentable to the convention.

I was received in the convention hall with loud acclaim, as all the delegates were men who had known me for a great many years. I believed that I had reached the very zenith of my political fortunes when I saw my picture in the windows of the shopkeepers of the district.

The rivalry between the Divver and Foley factions was still alive, although Judge Divver himself had passed away. Desiring to be what was called regular, the Divver faction hung a banner across Madison Street with my name on it. At that time there began to dawn on me the significance of the phrase—"politics makes strange bedfellows." Those who had been my enemies were now supporting me.

Former Judge Allison was at that time commissioner of jurors and he strongly advised me against taking the nomination. I can remember the basis of his argument. He said that a man who went to the legislature who was not a lawyer had very little chance, and that there were blocks and blocks of ex-aldermen and ex-assemblymen walking the streets of New York; a great many of whom seemed to have done nothing for the rest of their lives, after they had once served in the legislature.

I disregarded the old gentleman's advice, notwithstanding the fact that I was sure that he meant well and offered it in my own best interest, for he displayed a personal fondness for me, although he was a Republican.

Aside from the clubhouse itself, the district contained no meeting halls and the campaign was conducted entirely from the end of a truck. Being gifted with a loud voice and a good pair of lungs, I am told that I could be heard a block away, over the rattle of the horse cars on Madison Street.

I was elected by a very substantial majority. I was opposed in the election by Paul M. Kaminsky on the Republican ticket, and there were three other candidates besides—one on the Socialist ticket, a Prohibitionist, and an independent. The Republican received 1472 votes, the Prohibition candidate 5, the Socialist 106, and I received 4942 votes.

My mother and sister came over from Brooklyn early on Election Day and remained in the district until the polls closed, when there was a celebration in the Peck Slip house.

As an evidence of his good faith and good will to me, the commissioner of jurors looked up the statutes and found nothing in the law that required a county official to resign until he was ready to assume his duties at Albany. Accordingly, after my election I continued to serve subpœnas for jury duty up to and including December 31, 1903. That helped out the family, because I did not have to sacrifice two months' salary.

In the fall of 1903, after my election, Henry Campbell took me up to Brooks Brothers, a first-class clothing store at the corner of Astor Place and Fourth Avenue, and bought me my first cutaway and my first spike-tail dress suit, so that, as he said himself, "The old neighborhood would have as well dressed an assemblyman as the uptown folks have." The cutaway was for wear at the legislative sessions and the full dress for the governor's receptions and other special occasions. Dinner coats at that time were worn almost exclusively by waiters.

A SEYMOUR CLUB PICNIC AT FAR ROCKAWAY
Assemblyman Smith stands at the left holding his eldest son.

THE EARLY SCHOOL AND TUTORS OF THE SMITH POLITICAL CAREER

Henry Campbell.   *Tom Foley.*

The Down Town Tammany Club,
Madison Street.

CHAPTER V

Learning the Legislative Ropes

I was anxiously looking forward to the day when I would have a chance to see the Capitol of the state. I had never seen it. I had passed through the city of Albany five years before on my way to the Catholic summer school at Cliff Haven on Lake Champlain, where I took part in an amateur production for the benefit of the school. I transferred from the Albany night boat to the Delaware and Hudson train, and I had no opportunity to see anything except the water front of Albany.

I arrived in the capital city on the first Tuesday night of January, 1904. The thermometer outside registered fifteen degrees below zero, but I was warmed with enthusiasm and did not seem to pay any attention to the weather.

Were it not for the fact that I was blessed with a good strong constitution, I would not have felt so well on the morning of the first session of the assembly, for I had passed an extremely uncomfortable night at Keeler's old hotel at the corner of Broadway and Maiden Lane. My associate from the old First Assembly District, Tom Caughlan, who roomed with me, was older than I and engaged in the produce business. He came from the district of "Battery Dan" Finn.

"Battery Dan" Finn, so called because he belonged

down near the Battery, was a man with a great sense of humor. He had a great following, and was admired by men whose friendships were worth having. He was a man of strong likes and dislikes. He was a city magistrate at the time when a resolution was passed by the Board of Magistrates that all magistrates should wear gowns in order to impress the people who came into the police courts. "Battery Dan" arose in the meeting and asked if the judge in the night court would wear a nightgown.

A few days before the opening of the legislature, a number of people had been burned to death in a hotel fire in Chicago, and while reading the account of it in the evening paper I went to the window to see where our fire escape was. We were on the seventh floor and I found that the window of my room led on to a corridor. There was an enormous open fireplace on the first floor, and I had seen men piling wood on it as rapidly as they possibly could, to feed the flames, and I was unable to escape the fear of fire on my first night away from home in five years. With the harrowing story of the Chicago fire ringing in my ears and fresh in my memory, I persuaded Tom Caughlan to stay up playing pinochle with me until five o'clock in the morning, when we took turns at sleep for an hour or so up to breakfast time.

The Democratic minority of the assembly was very small and caucused in the assembly parlor, while the Republican majority used the assembly chamber itself.

Later in the morning, at eleven o'clock, I took my first oath of office, and very little did I dream that I would take seventeen oaths of office in that same chamber. I should hate to have to tell you my opinion of the mental condition of the man who at that time would have suggested to me that in that same room I would take the oath as governor four times.

After the preliminary business of organizing the assembly was finished, the regular business of the session began. The rules of procedure of the Assembly were so involved that it was difficult for a newcomer to understand just what it was all about. I was diligent in my attendance at the meetings, but I did not at any time during the session really know what was going on.

The speaker of the assembly at that time, S. Frederick Nixon, came from Chautauqua County and was of the old school. He had very little sympathy with any suggestion to modernize the rules or to make the procedure more understandable. New members of the assembly identified with the majority party had all they could do to get recognition. Members of the minority party found themselves in the last row, and it was difficult, at times, to distinguish them from visitors to the chamber. It is a matter of fact that the speaker of the assembly did not become acquainted with me until three days before the adjournment, three and a half months later.

I brought all the pending bills to the little furnished room on Broadway, in Albany, occupied by Tom Caughlan and myself, in an attempt to study them and understand what it was all about. On several occasions I spoke to him of my discouragement with the whole situation and my apparent inability to get a proper understanding of it. I was reading amendments to laws that I had never heard of before. In fact, I never knew there was so much law. My early school training under the Christian Brothers made me familiar with the Commandments and, consequently, familiar with the Penal Code, but all the rest of it was Greek, and appeared to be too much for me.

However, my attention to the constituency that elected me, and my willingness to serve them, brought about my renomination in 1904, when I was again elected by a large plurality and served in the assembly of 1905.

Immediately after I cast my ballot on the Election Day that I ran for the assembly for the second time, the furniture van came up to the door and moved us up to 28 Oliver Street on the third floor. In this house my second son, Arthur, was born in August of 1907, so that in 1928 he voted for the first time and had the pleasure of casting his first vote for his father for President of the United States.

My second term was as much of a blank to me, so far as knowledge of what was going on in the legislature was concerned, as my first one had been. I was still seated in the last row.

Precedence is as important in a state legislature as in Congress. The majority and minority leaders are seated on either side of the middle aisle, exactly opposite each other. The majority sits on the right. Naturally when I later attained first one and then the other of these seats, I became identified with them. So much so, that when I appeared once before a joint legislative committee hearing in 1922 when I was out of the governorship, there was a general agreement that I make my argument from the particular seat on the aisle which I had occupied as majority leader.

In the last few years I have often sat on the porch of the Executive Mansion and recalled Albany as it appeared to me a quarter of a century earlier. There were no automobiles, and in the winter all transportation aside from the trolley cars was on runners. Deliveries from the butcher and the grocer came by sleighs, and when, in 1904, I paid my first visit to the Executive Mansion to attend the legislative reception given by Governor Odell, a party of five of us went in a sleigh. I was not familiar with the legislative receptions and was under the impression that nobody was invited to them but members of the legislature.

Dressed in my spike-tail coat and a high hat, I was ushered in at the rear entrance of the Executive Mansion with my party. We were taken in hand by a soldier in uniform and led over to Governor Odell, who shook hands very pleasantly and very cordially introduced us to Mrs. Odell, who, in turn, presented us to the Secretary of State and the different officials and their wives on the receiving line. This performance occupied less than three minutes, when we found ourselves again in line on our way to the cloakroom, and I discovered that, aside from the legislature, there were five thousand other people invited and a brief visit was all that could be accorded to any of the guests not members of the receiving line. The whole performance occupied less than a half hour.

When the party returned to the Hotel Ten Eyck, I casually observed that if I was ever governor and gave a reception to the legislature, it would be for members and their families only, so that they might receive the full attention of their host. It is only fair to say that Governor Odell was following a precedent of many years' standing and all the governors succeeding him followed it until it came time for me to give my first reception to the legislature. I carried out the promise made fifteen years earlier in the Ten Eyck Hotel and entirely changed the procedure of the reception, so that the members of the legislature and their families might have a pleasant evening with the governor in his official home. Many of my advisers were against breaking down the old traditions or tearing up old precedents, but I did quite a bit of that as governor and found it worked as successfully in this case as in many others.

The session of 1905 brought forth a commission to inquire into the affairs of life-insurance companies; but aside from the great public interest displayed in delving into these affairs, the session was without importance. I was appointed to the Committees on Banks and on Public Lands and Forestry. At the close of the session I found myself in about the same position as in 1904, in so far as having any understanding of its problems was concerned. I knew nothing about banking laws and had never been in a bank except to serve a jury notice, and I had never seen a forest.

In the summer of 1905, I had breakfast one morning with Tom Foley at Holtz's Restaurant at Franklin Street and Broadway, and the question of my future came up for discussion between us. Mr. Foley had an opportunity to have me appointed to a position as Superintendent of Buildings under Mayor McClellan, and I was inclined to accept the offer, feeling fairly well convinced that the position of member of the assembly was a little bit too much for me. No decision, however, was arrived at during breakfast. I thought it all over and I just hated the idea that I should have to admit there was anything I could not understand. After thinking it over for several weeks, I decided to try the assembly for another year.

The year 1906 found me back in the legislature, but the procedure and rules had been materially changed under the leadership of James W. Wadsworth, who was elected Speaker that year. He evinced a personal interest in me and gave me committee assignments that put me in a position to understand better just what was going on. I found myself on the important Committee on Insurance in the year that the Hughes report came to the legislature. I still had little interest in the big affairs of the legislature, but I was struggling to learn and I liked the position my being an assemblyman gave me in my home district.

In this, my third year in the assembly, I became friends with James W. Wadsworth, called the "young Speaker of the Assembly." Though I disagreed strongly with many of his policies, I have always held him in high personal esteem. I admired him as a father and husband. I was greatly impressed by the scene that took place at the end of the steps leading to the Speaker's rostrum when Wadsworth dropped the gavel at the close of his first session as Speaker, and his wife emerged from the Speaker's room and publicly embraced him to indicate her satisfaction with the success he had made in his first year in that office. He had the respect and esteem of all the assemblymen without regard to party. So strongly did he influence them that he was able to hold the assembly in a quarrel over apportionment with John Raines, leader of the senate, until the matter was adjusted to his satisfaction. The Democratic assemblymen rallied to the support of Wadsworth and held the assembly in session until Wadsworth had his way about it.

Determined to make headway, I worked very hard during the winter of 1906. By working hard I mean to say that I went back to the Capitol at night and devoted every minute of my time to a study of what was taking place. I felt that I had made so much headway in that winter that I was eager for renomination.

Following the advice of Tom Foley, during the sessions of 1904-05 and 1906 my voice was not heard in the assembly chamber except to vote. Foley had said to me, "Don't speak until you have something to say. Men who talk just for the pleasure of it do not get very far." He also said, "Never promise anything that you are not perfectly sure you can deliver. Most people who come to public men are not looking for the truth. They like to be jollied. The safest practice is to tell them the truth, and after they have tried out a dozen other people, they will come to the conclusion that you were right in the beginning."

It was Foley's contention that "most political leaders try to tell the man who meets them what they think the man would like to hear and what would probably be forgotten before the next election, relying upon what they believe to be short memories." Foley himself practiced an entirely different course. He spoke the truth, no matter how much it hurt, and, as a result, probably enjoyed a greater degree of confidence among the rank and file of the men of his party than any leader in the history of Tammany Hall.

From 1901 to 1925, when Foley died, he was the complete master of the political situation of lower Manhattan Island. His leadership was never challenged. His greatest strength and greatest power came from the fact that he was himself absolutely unselfish, and aside from being elected alderman for one term and councilman for one term and sheriff for two years, he neither held political office of any kind nor received any pecuniary benefit from his interest in politics.

It is a fact that, although a good business man, he died without any money. In his humble home in Oliver Street the people who came to take a last look at him made an impressive sight. Men and women in every social stratum in our city visited the Oliver Street house. His memory is still green and all the young men who started with him in his career as leader a quarter of a century ago gather in St. James' Church every year to attend a memorial mass for him, and regular visits are made to his grave in Calvary Cemetery.

In the session of 1907 I took an active part in debates, particularly upon amendments to the New York City charter. My appointment that year as a member of the Committee on Affairs of Cities gave me my first great chance to make myself felt in the assembly. In that same year I was also appointed a member of the Special Committee on Revision of the Charter of Greater New York, which opened wider still the door of opportunity for study.

When I arrived in Albany, Governor Odell was in the last year of his second term. Nothing of importance or of a constructive nature occurred in 1904. There was pretty general dissatisfaction throughout the state with the administration of affairs at Albany and I think it is safe to assert that, had it not been for the form of the ballot, the Democratic candidate for governor in the fall of 1904 would have been elected. D-Cady Herrick, former justice of the State Supreme Court, a very able and prominent citizen of Albany, was the candidate on the Democratic ticket, running against Frank W. Higgins, Republican, who had been lieutenant governor during Governor Odell's term.

The ballot was arranged at that time so that the entire Democratic or Republican ticket could be voted by making a single cross mark in the circle underneath the party emblem. Theodore Roosevelt, then candidate of the Republican party for President of the United States, had his name at the top of the ballot. He was at the height of his popularity, and a great vote getter.

It is a known advantage to have one's name at the top of a ballot, and not unusual to find that the head of a ticket carries the rest of it with him. People do not always read to the end of a ballot. They mark a few names with which they are familiar at the top of the list and then seem to get tired. This was the reason for the reform of the ballot so that people could not vote a whole ticket by making one mark. In the Massachusetts form of the ballot now prevalent in most states, the candidates for various offices are grouped together under the heading of the office for which they are candidates. Even in this form of voting, it is noticeable that the candidate drawing first place on the ballot almost invariably has an advantage and rolls up more votes than his colleagues on the same ticket. Roosevelt, at the top of the ticket, carried the state by 175,500 votes. Frank Higgins, who was carried with him, was elected governor on the Republican ticket by only 80,000 votes.

Governor Higgins' administration was notable in the legislature for devising new state taxes to make provision for the support of the government. It was in his administration that two important legislative committees were appointed. One was to investigate the cost of production and distribution of gas in the city of New York for the purpose of fixing by law a reasonable rate to consumers and a proper return to the companies. The duty of the other was to investigate the business of life-insurance companies.

The first committee made two major proposals. One covered the creation by law of a permanent commission to study the cost of production and distribution of gas for the purpose of reporting to the legislature from time to time. Their report was to form a basis on which to fix the price to the ultimate consumer. The other recommendation fixed the price of gas definitely at eighty cents a thousand cubic feet. The people of the state were shocked to find that the legislature which passed the bill creating the commission to do the studying, failed to pass the bill fixing the price of gas at eighty cents.

Charles E. Hughes was counsel to both commissions. He made an enviable record in both investigations. The defeat of the eighty-cent gas bill and the revelation of official wrongdoing brought out in the course of the insurance investigation created such a strong public feeling against the Republican party that, when, in 1906, Mr. Hughes was nominated for governor, he was the only Republican on the state ticket who was elected. And when Governor Hughes was inaugurated on January 1, 1907, the lieutenant governor and all the other elected state officers were Democrats. The legislature however was strongly Republican.

When Governor Hughes had hardly begun his term, he incurred the hostility of the reactionary leaders of his own party. Many of the constructive reforms afterward accomplished by the Democratic party were recommended by Governor Hughes. He recommended, for instance, the shortening of the ballot by doing away with many of the elected officials. That was afterward accomplished in my administration upon my recommendation. He recommended a change in the form of ballot that made it necessary for every voter to choose between the different candidates for a given office, doing away with the possibility of voting a straight ticket with the single cross.

Early in the session, the legislature passed and presented a bill to him, fixing railroad fares by the state on the steam railroads at the uniform rate of two cents a mile. He vetoed that bill upon the ground that there were no figures before him which would indicate that the smaller railroads of the state would be able to give service at the price sought to be fixed by statute. The whole theory of fixing prices and standards of service for public utilities by law had fallen into disrepute. The action of the legislature on the report of the gas investigation foreshadowed what was to follow. Governor Hughes recommended—undoubtedly the oustanding achievement of his whole administration—the creation of the Public Service Commission and the delegation to that body of power to fix the standards of rates of payments by the users of public utilities. The bill was supported in the legislature by both parties and became a law on the first of July, 1907. To my mind it contained one error when it gave jurisdiction over the construction of subways in New York City to the state body. This remained unchanged

until July 1, 1924, during my second administration.
All of Governor Hughes' other recommendations, including the application of the direct nominating system instead of party conventions, went down to defeat. So strong was the feeling of the Republican leaders against Governor Hughes after his first term that, in convention assembled in the city of Saratoga Springs, in 1908, they had definitely determined not to renominate him. But Theodore Roosevelt, then President of the United States, was the big boss, and word came from Washington to the leaders at the Grand Union Hotel that the renomination of Hughes was very much desired by the national administration. The advice and suggestion of the President were accepted and Governor Hughes was renominated and re-elected.

Many things that he suggested in his second administration were accepted by the party leaders, but the outstanding progressive suggestions of his first term again went down to defeat in the second term. He succeeded in enacting laws against bookmaking and pool selling at the race tracks. He signed much legislation of benefit to the state of New York, particularly the bill reorganizing the courts of inferior criminal jurisdiction. I was a member of that commission and spent much time in studying all the operations of the inferior criminal courts.

Had Governor Hughes received the sympathetic co-operation of the members of his own party, his two administrations would have been noted for great constructive achievement. Early in his administration he realized how impossible it was for a governor, although charged in the public mind with responsibility, to have effective control of the administrative officers under him, since they were all appointed for terms longer than his own. In order to find out how the heads were running their departments and whether they were men of sufficient ability, he recommended and had enacted into law what is called the Moreland Act. This is an amendment to the executive law which gives the governor, through himself or any person designated by him, the right to inquire into the affairs of any board, bureau or commission of the state government and to require people to testify under oath and to issue subpœnas for their attendance. This amendment to the executive law has been useful to all governors since. I used it with great effect upon many occasions where there were indications of abuse of power or dishonesty in public office.

CHAPTER VI

Growing Up with the Legislature

AT the close of the session of 1907, I had so well established myself that renominations thereafter came practically as a matter of course and I felt my influence in the legislature growing year by year.

The children were growing up and the 28 Oliver Street apartment became so crowded that I had to sleep on the lounge in the parlor. In the fall of 1909, when I had just been elected to my fifth term in the assembly, we moved across the street into 25 Oliver Street, where we had a basement, parlor floor and second floor. As the houses were directly opposite each other I utilized the boys of the Downtown Tammany Club as the moving-van company to bring about the transfer of the Smith household property. A driver in the Street Cleaning Department carried over the stove and the ice box—the two heavy pieces. For the smaller things around the house we had the help of the small boys in the neighborhood. I venture that no modern up-to-date moving company could have made a more complete job of it inside of two hours.

In December of that year the youngest member of my family, Walter, was born at 25 Oliver Street. All five of my children went to St. James' School—the same school that I had attended and the same school that my mother had attended before me.

WITH THE TWO ELDEST CHILDREN
About 1902.

ASSEMBLYMAN SMITH AND HIS FAMILY
About 1910.

NO. 25 OLIVER STREET
The Smith home for many years.

MRS. SMITH AND THE CHILDREN
On the steps of the Oliver Street home.

These localities may not be familiar to all my readers, but I can sum the matter up in a few words by saying that my father, my mother, my sister, my wife, all five of my children and I, were born within five blocks of one another.

In 1911, while spending the summer at Far Rockaway, a friend of mine gave me a present of a team of goats and a carriage for the children. We had no trouble caring for them while in the country, but the problem arose of what to do about them when we came back to Oliver Street. I suppose I was just as insistent as the children that we keep them, and consequently I had a door broken through from the yard of the Oliver Street house into the side of a stable on Madison Street. Thus we had a private stall for the goats with a rear entrance into the yard of the Oliver Street house. You can imagine the popularity of a boy in the old neighborhood who had it within his power to ride children around in a goat wagon. Mine and the neighbors' children got all there was in the poor goats, and they worked on Sunday as well.

I never had less than two dogs, and one of them, when I lived in Oliver Street, was an enormous Great Dane. called Cæsar. They were quite a problem and I had a time training the dogs to be friendly with the goats, as they were all out in the yard at once. Cæsar had a speaking acquaintance with everybody in the neighborhood, despite his size and ferocious appearance. He was a good-natured, mild-mannered animal, and children took great delight in putting their arms around him because of his size. Not infrequently he went on visits all by himself to the homes of neighbors in the vicinity. When we left for Albany, it was a matter of concern to all the children that Cæsar should be on the train with us. My oldest son, Al, walked up with him from the Union Depot in Albany to the Executive Mansion and arrived at the front door of the mansion as I was shaking hands with the retiring executive, Governor Whitman, and his military secretary. Young Al, eager to get rid of the dog, unhooked his leash at the entrance of the house. Cæsar was excited after the long train ride, the first he had ever had in his life, and started through the ground floor of the Executive Mansion looking for me. He sprang from behind the entrance into the reception room and gave Governor Whitman and his secretary quite a scare. I said he was the Tammany Tiger arriving in Albany and taking possession of the Executive Mansion.

He had the free run of the mansion and became thoroughly acquainted with all the south side of Albany before I was compelled to have him put to death in the latter part of 1920 because of failing eyesight. When it was suggested that I agree to have him electrocuted, it was one of the hardest decisions I had to make during my first term as governor.

Governor Hughes did not finish out his second term. He resigned as governor on October 6, 1910, to accept appointment by President Taft, as Justice of the Supreme Court of the United States.

It was during Hughes' administration that the Allds

scandal broke. On the death of Senator John Raines in 1909, for years Republican leader of the senate, Senator Jotham P. Allds had been elevated to the leadership. Some of the members of his own party speaking in opposition to his elevation, made reference to an incident in his legislative career which brought about a charge of accepting a bribe to influence legislation. Allds sought public inquiry into the facts and after a long hearing before the full senate in which both sides to the controversy were ably and forcefully represented by noted counsel, he was found guilty.

The treatment accorded their own governor by the Republican leaders, plus the revelations of the Allds trial involving Republican county supervisors in shady deals with bridge-building companies throughout the state, so embittered the people of the state that in the fall of 1910 the entire Democratic state ticket was elected with John Alden Dix, a lumber merchant from northern New York, as governor at the head of it. Both houses of the legislature went Democratic for the first time since 1892.

When the legislature convened in January, 1911, I was selected as the leader of my party—then in the majority—and appointed Chairman of the Committee on Ways and Means. It must be borne in mind that the Democratic party came into power in 1911 for the first time since 1893 —eighteen years—and I found myself, as a result of the political upheaval, chairman of a committee on which I had never served—something unheard of before.

During my early years in the assembly the Democratic leader invariably came from up state, and George M. Palmer, of Schoharie County, was the minority leader. So well established was the precedent that Daniel D. Frisbie, who was elected to succeed Palmer as leader in the fall of 1910, was also from Schoharie County, and was selected as Speaker in 1911. It would not have occurred to the assembly of those days to elect a man from New York City as Speaker.

I have studied the legislature of recent years and compared it with the sessions I knew early in my service there, and I see a very marked difference. Interest in general legislation affecting the whole state reached more of the members twenty years ago than it reaches today. Debates were livelier. More men studied the issues than do so today. The legislature, it seems to me, has been anxious to adjourn early and is in a hurry to get away. The members have more outside interests. Twenty-five years ago the legislature continued into the latter part of April, or even into May. Twenty years ago the legislature adjourned as late as June, when the cost of supporting the government was about twenty millions of dollars and the activities of the state, by comparison with today, were very small. In recent years the legislature has attempted to transact the state's business in a shorter time than the legislature was able to do it in twenty-five years ago.

When I first went to the legislature the appropriation bill for the support of government was debated for hours. In recent years only a handful of men—probably less than ten—knows anything about the appropriation bill. Once reported from committee, it seems to pass automatically, and while the legislature will debate for hours the advisability of lengthening the season for shooting wild duck on Long Island, they will pass a $30,000,000 bill for the repair and maintenance of highways on a quick roll call. The clerk does not go through the formality of calling one hundred and fifty names. He takes the first name on the list, the names of the two leaders, the last name on the list, and the roll call consists of calling four names. The constitution requires that the roll be called. He calls it, but only calls out four names. "Now, is there no objection to Bill Number So-and-So?" and so forth. I have also seen it done this way: An appropriation bill is up.

"The clerk will read the bill."

The clerk reads, "An act providing for the repair, maintenance and construction of the state highways, $37,000,000."

"Read the last section," says the Speaker.

He reads, "This act shall take effect immediately."

The Speaker says, "Call the roll."

"John Adams, yes; Adolph Zimmerman, yes. One hundred and fifty ayes, no noes."

And that is the way they pass on the appropriation of $37,000,000.

This condition remained the same while I was governor, and I recommended biennial sessions of the legislature. Every second year nothing would be in order but bills making provision for the support of government, except by special message from the governor in case of emergency. I believe that recommendation to be sound. No board of directors of any corporation would appropriate twenty-five or thirty million dollars on the say-so of a handful of men. There is no better way of becoming acquainted with the business of the state than to study the appropriation bill. A man gets a good knowledge of his own business and his own undertakings when he checks up his bills himself.

The whole state of New York was shocked by the terrible catastrophe caused by a fire occurring on March 25, 1911, in the factory of the Triangle Waist Company, in which 148 employees, chiefly women and girls, lost their lives. There was an immediate conviction in the public mind that this appalling disaster resulted from neglect to enforce laws for the protection of the lives of people in factory buildings.

The fire started from a cigarette thrown among some waste material. Obstructed avenues of exit and a locked door were the direct causes of the great loss of life. The building itself was fireproof, and nothing burned but the contents of the rooms devoted to the making of shirtwaists, but the locked door and blocking of the aisles of exit caused this enormous loss of life in a very few minutes. The newspapers of the time contained the shocking details of women and girls jumping from the windows only to be crushed to death on the pavement.

A Committee on Safety was immediately formed to

meet the public protest. Frances Perkins, now Commissioner of Labor, was secretary of the committee. At one time Henry L. Stimson was the chairman and later Henry Morgenthau succeeded him. Among its members were Amos Pinchot, R. Fulton Cutting, and William McAdoo, later my opponent in the 1924 convention, but at that time an engineer interested in problems of public safety. Its treasurer was James Sheldon. Among the women on the Committee were Miss Anne Morgan and Mrs. Helen Hartley Jenkins. The Committee immediately called a mass meeting in the Metropolitan Opera House and a resolution was offered by Henry Moskowitz, then head worker in an East Side Settlement, calling on the legislature to make a thorough investigation of safety conditions in factories and to pass laws to prevent a recurrence of such a catastrophe. Prior to that year a number of beneficial statutes had been enacted for the protection of industrial workers, but they were entirely ineffective because the legislature had failed to make adequate appropriation for their enforcement.

John Kingsbury, who represented the Association for Improvement of the Condition of the Poor, and Henry Moskowitz for the Committee on Safety, carried the story to Albany. They sought me out and asked for help in the formulation of remedies to prevent future disasters. Conferences with them and with Senator Wagner, then leader of the state senate, developed the necessity of a thorough study. A commission was suggested. The bill to create it was introduced into the senate by Senator Wagner and into the assembly by myself. It was practically unopposed, although later there was severe opposition manifested in both houses to a great many of the measures recommended by it.

The commission was composed of two members of the senate, three members of the assembly, and four citizens appointed by the governor. Senator Robert F. Wagner was elected chairman and I was the vice chairman. The commission appointed Abram I. Elkus, afterward judge of the Court of Appeals, as chief counsel, and Judge Bernard L. Shientag, now of our City Court, as assistant counsel. Both of these men served without compensation and devoted practically all their time to the work and investigations carried on by the commission. The senate was represented by Robert F. Wagner and Senator Charles M. Hamilton of Chautauqua County. Representing the assembly along with me were Edward D. Jackson, of Erie, and Cyrus W. Phillips, of Monroe. The governor appointed Simon Brentano, of the well-known publishing house in New York City; Robert E. Dowling, prominent real estate man; Miss Mary E. Dreier, social worker interested in the welfare of working women and children; and Samuel Gompers, president of the American Federation of Labor.

As outlined in the act creating the commission, the scope of the investigation was very broad. Though it is true that the waist-factory fire led immediately to the creation of the commission, such fires are a rare occurrence, while industrial accidents, poisoning, and diseases will maim or disable thousands of people every year.

Considering insufficient ventilation, bad sanitation, and long hours of labor as menaces to the safety and health of industrial workers, the commission did not limit itself merely to the study of the fire hazard in factory buildings but extended its activities to the conditions of employment of women and children, sanitation, accident prevention and industrial poisoning and diseases. In brief, it was the aim of the commission to devote itself to a consideration of measures that had for their purpose the conservation of human life.

So lax had the state been prior to 1911, that the commission hardly began its labors when it was discovered that there was no way for the state even to know when a factory was started. A man could hire a floor in a loft building, put in his machinery, and start his factory. There was no provision of law that required him to notify the state that he was engaging in a business which came under the supervision of a department of the state government.

Factory-inspection forces were so small that the inspections in some cities were made only once in two years and in others once a year. Factory managers knew just about when to expect an inspection, and consequently, during the day of the inspector's visit everything was in ship shape. The rest of the year it was allowed to run haphazard, there being no fear of detection by the authorities in charge of the Department of Labor. Once an inspector arrived at a factory a day ahead of time. There were children under the legal age employed in that particular factory and these were hastily put into the elevators, the cars were run between the floors and kept there until the inspector left.

A competent staff of experts was organized by the commission including Dr. George M. Price who set up the standards of sanitation and safety, and a group of investigators and advisory members representing every phase of the industrial life of the state. Many of the inspections incident to the work were conducted by the commission itself. I was not only at every public hearing but I took an actual part in the investigations and visited many factories. I became convinced that a majority of manufacturers were in favor of the reforms suggested by the commission and many of them would undoubtedly have been installed without law had the heads of the concerns themselves been a little more familiar with what was going on in their factory buildings. One prominent business man in an upstate city was present at a hearing before the commission when a report was being made upon his own factory, and he publicly rebuked his superintendent for permitting such things to exist. He admitted frankly before the commission that he never went through the factory himself.

During all the years that the state was directing its attention to the employment of children in factory buildings, no attention was given at all to manufacturing in tenement homes, where women and children of tender age were engaged in lines of manufacture detrimental to their own health, not to speak of the possibility of the spread of contagious disease where clothing was made in the home—particularly children's clothing.

This, of course, was a difficult problem to tackle. Thought and consideration had to be given to the fact that in many instances a large part of the family support came from the ability of the children to help the mother in home manufacturing. The commission was careful to limit its activity only to such manufacturing as was definitely stated by competent authority to be detrimental to the public health or to the future health and welfare of the children themselves.

Probably nowhere were there more shocking revelations than in the factory commission's investigation of the canneries, where women and small children worked as many as sixteen hours a day. It is a surprising fact that the owners of the canneries of this state for a great many years wielded powerful political influence. Their establishments were entirely free from state regulation of any kind.

At one of the sessions of the commission held in the assembly parlor of the Capitol at Albany, the superintendent of a well-known cannery denied the testimony brought out by counsel. The commission immediately confronted him with Mary Chamberlain, a young girl whom he recognized at once and admitted had been employed in his cannery. She was a student at Vassar College who had been sent to the cannery by the commission to work on the same basis and under the same conditions as the others. In the face of such overwhelming testimony he broke down and admitted the charges were true.

When the legislature passed the one-day-of-rest-in-seven law, requiring all manufacturing and business establishments to give their employees at least one day's rest out of a week, the cannery owners, through their political influence, sought by a special enactment to have the canneries exempted. In opposing that bill on the floor of the assembly, I made probably the shortest speech on record when I said, "I have read carefully the commandment, 'Remember the Sabbath Day, to keep it holy,' but I am unable to find any language in it that says 'except in the canneries.'"

It was during the course of the investigations made by this commission that I got my first good look at the state of New York. The commission met in practically every city in the state. I afterward derived much benefit from the personal inspections we had made, because, as leader of the Democrats in the assembly, it was up to me to lead the battle for the enactment of these statutes in the lower house.

The newspapers often referred to Al Smith's Gang during my years in the legislature. That meant all my children, my wife, some of my sister's children and, on some occasions, my mother. I brought them all to Albany as often as I could. It was lonely for me and for them to be separated throughout the session. So whenever I could I took some or all of them with me on my trips.

Growing Up with the Legislature

We have always had, in both houses of the legislature, senators and assemblymen who represent counties in the state which have no factories in them, and they opposed many of these laws. In fact, after the close of the Factory Commission's work, a manufacturers' association was organized which maintained a paid representative at Albany, and still does, to oppose the enactment of laws regulating and prescribing conditions of labor.

In the first year of its existence the commission proposed and passed laws controlling the sanitary conditions of factories, regulating the labor of women and children, and providing fire-prevention measures and regular fire drills. One of the important statutes resulting from our investigation was the prohibition of night work for women in factory buildings.

An important study of wages was undertaken by the commission, and the creation of a wage board with power to suggest minimum wages in accordance with location, industry and general cost of living in a particular section of the state was proposed by the commission. Strange to say, there was division of opinion inside the commission itself upon the principle of a minimum wage fixed by law or even by suggestion, and the opposition came from Mr. Gompers himself. I made a speech and appealed to the commission for such a board. My argument was based solely upon the health and well-being of women workers. Placed upon that ground, I had no trouble in winning the venerable president of the American Federation of Labor to my side of the argument. He then confessed that he was looking at it from an economic rather than from a health standpoint. In later years I had many occasions to meet and work with Mr. Gompers. He was always fair and reasonable, and often assisted in straightening out labor tangles in New York. He liked to sit and talk, smoking a cigar and drinking his glass of beer.

It was interesting to me to see how the reactionary legislator who was unfriendly to this kind of legislation would always manage to find such strong legal and constitutional arguments against it. Always declaring in favor of the principle and being in complete harmony and sympathy with what was sought to be done, the clever debater could invariably find a way of explaining that, in his opinion, the proposed enactment would not bring about the result desired. Although he himself had no suggestion to cure the wrong that was so apparent from the studies of the investigating commission, he could always find such legislation was either in opposition to the constitution or improperly drawn.

CHAPTER VII

In and About the Legislature

ONE morning at four o'clock, during the session of 1911, the telephone bell rang in my room. I hastened to answer it and was informed that the Capitol was on fire. Always being ready for the practical joker, I went first to the window of the Ten Eyck Hotel and looked toward the Capitol. The red clouds in the sky indicated that the news by telephone was correct.

Being an old time "Buffalo" around the engine house I always liked to see a fire and you can imagine the haste with which I dressed myself and rushed up Capitol Hill. On the way I met Judge Addington, the County Judge of Albany County. We were admitted through the fire lines and went into the building. The fire was in the north wing of the Capitol. We went upstairs and stood at the entrance of the assembly chamber and saw the firemen in the well of the chamber playing the hose against the ceiling. The whole floor above the assembly chamber was gutted out.

The ceiling of the chamber was one of the curiosities of that fire. When the Capitol was originally built, specifications called for an oak ceiling. The contractor substituted plaster and painted it over and, evidently, got by, as nobody detected the plaster ceiling until years afterward when a piece of it fell down. But in 1911 the plaster ceiling was a blessing to the state. It resisted fire and saved the assembly chamber.

The Judge and I walked around to the northerly end of the building and watched the giant slabs of granite, burned by the heat, dropping down into the yard at the rear of the Capitol. It was a cold winter morning and a café on the opposite corner was doing a rushing business. I went in with the Judge. The proprietor recognized him and, as the Judge was a Republican, he desired to curry favor with him. He did not recognize me and had no idea who I was, but he proceeded to give the Judge immediate attention, during the course of which he remarked, "The Democrats were unable to take the Capitol away with them so they decided to burn it down."

In 1920 when I was governor we were again close to disaster from fire in the Capitol. It occurred right in my own office. I could smell smoke but was unable to detect its source. Finally I saw a thin cloud of smoke coming up from the floor right at the entrance to the room. My secretary telephoned to the nearest fire company and two men came with an extinguisher. They pried loose the hard wood flooring and there was a rush of flame caused by defective insulation. The wiring of the Capitol was a difficult job because it had to be done after the building was completed. When the building was originally planned, no electricity was installed and the Capitol was entirely lit by gas. I have often since wondered what might have happened had the fire in my office occurred in the nighttime.

In and About the Legislature

The session of 1911 was prolonged. Much bad feeling was generated among the Democrats by the fight over the election of a United States senator. The amendment to the Constitution providing for direct election had not yet been adopted at that time, and the legislature had to elect the successor to Chauncey M. Depew. The Republicans renominated him. The Democrats, in caucus, voted to support William F. Sheehan, former lieutenant governor and hitherto a resident of Erie County, but at that time connected with a New York law firm. Upward of twenty Democratic legislators bolted the caucus and refused to support Sheehan, and thereafter followed two and a half months of wrangling. The Sheehan men held steadfast and the so-called insurgents stood by their guns.

The term of Chauncey M. Depew expired on the fourth of March. The lieutenant governor, who presided over the daily joint sessions, announced on the third of March that the purpose of the joint session was to elect a successor to the Hon. Chauncey M. Depew, and added, "whose term of office expires tomorrow." We met again on the fourth of March, and he said, "whose term of office expires today." On the fifth of March, he remarked, "whose term of office expired yesterday."

No one candidate receiving a sufficient number of votes, adjournment was taken from day to day. The Republicans stood by their man, although his election was hopeless. The insurgents changed from day to day and voted for various leading Democrats throughout the state.

The leader of the insurgent group was the present governor of New York, Franklin D. Roosevelt. They held their meetings at his house and their plans were formulated there. He was then a member of the state senate from Dutchess County.

The legislature met daily in joint session to ballot for the United States senator. Finally, about the middle of April, after two and a half months of wrangling, Senator Wagner and I succeeded in bringing the insurgents back into caucus when the name of Justice James A. O'Gorman of the Supreme Court was suggested in the caucus and agreed upon, and the long-drawn-out fight was ended. It was finally settled in the Albany County court house, which was the temporary meeting place of the legislature because the assembly chamber had been partially destroyed by water and fire.

The legislature immediately went into recess until such time as the assembly chamber could be prepared for its use. The first night the assembly met in the chamber after its temporary repairs had been made, I stood up on the floor to speak as majority leader, making the preliminary motions to adopt the minutes, but nobody could understand what I said. We were all at a loss to know what was the matter with the chamber, when finally somebody discovered that the workmen had forgotten to install the sounding wires. We were compelled to adjourn immediately in order to give the man time to put them in.

Many prominent members of the legislature lived at the Tub. There were four floors of furnished rooms, a restaurant on the first floor, and a Turkish bath in the rear. I lived at the Tub for a year and at Keeler's Hotel for a year. Then I lived another year at the Kenmore Hotel. The balance of the time until I became governor I lived at the Ten Eyck Hotel.

In those early days in the legislature I was ably assisted by a friend and neighbor of many years' standing, then State Senator Daniel J. Riordan. Later he was the representative in Congress from my congressional district, which was composed of the lower part of Manhattan Island and Staten Island.

During my long years in Albany I rode up and down beside the Hudson River so often that I can look out of the car window at any place and tell you exactly where we are, how far we are from different points, and about what time we ought to be in the depot, barring accident. In my earlier days I spent most of my time between New York and Albany reading either committee reports or proposed legislation. In my latter years I took advantage of the three-hour trip to write messages and prepare statements and sometimes to dictate letters.

While I was in the legislature I would go up to Albany on Monday and return on Thursday during the first two months of the session and come down on Friday for the remainder. I spent my week-ends, Friday and Saturday nights, at the district headquarters, where there was always a line of people waiting to see me.

There were all sorts of duties devolving on young politicians. There was attendance at the Club House, for me the Downtown Tammany Club on Madison Street. Here everybody came who wanted anything, a mother whose husband was out of work or whose boy had been arrested, civil employees who wanted to be transferred from one city department to another, or wanted an increase in pay, or somebody to tell of a family in distress in the district. There is no end to these requests, and politicians, young or old, must do their party chores.

For ten years or more after civil service became an established fact and examination was required for appointment to offices, a large part of the time of minor elected officials was given to an examination of the papers of applicants who felt that they had been unfairly or unjustly dealt with by the civil service authorities. The examination papers disclosed interesting sidelights on the ideas people have of their fitness for positions.

After the examinations were over and the papers had become public property, we would look them over to find out whether any people in whom we were interested had received improper ratings. One boy took an examination for office boy. He identified James G. Blaine as follows: "He had discovered gold and had organized a club under his own title and had been very successful in his undertaking." There was a neighborhood political club called the James G. Blaine club.

A young clerk taking an examination for stenographer, under the part of the examination devoted to civics said: "The mayor of New York has to see to all private residences in the city of New York."

In and About the Legislature

Another young friend of mine took an examination for assistant fire marshal, and was greatly disturbed to think that he did not pass the examination. He asked me to look up his papers. One of the questions called for a definition of three degrees of arson.

He said: "There are three degrees of arson. The first degree is where a person who is sane commits arson. The second, when a person is slightly unbalanced and has a mania for fires. The third, where a person is entirely insane and commits arson."

In the same examination another candidate answered the same question as follows:

"There are three degrees of arson. First degree is caught in the act of applying the match. Second degree is caught leaving the building after the fire was discovered. Third is known to be a fire fiend. Could be convicted on past record if seen in vicinity of fire."

In an examination for doorman in the Police Department a man complained to Congressman Riordan that he had been dealt with unfairly. He should have passed the examination, he said. The congressman and I read his answers over together. He was asked: "What would you do in case a prisoner in your care attempted to hang himself?" He answered: "I would cut him down and try to make him feel happy until the doctor arrived."

The next question asked of him was what he would do as a doorman in the Police Department if he found there were more prisoners than cells, and he answered:

"I would put two in each cell—namely, a sober and

105

an intoxicated person, and likewise a female, in case of lack of room."

One time while I was governor and we were at the height of the excitement over the housing shortage and the rent extortions, my telephone rang at the Executive Mansion on a Sunday morning.

I finally went to the telephone to hear an excited person at the other end of the wire say: "Is this the governor?"

I answered, "Yes."

"Well, I want to tell you that my landlord raised the rent and it's against the law and I want you to tell him he should let me stay."

It was difficult to explain over the telephone that complaints should be lodged with the Municipal Court of New York City, instead of with me.

Just recently I received a telegram from a place in Arkansas which read:

BLANK FISH COMPANY AT BLANK STREET OWES US SEVEN HUNDRED EIGHTY DOLLARS FOR FISH STOP PLEASE COLLECT AND SEND OUR MONEY AFTER TAKING OUT FOR YOUR TROUBLE STOP

The telegram was signed by a fish company evidently doing business in that town.

Sunday I gave to the family. My Sundays during the winter were practically all alike. After mass, in company with several companions and at least two dogs, I walked over the Brooklyn Bridge from the Oliver Street home to 9 Middagh Street, where my mother lived.

She looked forward to that visit every Sunday, as I was away from New York during the week. Up to the time of her death she had a very keen mind and a very good memory, and she walked every morning before eight o'clock to the Brooklyn entrance of the bridge to get the newspapers and read the Albany news. When I arrived at her house on Sunday she had a line of questions all ready for me.

Returning from Brooklyn, we had dinner in the middle of the day when the children were growing up and a light supper in the evening. Sunday afternoons between dinner and supper were usually given up to a visit to somebody who was sick either at home or in the hospital. I usually spent Sunday night in the house with the neighbors. I was one of the first on our block to own a victrola, and I had all the neighbors in in relays on Sunday night to hear it played.

The nights of my arrival in New York, in my early years in Albany, I was usually met by Mrs. Smith and some of our friends at the Grand Central Depot, and we would go to dinner and attend the theater.

I was appointed a member of the New York State Commission to the San Francisco fair, and though I did a great part of the work in and around New York, to prepare our part in it, I was the only member of the commission who did not attend the fair. My children were growing and I hesitated to leave them for so long a time. Instead, I spent the summer with the family in a little cottage at Far Rockaway.

Probably one of the most interesting characters that I met in my long legislative career was Edwin A. Merritt, Jr., who represented St. Lawrence county. Coming from a solidly Republican district, he worked his way up through long years of service from membership in the assembly to the speakership in 1912. He was chairman of the Committee on Ways and Means from 1908 to 1910. Afterwards he was majority leader. During 1911 when I held the position of majority leader, Merritt was minority leader, and we sat across the aisle from each other in the assembly chamber. Although a strict organization Republican he had very liberal ideas and broad sympathies and favored most of the progressive measures that came up during his time.

Ed Merritt always claimed that I helped him considerably in his understanding of New York City's great problems. He and most of the other legislative leaders, instead of returning home to their small villages in the country sections of the state during the session, often spent the week-ends in New York City. On several occasions I met him in New York and took him through the East Side to show him the thickly populated tenement sections of Manhattan Island. He frankly said that the great population of New York was a revelation to him. The village of Potsdam in which he lived contained 3,950 inhabitants.

I cannot estimate what Ed Merritt meant to me better

than by quoting from the speech I made at his funeral in Potsdam in 1914.

"I met him in 1904 when I entered the assembly chamber for the first time. He was then a prominent member of the majority side of the House. I served with him through the years until 1912 when he was elected Speaker, and in that time I developed for him as strong an affection as it is possible for one man to have for another, not of his own relationship. . . . He was a good friend. . . . He helped me to success when my failure might have meant something of advantage to his party. Public life makes many fair-weather friends. Many there are who shake your hand and pat your back when you are in the heyday of your power; but Merritt's friendship was of the kind that was much stronger when the clouds of political adversity frowned upon you."

Among other interesting characters in my time in the legislature was Senator Elon R. Brown. Senator Brown was a powerful debater, a man of good judgment, a very able lawyer and a quick observer. He was in the insurgent group of Republicans in 1907 and 1908 in the senate backed by Senators Brackett and Elsberg, who opposed John Raines.

Thaddeus C. Sweet, known to all the boys in Albany as "Tad," and Speaker of the assembly from 1914 to 1920, was the owner of a large paper mill in Oswego County and lived in the village of Phoenix. He was another of the leading characters of the assembly. Throughout his whole career as Speaker of the assembly, Sweet established a reputation for absolutely fair play. He had the respect and I might even say the affection of the whole assembly. He was a strong partisan but you always knew exactly where he stood and his word was as good as his bond. I joined with all of his friends in Albany in the expression of sympathy at his sudden and accidental death in an airplane while he was serving in the national legislature to which he was elected at the end of his speakership.

Service in the senate and assembly was not without some amusing incidents. Though it is hard, grinding work on those who devote themselves to it, nevertheless, there is a lighter side. There was an assemblyman representing Washington County by the name of Pratt, and he was obsessed with the notion that the local papers of his county should from time to time record the fact that he asked some embarrassing questions of the Democratic leader, to whom he always referred in debate as the "Tammany leader." On one occasion I was debating certain amendments of the Workmen's Compensation Act and he arose in his place and asked of the presiding officer that he be given the privilege of asking me a question, to which I immediately agreed.

His question was, "Mr. Tammany Leader, what good is the Workmen's Compensation Act to the three hundred and fifty thousand men that are out of work on account of President Wilson?" There was a ripple of laughter around the chamber. It was in the late hours of the night, and in order to relieve the situation I said, "Mr. Speaker, I was walking down Park Row one night and a man came up and hit me on the shoulder and said, 'Hello, Al. Which would you rather be, a hammock full of white door knobs, a cellar full of stepladders, or a piece of dry ice?' I said I would rather be a fish, because no matter how thick plate glass is, you can always break it with a hammer."

Whereupon Pratt sprang to his feet and said, "I don't get the point of the gentleman's answer."

I replied, "There is just as much point to my answer as there is to your question."

The session of 1911 had a moment when partisanship on both sides of the house was running high. Ed Merritt, Fred Hammond and Jesse S. Phillips, representing the Republican side, and I, representing the Democratic side, were engaged in a cross-fire of debate on a bill that had to do with the removal of the Commission of Jurors in Niagara County. There was considerable hard feeling on both sides of the chamber when Assemblyman Wende from Buffalo arose in his place and asked the privilege of interrupting. It was readily granted.

Mr. Wende said, "Mr. Speaker, I have just heard that Cornell won the boat race."

Merritt said, "That doesn't mean anything to me. I'm a Yale man."

Hammond said, "It doesn't mean anything to me. I'm a Harvard man."

Phillips said, "It doesn't mean anything to me. I am a U. of M. man."

I was all alone, the only one of the quartet left standing,

so I said, "It doesn't mean anything to me because I am an F. F. M. man."

Assemblyman Hoey shouted out, "What is that, Al?"

I said, "Fulton Fish Market. Let's proceed with the debate."

There was a strong comradeship in the legislature, and when the political debates were over, Democrats and Republicans were "pals" together as though there was no political difference.

When the first Socialist was elected to the assembly, he represented Schenectady County and came from the city of Schenectady. Merritt was Speaker at the time and he was confronted with the problem of the treatment that he should give to the Schenectady assemblyman, in that he represented a political party with a place on the ballot. I advised him to recognize him as a party leader. This he was reluctant to do. I convinced him that under our system all parties are equal in their rights in accordance with their numerical strength. Merritt finally consented and gave him his choice of committee assignments and permitted him to select his seat in the chamber when the Republican and Democratic leaders were picking those for their party members.

After the session had progressed a few months I met the Socialist in the corridor one day and I said to him, "Well, what do you think about it?"

"Well," he said, "everything is all right. I find that a majority of the elected members can do anything they want to. It is pretty hard to quarrel with majority rule."

CHAPTER VIII

Lobbies, Issues and Legislation

IN my first three terms in the assembly I knew nothing about lobbying, or anything else that was going on, for that matter. The revelations of the Hughes insurance investigation silenced the so-called Black Horse Cavalry and put an end to the open operations of the lobby. Most important and startling of the revelations before the committee was the maintenance in Albany of a resort known as "The House of Mirth," paid for by the insurance lobby. Here legislators were entertained and here the insurance lobby put in its fine work.

A lobby, as such, is not necessarily to be held in suspicion. Lobbying came into public disrepute when it conspired against the public interests and tried to defeat the public will with the use of funds. There is a great difference between a lobby active to defeat measures to protect policy holders in an insurance company and a lobby actively promoting the creation of some public agency of general public good. I lobbied myself, in 1921 and 1922, for the reorganization of the state government and also for the creation of the Port of New York Authority and the adoption of its comprehensive plan.

Amateur and non-salaried lobbyists caused some amusing situations at times. No lobby, in my time, was as strong in point of numbers as the lobbies for the promotion of equal pay for men and women teachers, the adoption of the suffrage amendment to the Constitution, and in favor of local option and the ratification of the Eighteenth Amendment.

The Anti-Saloon League maintained an active and vigorous lobby at Albany at all times and exercised a widespread influence over the representatives of country districts. The lobbyists were paid and felt they had to earn their salaries at least to some degree. They therefore made it their business to stir up something every year. Not one, but probably a dozen men from rural sections have said to me in private conversation that they did not believe in a given excise or local option bill, did not believe it was in the best interests of the state, and did not believe it would accomplish what was sought by the sponsors, but were afraid to vote against it for fear of the consequences on Election Day. In fact it was largely a campaign of intimidation.

Some of the warmest arguments in the legislature in those days occurred over what were called "ripper" bills. The party in power would legislate their political opponents out of office and provide for some new method of appointment. These bills were pretexts for patronage. Prior to the time that the appointment of the commissioner of jurors was given to the judges of the Appellate Division in Brooklyn, the appointing power was changed every two years to suit the complexion of the officers. When the Democrats elected enough men to appoint the commissioner of jurors, the Republicans would change the law, and vice versa.

Under the pretense of reorganization, whole departments would be abolished and established all over again. The state Fair Commission at that time consisted of the lieutenant governor, the commissioner of agriculture and two appointees of the governor. The lieutenant governor and commissioner of agriculture were Republicans. The two appointees of the governor were Democrats. In 1915 a bill was introduced bringing an end to the terms of the two Democratic commissioners but the power of appointment by the governor was left undisturbed. This was the premier ripper bill of our state history. This type of legislation could not be enacted today under the reorganized government, because the departments and the manner of bringing them into existence are fixed in the constitution itself.

In the 1911 session of the legislature I occupied what afterward became two distinct positions. I was not only the majority leader but I was also chairman of the Ways and Means Committee. The 1911 session demonstrated that that was too much work to put on any one man and, in 1912, at the suggestion of Ed Merritt, who was then Speaker, the rules of the assembly were changed so that the Speaker could appoint one man as the majority leader and another as chairman of the Ways and Means Committee.

Because of my dual capacity in 1911, I was limited in the number of statutes I could introduce and keep track of and defend. As majority leader I gave many of the bills

115

to the chairmen of the different committees and assisted them in their defense of them on the floor. I introduced three classes of bills that year—those that carried out the party platform; those that were upon some subject of which I had an intimate personal knowledge, such as our inferior criminal courts, because of my service on the commission to study them; and finance bills for the support of government.

The first bill I introduced that year was the bill to ratify the amendment to the Federal Constitution to establish the levy of a tax on incomes. The promise to ratify it was part of the Democratic platform of that year, and accordingly, Senator Wagner, then president pro tem of the senate, and I introduced and defended the bill.

Probably one of the most important bills introduced by Senator Wagner and myself was the one setting up the Department of Conservation. It was drawn up by Senator Wagner and passed both houses under his name. It merged in a new department known as the Conservation Department the old Fish and Game Commission, the Forest Preserve Board and the State Water Supply Commission. The department has never been changed since that date except to put it under a single commissioner when the reorganization of the government took place, but it was the first consolidation of allied activities into a single department. I was evidently interested in the consolidation of state departments not only before I became governor but long before the suggestion of consolidation was made in the constitutional convention.

The 1911 session of the legislature was notable too for the strong difference of opinion between the members of the majority party. It began with the defeat of William F. Sheehan for United States senator and continued throughout the session. This may be explained, I think, by the fact that a great many of the upstate Democrats elected to the assembly and the senate in the fall of 1910 were really not in sympathy with the big majority of the party coming from the cities. They represented rural communities having nothing in common with New York City.

Something which occurred in connection with an amendment to the excise law, the provision forbidding a saloon to be established within two hundred feet of a church or school, is an apt illustration. It was intended by the framers of this law to mean that if the church or the school located first, a saloon could not locate thereafter. A decision of the Court of Appeals in 1910 held the wording of the statute to be such that no license could be reissued or renewed to any saloon for the sale of liquor within two hundred feet of a church or school, even if the latter established itself after the saloon had already been there. Therefore, anybody could establish a church or school within two hundred feet of the Waldorf-Astoria Hotel, which had been in operation for years, and the hotel license to sell liquor could not be renewed. The Court of Appeals, in its decision, spoke of the harshness of the law and suggested in so many words that relief be sought by legislation. Having in mind the great investment in hotel, restaurant and café property in all the

117

cities of the state, the legislative leaders on the Democratic side entered into an agreement to give the relief suggested by the Court of Appeals.

The bill had no trouble in the senate, as the great majority of Democrats in the senate came from the big cities. Although there was agreement on it when the bill came on the assembly calendar for final passage, I discovered, coming close to the end of the roll call, that it did not have the necessary seventy-six votes to pass it. I asked the Speaker if he had excused anybody from what we call a "close call of the roll," but he said "No." I scurried through the assembly parlor and all of the assembly enclosure to find out what had become of the missing members. I went to the men's washroom, and the old colored porter there, being a friend of mine, motioned toward the window. I opened the window and saw five Democratic members of the assembly standing outside on a scaffold that was being used for repair work on the burned part of the Capitol. As leader of the majority, I insisted that they come under the influence of the house and cast their votes, informing them that it made no difference which way they voted, but that they must vote. The bill was passed.

In the recent campaign attempts were made to put the idea into the minds of the American people that while I was in the legislature I voted for all kinds of laws intended to break down the salutary provisions of the excise law. Nothing could be further from the truth. A large number of the amendments referred to in the circulars printed against me were department measures and were recommended by the excise committee of the legislature itself, to clarify the law and to meet court decisions.

All the talk about churches and schools and saloons and the number of bills introduced on that subject would lead one to believe that there was a widespread attempt to do away with the provision of the excise law prohibiting the establishment of saloons within two hundred feet of a school or church. The truth of the matter is that all these bills related to a single instance in the city of New York.

When the Hotel Gotham on Fifth Avenue, one of New York's first-class hotels, was first opened, it was known by the owners and by the promoters to be within two hundred feet of a church. Rumor had it that the hotel was backed by influential public leaders and that they would remedy the difficulty by getting a law passed. They actually undertook to do it. The bill met with vigorous opposition from rural sections.

The condition is readily understood. The situation was the exact opposite of the one for which the Court of Appeals had recommended legislative relief. The owners of the Hotel Gotham had gotten a decision that wine and liquor could be consumed on the premises providing it was not sold in the hotel. So the hotel proprietors hired a private house outside of the two-hundred-feet limit and set up a well equipped dispensary. The guest ordered whatever he wanted, and a bellboy went down the street with a basket, bought the bottle of wine and brought it back to the guest who drank it with his dinner.

When I made my decision to vote for that bill, I thought it was far better for the state from every standpoint that, if the liquor was to be consumed on the premises, it should be sold there rather than that the public be treated to the hypocritical performance of having a boy walk through the street with a basket in his hand filled with wine.

It always seemed a curious part of this whole situation concerning the sale of liquor that the men in and out of the legislature who interested themselves most in the suppression of the liquor traffic never took much interest in social legislation such as reform of the Factory Code, workmen's compensation, pensions for widowed mothers, public health or parks. The fact is that a great many legislators from the rural districts who were loudest in their cry for prohibition and for local option opposed humanitarian measures, either because they lacked knowledge concerning them or because of the reactionary attitude of their constituents against most new legislation unless it followed one line.

When the Greater New York Charter came up for adoption in 1911, the city-against-the-country attitude, or the country-against-the-city attitude, was again clearly reflected. It broke down party lines. Needless for me to say, none of the so-called insurgent assembly group, or very few at least, were returned from their constituencies that year, fall of 1911, and that accounted for giving the assembly back to the Republicans after the first year of Democratic ascendancy in the body in sixteen years.

Although I had met Mr. Murphy, the leader of Tammany Hall, while I was spending a summer at Good Ground, Long Island, in 1908, it was a casual meeting out on a sand bar when we were swimming at Quogue. It was not until 1911, when I was majority leader, that my intimate acquaintance with Mr. Murphy began. He took keen interest in the affairs of the party, so far as it promoted the interests of the state. Every week-end he met at Delmonico's Restaurant a group of legislative leaders and men in whose judgment he had confidence. In this group were men like Martin Littleton, Congressman Tom Smith, Senator Wagner, and myself; and from time to time individuals were called in who had special knowledge or information on some piece of legislation. These meetings were largely for the purpose of discussing measures of benefit not alone to the city but to the whole state, and to map out party strategy.

Mr. Murphy, being a man who himself had come up from lowly surroundings, took a keen interest in bills embodying social legislation. The Factory Investigating Commission's bills, the widows' pension law, and similar bills had his unfailing and enthusiastic support.

Contrary to the general belief, Mr. Murphy was not what is commonly called The Boss. He was a good adviser, and if he placed his confidence in a man he allowed that man to make the decision. The Democratic attitude in all major proposals was determined by the group of men he called around him. They being usually leading lawyers and well-trained business men, his familiar expression was, "If these men do not understand this thing, who does?"

In the session of 1912 the assembly was in control of the Republicans and the senate in control of the Democrats. The session was short and uninteresting. The only outstanding constructive achievement was the passage of the resolution proposing an amendment to the state constitution to permit the enactment by the legislature of a workmen's compensation law and certain of the recommendations of the Factory Investigating Commission which had been in active operation for more than six months. Senator Wagner, being leader of the senate as well as chairman of the commission, naturally put the bills through the upper house. As I was vice chairman of the Factory Investigating Commission, it fell to my lot to push them and debate them in the assembly, and I was successful with a great majority of them, due to the liberal attitude of Speaker Merritt.

Much of the opposition to these bills was due to a complete misunderstanding of what they sought to do. There was talk of the exercise of outside influences on the legislature, because manufacturers generally throughout the state were beginning to organize in opposition to some of the statutes, which they regarded as too drastic. Once they had been put into operation, manufacturers themselves would be the last ones to suggest repeal. The revelations of the Factory Investigating Commission convinced the large employers of labor that an employee who was sound in health was an asset, and when all is said and done, these measures largely provide for what might be called decent, clean housekeeping in places where large numbers of people are employed.

In that year, also, the first attempt was made to supply power, energy and electricity from hydro-electric plants owned and controlled by the state to the various municipalities of the state. It passed the senate but went down to defeat in the assembly. It caused long debates in the lower house and was really the first move made to carry out the mandate of the statute enacted in 1907 which had brought about the 1911 Conservation Commission charged with preparing and submitting to the legislature a comprehensive plan of development of water power under state ownership and state control.

Adjournment occurred on the twenty-ninth of March, which was the earliest date of adjournment of any session of the legislature in which I had served up to that year.

Although John Alden Dix was a candidate for re-nomination in 1912, the majority of Democratic leaders throughout the state were of the opinion that it would be difficult if not impossible to re-elect him. They believed that William Sulzer, then serving in Congress, could be elected. Personally I did not favor the nomination of Sulzer and never voted for him in the convention.

There were three candidates in the field in the state election of 1912. This was the year in which the Progressive party made its great fight. Oscar Straus was its candidate for governor. The Republicans on the regular ticket ran Job E. Hedges. With the Republican vote split two ways, there was a Democratic landslide in the state. It was easy for the Democrats to elect their candidate, and Sulzer became governor.

The senate and assembly were overwhelmingly Democratic. Of the one hundred and fifty members in the assembly, one hundred and five were Democrats. Strange to say, the only Republican legislators who survived were from the small counties, where the Republican machine, because of its local patronage and the comparatively few voters, had such an overwhelming control that the Republican candidates could be victorious even with the party split in half. Not a single Republican was elected to the legislature from Montauk Point to Westchester County.

As the unanimous choice of the majority for Speaker of the assembly I was duly elected at the caucus the night before the legislature convened. Immediately after my election I ran into my chief difficulty in an effort to find sufficient committee places for one hundred and five men. I found myself one general who wished he did not have so many soldiers.

When I ascended the rostrum to preside over the assembly, I believed that I had reached the peak of my political prominence. My elevation to the speakership was a joy to me and to my family. My wife, my mother, my five children and all my friends were present the day that the assembly convened. The Speaker of the assembly wields a great power over that body. The chairmen of all committees are his appointees. They form his cabinet. His advice is sought with respect to all legislative proposals. All the Speakers of the assembly in my time felt the weight of the responsibility.

Ten days before adjournment all committees of the assembly are discharged, and thereafter till adjournment all legislation is in the hands of the Committee on Rules, of which the Speaker is chairman. There has been considerable criticism of the Committee on Rules. It has been called arbitrary, tyrannical and as many other phrases as anybody could, in decency, call it; but, in my opinion, the real fact of the matter is that the assembly could not operate in the closing days without the Committee on Rules. The body is too large, there are too many committees, and it would be impossible to print the calendars, if all of the various committees of the assembly were in continuous operation right up to adjournment.

There is probably no harder-worked man in the whole state government than the Speaker of the assembly while that body is in session. In the last ten days of the session it is a day-and-night job. The Committee on Rules often sits until the small hours of the morning, requiring everybody to be back in the chamber before ten o'clock the next morning. The public printer keeps the presses running night and day, as the calendar of bills reported favorably sometimes does not reach him before three in the morning and has to be on the desks of the members by ten. During the long session of 1913 I never missed a day.

My year as Speaker was a year of turmoil. Yet it is strange that during that year some of the most comprehensive reform legislation in the history of the state was enacted. The Workmen's Compensation Act, the reform of the ballot, and the ratification of the amendment to the Federal Constitution providing for the direct election of United States senators were all put on the statute books while I was Speaker.

Among other things that year, the resolution to amend the Constitution to permit the granting of suffrage to women was passed. I have often been asked what my attitude to women's suffrage was and I have stated it frankly several times. I opposed the suffrage amendment as an assemblyman representing a single assembly district and my opposition was in thorough keeping with the sentiment of my district. Very few women in the old Second Assembly District were anxious to vote. I remember being called upon once by some of the suffrage leaders, and I told them that I would be for suffrage when I should become convinced that the majority of women in my district were in favor of it. They then began to petition me, and I was greatly amused by the petition. Half of the people on it had no existence at all and some of the addresses indicated numbers that would require the city to build out into the East River. When my party as a whole declared in favor of the submission of the amendment, I led the fight for its passage in the assembly, as, in that instance, I believed that my own constituency had to bow to the will of the majority as expressed in the platform adopted by the party at the state convention.

While I was Speaker recommendations of the Factory Investigating Commission were practically completed.

An honest direct-primary act based on recommendations originally made six years earlier by Governor Hughes, but which he had been unable to convince the legislature to pass, became law.

A water-power bill setting up a hydro-electric commission for the Capitol district to take advantage of the use of the surplus waters of the Erie Canal for hydro-electric purposes at a place called Crescent Dam and at Vischer's Ferry, was passed, but vetoed by Governor Sulzer. It was not until some years later that power plants were built by the state for the generation of electrical energy at these two points.

While I was Speaker in 1913, Sophie Irene Loeb, Mrs. William Einstein and several other progressive people came to the legislature with a proposal that the children of widowed mothers should no longer be objects of charity. They proposed a pension for widowed mothers so that children might remain at home under the care of their mother, instead of being sent to institutions. It was not possible to put through such an important reform at once, especially as it was opposed even by some of the charitable relief organizations. Instead, a commission was named, consisting of five assemblymen, three senators and five persons to be named by the governor, to inquire into the question of relief for widowed mothers. As a result of the labors of this commission the present Child Welfare Act in its original form came before the legislature

127

of 1914. It passed the assembly, but met defeat in the senate.

In 1915 it was again introduced, but after four or five years of progressive forward-looking social legislation the pendulum began to swing in the other direction and reactionary influences gripped the session of 1915. Though the bill passed the senate unanimously, the reactionary spirit of that year was shown on the floor of the assembly. The majority leader and a number of his companions showed vigorous opposition and, curiously enough, the arguments put forth by them in opposition were identical with the language used later that same year by William Barnes, Jr., as leader of the Republican party at the Constitutional Convention. So it was easy to detect the source of the inspiration. Incidentally, the leader of the assembly also came from Albany, which was then regarded politically as a principality within a republic ruled by William Barnes, Jr.

It fell to my lot, as minority leader, to urge the passage of the Child Welfare measure. I was interested in the subject from the time I appointed the members of the assembly who served on the commission.

In the course of my speech in the debate on this bill I put the matter on a plane on which it had not before that time been considered. I said:

"What must be her idea of the state's policy when she sees these children separated from her by due process of law, particularly when she must remember that for every one of them she went down into the valley of death that a new pair of eyes might look out upon the world? What can be the feelings in the hearts of the children themselves, separated from their mother by what they must learn in after years was due process of law, when they must in after years learn to know what was the state's policy with respect to their unfortunate system?"

I then indicated what the new policy would be if the bill passed and how the state recognized in the children a resource to be taken care of "not as a matter of charity, but as a matter of government and public duty."

I concluded:

"We have been in a great hurry to legislate for the interests. We have been in a great hurry to conserve that which means to the state dollars and cents. We have been slow to legislate along the direction that means thanksgiving to the poorest man recorded in history—to Him who was born in the stable at Bethlehem. . . .

"We are sending up to Him a prayer of thanksgiving for the innumerable blessings that He has showered upon us, particularly in the light of the words of the Saviour Himself, who said: 'Suffer little children to come unto me, and forbid them not, for of such is the kingdom of heaven.' "

Viewing the bill in that light, a sufficient number of Republican assemblymen rallied to its support to pass it.

Having lived all my life in the poorer section of New York City, I was able to know at first hand the hardships of the mother and the despair of the children when, at the death of the father, they are taken to court, the mother to be separated from her children and the children committed to an institution. I cannot help thinking how close I came to that experience myself. Had my mother not been in the enjoyment of good physical health,

I would probably have found myself in the same position.

When I was governor I signed many bills extending the benefits of the original act. I regretted that I left Albany without securing legislative approval of a proposal which would encourage backward counties to establish boards of child welfare. I wanted the state to subsidize such localities.

Though many men and women took a keen interest in the progress of this legislation, one figure stands out above all. Sophie Irene Loeb, who died recently, was the great driving force behind the Widow's Pension and Child Welfare Bills and kept the group together, including myself, until child-welfare laws similar to our own in this state were enacted in all but four states in the country.

That session of 1913 was the longest and stormiest in the history of the legislature. They were still in session in the month of December. They did everything the constitution gave them the power to do. They put a Supreme Court judge on trial, jailed a newspaperman for contempt of the assembly, and impeached the governor of the state.

The Supreme Court justice was exonerated, but the newspaperman went to the Albany County Jail. He had written an article in a newspaper making the bold statement that money had been paid for votes to bring about the impeachment of the governor. He was subpœnaed before the House Committee on Judiciary, repeated his charges and defied the committee. The committee thereupon recommended that he be brought before the Bar of the House and charged with contempt. He had a family of children and I was unwilling that anything be done to punish him, but his open defiance of the assembly itself, while in session, so incensed the members that I was powerless to be of any assistance to him or to his family, and he found himself one fall morning in the Albany County penitentiary. The state interposed no objection when he was released just before Christmas on a writ of habeas corpus.

Governor Sulzer called the legislature into extraordinary session in an effort to force through the enactment of a direct-primary measure. Under our state constitution no measures may be proposed and nothing is in order in an extraordinary session except on recommendation from the governor by special message.

Governor Sulzer sent a message to the legislature relating to an amendment to the Corrupt Practices Act, whereupon a Republican senator arose in his place and offered a resolution to investigate the governor's own campaign funds.

A committee was appointed to conduct an investigation. New York State has a Corrupt Practices Act with severe regulations, requiring an accounting for campaign funds. Within twenty days after election every candidate for office is required to file, under oath, a detailed statement of all moneys received and expended by him. This provision of law also applies to political parties, state committees or individual committees created for the purpose of assisting in the election of any candidate for public office. The facts disclosed concerning the Sulzer campaign fund brought about the impeachment of the governor by the assembly.

His trial before the Court of Impeachment, which is made up of the judges of the Court of Appeals and the members of the state senate, clearly established the accusations as true. The governor himself did not take the stand and made no defense. He was found guilty by the Court of Impeachment, and his removal from office automatically followed. In accordance with the Constitution, he was succeeded by the lieutenant governor, Martin H. Glynn, of Albany County.

The impeachment of the governor caused widespread comment and ill feeling throughout the whole state. The Republican party sought in every way to capitalize the impeachment of the Democratic governor by the members of his own party.

The session which followed in 1914 was not productive of much beneficial legislation. It really resolved itself into a political quarrel between the Democratic senate and the Republican assembly. Disagreement between them on the appropriation bills resulted in their adjourning without having made provision for the support of government. Governor Glynn thereupon called them back into extraordinary session immediately, and the appropriation bill as finally passed represented a compromise between two contending political factions.

In the fall of 1914, Governor Martin Glynn became

the Democratic candidate. He was defeated and Charles S. Whitman was elected.

Out of power for four years, the Republican party came back into full control of all of the machinery of the state government on the first of January, 1915. At a victory dinner in December, 1914, after Whitman had been elected as governor, a prominent member of the Republican party referred to the fact that the party which gave the people not what they wanted but what the party thought they ought to get had been returned to power. The reactionary tone and character of that speech were reflected in the operations of the legislature of 1915. That session was noted for the number of ripper bills appearing upon the calendars of both houses.

Special interests seeking governmental favor were busy. The lobby was revived and became active against water-power developments and against all amendments to the labor laws. They successfully blocked progress and succeeded in writing into the statute books many of their reactionary measures.

Under the guise of reorganization, the Conservation Commission, charged with control and development of water power, was legislated out of office and a single commissioner substituted. He was to hold office with the unique provision that he could not be removed by the governor without the consent of two-thirds of the members of both houses of the legislature. There was also a provision written into the law that no plan for the comprehensive development of the water powers of the state under state ownership could be effective without the approval of the attorney general and the state engineer and surveyor. The water-power interests of the state admitted that these provisions were intended to curb any repetition of the attempts made between 1911 and 1914 to give legislative approval to any plan of state development.

A concerted attempt was made in that session to break down the labor laws. Bills were introduced to lengthen the hours of labor of women and children employed in the canneries of the state. The most outstanding piece of reactionary legislation was the attempt to weaken the Workmen's Compensation Act under the guise of reorganizing the Labor Department. This legislation, as written into the law of 1915, did away with the supervision by the state of settlements for injuries and thereby took away from the workers the protection given them by the state. This amendment provided for private settlements between the injured persons and the insurance companies.

No living person today, employer or worker, would have the hardihood to suggest that we go back to the old method of compensation after injury—the long-drawn-out lawsuit, a large part of the recovery being paid to the lawyer, the injured person dying before the case reached the Court of Appeals, and all the old legal arguments of "assumption of risk" and the "fellow servant" rule of contributory negligence set up as defenses. The minority in both houses vigorously opposed and fought the proposal for direct settlement.

Senator Wagner and myself, leaders of the minority, succeeded in defeating the first attempt to put through this legislation when it was put into the appropriation bill as a rider, but the Republican legislators marshaled their forces and then put in a bill providing for a reorganization of the Workmen's Compensation Commission. This bill wrote a provision for direct settlements into the law. During the debate a telegram was received from the president of the American Federation of Labor, Samuel Gompers, calling the attempt to change the law in this way "reactionary and detrimental to the interest of the workers of the state." The production of the telegram created quite a scene in the assembly as it had been stated in debate in defense of the measure that it met with the favor of the president of the American Federation of Labor. Many of the Republicans disliked this particular bill, but they remained with the party, anyway, under the whip of the party leadership. The same sharp leadership produced executive approval by the governor.

When the legislature adjourned in 1915, I did not dream that it would be the end of my legislative service. As I close the period dealing with my legislative career, looking back over the years, I am prepared to say that the legislature is a great university of learning for the young man who is willing to give it his full time, his entire attention and close study. In no other place in the world can you make firmer or warmer friends. There is a comradeship between members of the legislature certainly not equaled in business and perhaps not even in schools or in colleges. To the young lawyer, service in the legislature is most valuable. They say that no man knows the engine like the man who works in the plant where it was built. No man knows law and the reasons for it, what made it possible and the forces opposing it, better than the member of the legislature who gives his work study and proper attention. I loved the assembly. It was a great institution to me. It made me acquainted with people all over the state and gave me a breadth of vision that I could obtain in no other way.

Above everything, I still like to think of the opportunity it gave me to do something to help large numbers of people, something I would have been unable to do in any other way. When the session of 1916 convened I deeply regretted being sheriff of New York, because I realized that in that position, outside of giving advice, I would be helpless to raise my voice on the floor of the legislature for the protection as well as the advancement of the beneficent laws in the enactment of which I had aided.

It is needless to say that the experience of my twelve years in the legislature was of inestimable benefit to me when I became governor, particularly the knowledge I had acquired of the state's fiscal system and the appropriation and handling of state funds.

Equally helpful in other constructive measures I later advocated was my knowledge of what had happened to bills in other years and my memory of the forces that had previously brought about their defeat.

CHAPTER IX

Making a New Constitution for the State

A Constitutional Convention is called every twenty years to consider the state constitution as a whole. The previous one was held in 1895. Delegates were chosen in 1914 for the convention to be held in 1915. I was elected a member to represent my senatorial district.

When the Constitutional Convention met in the assembly chamber in April, 1915, it was overwhelmingly Republican although the leading men of both political parties were elected to it. Senator Elihu Root was made chairman. Judge Morgan J. O'Brien was selected to lead the Democrats, and George W. Wickersham, former attorney general of the United States, was selected to lead the Republicans. I looked forward eagerly to the sessions.

The convention began its duties after an opening speech by Senator Root wherein he stated that the constitution contained considerable obsolete matter and should be brought up to date. He found fault, in the first instance, with the size of the constitution and the number of words employed in it, and suggested that with proper revision it could be reduced to a small-size book that could be carried in your vest pocket.

LeRoy Austin, a young lawyer from Greene County, was appointed chairman of the Committee on Revision and ambitiously set his committee to work at once studying the older provisions of the constitution to see how much of these could be left out. The first section the committee lit upon occurred in Article I, which had to do with the abolition of feudal tenures, allodial tenures and leases of agricultural lands. These provisions were put into the constitution in the early days of the state because of the practices of the holders of large tracts of land in the Capitol district known as the Rensselaer-Wyck estates, and after considerable study the committee came before the convention with a proposal to eliminate these passages from the constitution.

In the body was a lawyer from Brooklyn who specialized in title searching. He started to speak against striking out these sections of the constitution after recess on Tuesday. He talked until adjournment and started in again when we reconvened on Wednesday morning, talked all day Wednesday, and on Thursday the convention voted on the proposal. They voted to leave the sections in. The lawyer had created sufficient doubt in the minds of the members as to whether their removal might not, in some way or another, affect title to property. It can readily be imagined, after that performance, how difficult it became to take anything out of the constitution.

In spite of the speech of the presiding officer and the endeavor on the part of the Committee on Revision to reduce the size of the constitution, the final document emanating from the convention assumed the proportions of the New York Telephone Directory.

During 1914 and 1915 a decidedly reactionary element

in the legislature and in the state had been actively bent upon attempting to stop what they called socialistic legislation. They included workmen's compensation and many of the factory laws and the provision for pensions for widowed mothers in that grouping. By a cleverly worded amendment to the constitution introduced by William Barnes, Jr., then state leader of the Republican party, it was sought to prohibit the legislature from passing any more measures of a similar nature. The full purport of the proposed resolution was not understood for sometime because of the subtle wording. To the best of my recollection, it ran as follows: "The legislature shall not pass any bill granting hereafter to any class of individuals any privilege or immunity not granted equally to all members of the state." I was a member of the committee to which this resolution was referred, and I fought it in the committee as vigorously as I knew how. I was beaten on the question of reporting it to the convention, by the strong support Mr. Barnes was able to hold under his leadership.

The resolution came on the calendar of the convention for debate at a night session. We were debating under a rule that limited the members to ten minutes, with a half hour for the majority and minority leaders. The danger of such an amendment to the constitution was fully realized by the more liberal-minded delegates on the Republican side, and Mr. Wickersham, the Republican leader, gave me twenty minutes of his half hour, using only ten minutes himself, and permitting me to devote a half hour to opposition of its adoption. The call of the roll showed the Democratic minority solidly against it. With them in the same voting column were the liberal Republicans, including their leader. The resolution was defeated; but it indicated the trend of the times on the whole question of social legislation.

Barnes himself was a man of unusual ability, a good talker with a broad knowledge of affairs, but he was probably as reactionary a man as I ever met. He came by his convictions honestly. In the course of his speech in favor of his unique proposal to stifle all social legislation, he blamed the war on the socialistic tendencies of the German Empire. He said that socialistic bills and socialistic proposals had so gripped the people of Germany that they had ceased to consider that the government existed for them and were forced to the belief that they existed for the government.

He referred to a speech made by Prince Bismarck before the Reichstag in 1873, and quoted Bismarck as having said: "Take care of the widowed mother; provide insurance against sickness and old age, and they"—meaning the Socialists—"will have sung their swan song."

Though I disagreed with him on his political theories as bitterly as I could, I always had a sincere regard for him and for his ability, and I am reasonably certain that it was reciprocated.

The chief debates in the convention occurred upon the proposals to amend the constitution to bring about the shortening of the ballot and the reorganization of the state government, the adoption of an executive budget, the adoption of a proposal to amend the constitution to require a literacy test for voting, and upon the proposal to set up a Conservation Commission of twelve members, one from each judicial district.

I favored the reorganization of the government and the short ballot with a modification calling for the election of the attorney general, and not for his appointment, as the amendment submitted proposed. I felt that the state's chief law officer in advisory capacity to the legislature as well as to the executive departments should be elected in order to preserve the absolute independence of the two branches of the government.

Because of the wording of the resolution, I opposed the adoption of the executive budget. In the form in which it was submitted in the convention it did not cover the whole field of appropriation of public moneys, as I believed it should. In underlying theory I declared that I believed it to be right. I believed then, as now, that the responsibility for recommending the appropriation of public money should rest upon the governor in the first instance, while in no way depriving the legislature of its power to make the actual appropriation. Although I opposed it in the Constitutional Convention in 1915, I accepted it in 1926 in the form in which it was then offered in the convention. But in 1920, in my first term as governor, I urged it in the way that I believed it should have been worded.

In the convention I opposed the literacy test for voters

upon the theory that men and women who come to this country, work hard, send their children to school, take an oath of allegiance to our Constitution and to our flag, and obey our laws, are good citizens and, because of the handicaps of early life, should not be deprived of a voice in the government under which they live. This amendment was defeated in the Constitutional Convention, but was afterward adopted by the legislature as a proposal and put to a state referendum. In the course of the debate on the literacy test I held that the ability of a man to write was no indication of his character. I referred to the number of sojourners at Sing Sing prison who were not only able to write their own names but found their way in there because of their ability to write somebody else's name.

The proposal to set up by judicial districts a large, cumbersome, irresponsible, constitutional body for the conservation of our natural resources looked to me like an attempt on the part of the power interests of the state to prevent any state development or state ownership of our great water powers, and I opposed it.

Another measure which provoked considerable debate was offered by Seth Low, former mayor of Greater New York, who was chairman of the Committee on Affairs of Cities. It was the home-rule-for-cities provision. This proposed amendment was afterward adopted during my governorship and is now part of our constitution.

I sought to write into the constitution a provision permitting the creation by law of a minimum wage board with power to fix minimum wages for women and children in industry in accordance with legal conditions and local necessities. On roll call it failed of adoption. I debated it with one of our foremost constitutional lawyers, Louis Marshall. Though we disagreed sharply, I have to this writing enjoyed the pleasure and benefit of his friendship. In my later years as governor I often found myself working hand in hand with him against the forces we had both been fighting in the Constitutional Convention. Together we have resisted encroachments by the power interests on the Adirondack preserve, developed the State College of Forestry, and protected minority rights.

The various sessions of the convention were crowded with people on vacation and those traveling through the state, who stopped off at Albany. The debates were interesting and the night sessions were fairly well attended. Mrs. Smith and the children spent some time in Albany during the sessions of the convention and my eldest son, Alfred, acted as volunteer page boy.

During all the debates in which I engaged I am unable to remember that I took as personal anything urged against me, and I trained myself to give every adversary the benefit of believing that he was conscientious and came by his opinions honestly. I never opposed men. I opposed principles.

Nobody opposed Senator Brackett in the Constitutional Convention as bitterly or as vigorously as I did and in 1918 he supported me for governor. In turn I joined hands with him and the Saratoga Chamber of Commerce to clean up gambling and vice conditions in his city in the summer of 1920. I visited him during his last illness and was with him a short time before his death.

In the state campaign of 1914 when Martin H. Glynn ran for re-election as governor a strong religious attack was directed against him culminating in an organization known as the "Guardians of Liberty." Their great numerical strength was in Erie County. Like all such movements it did not die at once and it made itself apparent in the Constitutional Convention when the Guardians of Liberty circularized the convention against the Catholic Church. One of the delegates from Erie County, operating frankly in the interests of the Guardians of Liberty, introduced a proposed amendment to the constitution to compel the taxation of all church property and to prevent the legislature from exempting any of it in the future. Taking advantage of my legislative training and experience I introduced an amendment to the constitution taking out of that document the clause prohibiting the legislature from making appropriation to sectarian schools and institutions. That would have meant that the state could have made direct appropriation of its public funds for sectarian educational purposes.

George Wickersham said to me, "Al Smith, that proposal will create havoc in this convention." I said to him, "General, that's what we call a little legislative bludgeon. I have no intention of moving that resolution to passage. No church wants it and I can state to you that the Catholic Church which I attend does not want it. Catholics desire to supply the money themselves for their educational and charitable endeavors. It has been a great satisfaction to them to do it in the past and we shall continue to do it." He then asked me what I meant by a legislative bludgeon. I referred to the resolution offered by the Guardians of Liberty and I said to him, "General, if that resolution is released from committee I will insist upon this one of mine. If on the other hand that is allowed to slumber itself to death this one dies with it." He thereupon assured me that the other legislation would never be reported and it never was. Consequently there was no reason for disturbing mine. This will probably be the only opportunity that I will ever have to explain my object in introducing that resolution. It was used against me by opponents in the last election.

Near the close of the convention, which had lasted until well into September, I had a long talk with Senator Root. He asked me my opinion of the constitution as completed, and what chances there were of its adoption by the people. I told him, frankly, I did not think it could be adopted for various reasons.

First, it had taken the best lawyers in the state nearly four months to put it together, and now it was proposed to give the people of the state only six weeks to digest it. I further told him that I thought it was a mistake to submit it in a single document. If its submission had been delayed one year and it had been brought out in sections so that the people of the state could vote for the sections they liked and against the ones they disliked, the larger part of the revisions might have been adopted.

I explained to him that the chief underlying difficulty was that the proposed constitution was a compromise. I said, "There is too much in it that tries to please everybody." From the moment it was completed it was bound to make more enemies than friends, because we must bear in mind that constructive reforms are often bitterly opposed by just those people who may be beneficiaries of the system whose reform is sought.

An occurrence which took place at the opening of the session indicates the spirit of compromise that permeated the whole body. A man from the central part of the state offered a resolution that the clerk be instructed to buy for the members drinking water bottled in his section of the state. Quite unexpectedly it provoked a strenuous argument. Senator Brackett sprang to his feet and said, "The state of New York is owner and entitled to the waters of the Saratoga Springs, and they are the best drinking waters in the world. I regret and deplore the passing of a resolution declaring it to be the purpose of the convention to use privately bottled waters." Whereupon compromise started and the resolution was amended to buy both waters and let the members of the convention take their choice. They even compromised on the drinking water.

Employees of the cities of the state were opposed to the new constitution because of the home-rule amendment. Had it been adopted at that time, it would have taken from large groups of employees the protection they were enjoying by having their salaries fixed by state law.

The conservation article had roused the opposition of students of conservation and organizations for the protection and preservation of the Adirondacks.

The same reactionary influences, particularly in the small upstate counties, which had for political reasons voted against the submission of the executive budget and the reorganization of the government, lined themselves up in the ranks of those opposed to the constitution for other reasons.

The article of the constitution apportioning the senators and assemblymen to the various counties met with vigorous opposition in New York City. Largely because of that article, I voted against the adoption of the constitution myself. I held it to be, at that time, and I assert today, that that constitutional provision is a denial of the theory of representative democratic government. Under its provision, if you live in the city of New York you are one of 125,000 or 150,000 people entitled to one representative in the Assembly, but if you live in Putnam County you are one of only 10,000 entitled to the same representation. It is this particular provision of the constitution that has given the Republican organization such a grip upon the assembly that, in 1922, when I was elected governor by a plurality of 387,000, the assembly still remained Republican.

The debates on the apportionment article were very bitter. Senator Brackett arose in his seat and said, "Let's

147

have an end to this bickering back and forth between the Democrats and Republicans, and let us Republicans frankly say that we propose to keep control of the legislature upstate and that we are not going to let one little corner of the state of New York control the whole state."

Probably the worst blow dealt to the new constitution came from the ranks of organized labor because of a proposed amendment to the Bill of Rights. The European War was going on in 1915. The amendment to the Bill of Rights brought forth a storm when Judge Cullen, former chief justice of our Court of Appeals, in speaking about the proposed constitution, said that "there should be no drum-head courts in times of peace." Probably no man in public life in this state commanded more widespread respect than did Judge Cullen, and countless thousands of people, without inquiring into the matter at all, proceeded on the theory that the amendment to the Bill of Rights was so revolutionary as to give military control in time of peace. The trade unions led the opposition to the new constitution and succeeded in defeating it by a majority of half a million.

Just at the close of the convention William Barnes, Jr., who was the most consistent foe of the direct nominating system you probably could find in the length and breadth of the state of New York, gave the delegates a laugh. When the Tammany Hall executive committee made its designation of me to participate in the primary for the office of sheriff, Mark Eisner, then a delegate to the Constitutional Convention and a great friend of mine, re-

AN OLD HOME NIGHT
Election night, 1915, at the Oliver Street flat.

THE FAMILY GROUP AT THE INDUCTION OF SHERIFF SMITH IN 1915

ceived that word by telephone. He rushed into the assembly chamber and asked for recognition by the chairman. In his excitement he failed to say that the Tammany executive committee had "designated" me to run in the primaries for sheriff. He stated that the Tammany executive committee had "nominated" me. After the applause died down, William Barnes, Jr., arose in his place and said, "Mr. President, I thought we had direct nominations in this state."

The intimate associations of the five months in Albany made for me a large number of what afterward became personal friends and they have since been, at different times, in communication with me on all kinds of subjects affecting the state government. From that time up to the present day I have enjoyed the personal friendship of many whom I met there.

All through my governorship I had the support and friendship of Judge Alphonse T. Clearwater, one of the leading members and one of the brightest minds of the convention. He has had a deep and helpful interest in parks and in the reorganization of the government.

I have since then enjoyed also an intimate friendship with Senator Root, the presiding officer. It gives me great pleasure never to forget to send him greetings on his birthday. George W. Wickersham, Jacob Gould Schurman, former president of Cornell University, Henry L. Stimson, and others have all aided me when I made personal appeal to them during my governorship for assistance in the adoption of the amendments favored by them in the Constitutional Convention.

One of the most delightful characters in the Constitutional Convention was Delancey Nicoll, an able debater, a man of sound sense and understanding and of great ability, as were also the late John B. Stanchfield, then one of the leading legal lights of the country, and John Lord O'Brian of Buffalo.

The adjournment of the Constitutional Convention resembled the graduating class of a university bidding one another good-bye at the close of their labors together. The year 1915 probably presented me with what was, up to that time, the hardest year's work I had ever done. And when I left Albany I plunged right into the campaign for sheriff without rest or vacation of any kind.

CHAPTER X

From Sheriff to Governor

THERE was regret expressed at my leaving Albany, and it was certainly gratifying to have Republican newspapers express it editorially, as the *Tribune* did, and also to have a non-partisan organization, The Citizens' Union, support me for the new office.

The fall of 1915 found me for the first time engaged in a campaign that appealed to the county and not just to my home district. I was running for sheriff.

It was a unique campaign. I probably made more speeches than any candidate for that office who had ever preceded me, and the joy and satisfaction over my nomination was at so high a point in the old neighborhood that Old Home Night was celebrated on Oliver Street with bands of music and a display of fireworks. The windows were illumined with Chinese lanterns, and it seems to me that in the course of four hours I shook hands with every man and woman in the old district. My district had more nationalities than any other in the city. Large delegations from every civilized country in the world passed in front of the old house during the party. Chinamen, although not voters, were enthusiastic rooters, and the gay colors and lighting effects from Mott Street, in Chinatown, were moved over for the night into Oliver Street.

The early election returns indicated an overwhelming

151

victory and with the prospect of a large income ahead of me, I proceeded the day after election to build an extension on the Oliver Street house, although the property did not belong to me. It was difficult to house a family the size of mine on Oliver Street.

The extension was ready by the first of January, and the new sheriff of New York held forth in the old homestead after the inauguration, and I suppose I was visited by the whole neighborhood. At the sheriff's office that day I was surrounded by my wife and children, my mother, my sister, her husband and all of her children. There was no room in the big reception hall for anybody else. I was presented with a handsome revolver with an ivory handle. I thought at the time that it must have been given to me upon the theory that all sheriffs carried pistols. During my term of office I carried it once, and that was the night I went up to shoot off a blank cartridge to start the bicycle race in Madison Square Garden.

When I entered the sheriff's office the salary was twelve thousand dollars a year and one-half of the fees collected by him during his term of office. The other half went into the county treasury. My fees for the two years I was sheriff amounted approximately to $105,000. While I was in office the legislature amended the law and did away with the fee system, so that today the sheriff receives only his salary.

I was well recompensed as sheriff and probably it made up for the financial sacrifices I was compelled to make during my long service in the assembly. It gave me an opportunity to bring to the family, then fairly grown, the luxury of an automobile and a better and more pretentious summer home. More than anything, it relieved my mind of the constant anxiety about what might happen in the event of sickness and the many other troubles that come to a man at the head of a big family.

Compared to the twelve years in Albany, the sheriff's office was calm and tame. It offered strictly routine work, not so much to my taste as my legislative career had been. I gave much time to outside public activities and in 1917, after the United States entered the war, I gave considerable time to the sale of Liberty Bonds and to public speaking on behalf of the government loans. I invested more than 80 per cent of my income from the sheriff's office in Liberty Bonds.

In the summer of 1917 the struggle for the mayoralty election in the fall of that year began. I spent much time that summer at Delmonico's conferring with the leaders of the party over the outcome and the nominations to be made for the various city offices. By men not included in these conferences, it has often been said that I was a candidate that year for the nomination for mayor. There is no truth in that statement, because before anybody was selected or before any names were mentioned, it was definitely settled as a matter of political strategy that the nomination was to go to Brooklyn, the nominee to be selected later.

The occasion for the large number of conferences as well as for the large number of people called into them was the desire upon the part of the leaders to ascertain as closely as possible just what chance there was of defeating Mayor Mitchel for re-election. Besides, there was great anxiety as to just what the Republican party would do. There was widespread dissatisfaction with the administration of Mayor Mitchel among the rank and file of the Republicans. They felt that he had overlooked them in the distribution of patronage and many of the small fry were incensed because he had supported me for sheriff.

The outcome of the primary elections, when a straight Republican was nominated, making it a three-cornered fight, with John Purroy Mitchel running as an Independent, justified the apprehension of the Democratic leaders. Mitchel had a large and powerful independent following. He was a man of unquestioned ability. He brought about many desirable reforms in the administration of city business, but the loose cog in the wheel happened to be the fact that he held a political position and was a thousand miles away from being a politician. He did not know how to handle people and did not know how to deal with them or how to get along with them. He had a hot temper and he vented it too often for his own political good.

Not being a politician, he was lacking in knowledge of the human element. That was illustrated by one of his earliest actions in office when he attempted to have the legislature amend the city charter so as to take away from police officers the right to the writ of review, which would deprive policemen removed from office of the right to have their cases reviewed by the courts. He was defeated in that move by a Republican legislature, the New York members of which, at least, had vigorously supported him in his contest for the mayoralty.

There was uncertainty in the minds of the Democratic organization leaders about the result of the impending election occasioned by the fact that the so-called Independent, or Wilson, Democrats were behind Mitchel. He had been honored before his nomination for mayor by appointment at the hands of the President to the collectorship of the Port of New York. The leaders feared a house divided against itself. Another factor taken into consideration was the tremendous growth of the vote in South Brooklyn.

Practically all political selections are finally made up and decided by a process of elimination. The leaders hit upon John F. Hylan, then county judge of Kings County. As in all other political campaigns, some outside organization took a hand. To offset the Mitchel Business Men's League, another Business Men's League was formed under the chairmanship of Preston P. Lynn, then general manager of Wanamaker's store, and that league under the leadership of Lynn first mentioned the name of Judge Hylan.

After my overwhelming victory in the county of New York two years before, the leaders were anxious that I accept the nomination to the office of the president of the Board of Aldermen. It had certain attractions for me in that it was not an executive but rather a legislative position. My Albany experience made that much more to my liking.

Many estimates have been made of the influences affecting the 1917 city campaign. We were in the midst of the World War. That caused a natural uneasiness and apprehension which perhaps is best evinced by the large vote cast for the Socialist candidate, Morris Hillquit. He received 141,178 votes, the largest ever cast for a Socialist candidate for mayor in the history of the city. Probably, this large Socialist vote was a protest against the war.

Another thing which roused the ire of the rank and file of the people of New York during the Mitchel administration was the importation of men from other parts of the country who were called municipal experts. New York City has great and perhaps rather provincial pride. It believed that it had within its own families the ability to manage the affairs of the city. It resented also the attempt to convey the impression that ordinary men were unfitted for minor positions in the city government and that a corps of experts was what was required.

The condition in the public schools was another cause of dissatisfaction. Due to the scarcity of labor, even before we entered the war and just after it, it was impossible to erect enough school buildings to keep pace with the growing school population. Children were getting only a few hours a day in school.

In the last analysis, the defeat of Mitchel was nothing more or less than history repeating itself. After all, Tammany Hall for a century has been the dominating political party in the city of New York. No fusion administration of the city ever succeeded itself. No fusion administration, to my knowledge, was ever elected in the first instance on the merits of its candidates. Most of them were unknown. A fusion administration usually came into power when the people were so minded as to desire to rebuke Tammany Hall for grievances, real or imaginary.

When I was inaugurated president of the Board of Aldermen on January 1, 1918, quite naturally there was a great celebration by the old neighbors. The City Hall was in my own district and is only three minutes' walk from Oliver Street. I was deluged with flowers and congratulations.

It happened that for the first time there were a number of Socialist members of the Board of Aldermen, and at the first meeting over which I presided I said:

"To the majority party, I desire to say that the people of this city in no uncertain terms placed upon us a grave responsibility. The glory that comes from what we do of benefit can be claimed by everybody. Those things which are neglected constitute our sins of omission.

"I have a keen understanding of the relationship to the body of the minority and the minor minority—meaning the Socialist members. The people rule negatively as well as affirmatively, and a good, healthy, vigorous minority is the necessary check on great power.

"The rules of the board are intended for the protection of the rights of the minorities as well as to expedite the business of the majority. In that spirit, I will interpret them with a desire to do equal and even-handed justice to all."

During that winter in the absence of the mayor I was acting mayor at the time of the coal shortage. The Hudson River was blocked with ice and thousands of tons of coal were stored in the break-up yards in New Jersey, but we were unable to get it over to New York. It was then that the necessity for some development at the port of New York that would make such a thing impossible in the future impressed itself upon me. Later, when I was governor, it furnished the principal argument for me to accept the proposal to build a vehicular tunnel under the river between New York and New Jersey. Even at this time discussion was going on about methods of unifying the operations of freight in the port of New York, and it finally led to a comprehensive plan for the development of the port and the creation of the Port of New York Authority.

Operation of the government of the city during the war was difficult. Severe regulations required the Navy Department to close off the harbor at night. The city therefore found itself in an awkward predicament over garbage removal, because the garbage scows were unable to go to sea as frequently as they should. Consequently garbage had to be dumped along the water front. Similarly ashes because of the ice conditions on both rivers accumulated so rapidly that it was necessary to use the excavations then being made at the side of the new court house to bring relief to the downtown office buildings and to business generally.

City officials gave much time to war activities. I urged

158

the purchase of Liberty Bonds and visited the various schoolhouses where the soldier boys were gathered to bid farewell to their parents. Frequently I made as many as three or four speeches a day in different parts of the city and reviewed the departing men from the City Hall steps as they started from lower New York for Hoboken where the *Leviathan*, used exclusively as a troop ship during the war, was docked.

I had settled down to a four-year term as president of the Board of Aldermen. Upon assuming the presidency I led a movement to bring the rules and procedure of the Board of Aldermen up to date and to make its deliberations more understandable and more dignified. Had I remained for the full term I might have accomplished much, but I was scarcely well acquainted with the routine business of the city when I was plunged into another campaign—this time for the governorship of the state.

Charles F. Murphy, leader of the city Democracy, was anxious that the upstate leaders should select a man who they believed would be best equipped to win in the upstate sections. A committee was formed which met in Syracuse at the home of William F. Kelly, the leader of Onondaga County. It was apparent, after two or three sessions of the committee, that they could not agree on any candidate from the upper part of the state, and after further conference in New York it was agreed that a Tammany Hall man would be acceptable, provided upstate would declare in his favor first.

159

Some fifteen or twenty names appeared upon the list of possible candidates and by a process of elimination my name was the last one left on it. That information was conveyed to the leaders prior to a conference at Saratoga which occurred in the early part of August. Nominations for state officials were still made by the direct-primary system at that time and unofficial conventions of the party were called for the purpose of designating the candidates to run in the primary election. The Saratoga conference was to decide who was to be designated. It was in session for three days and at its close I was chosen as the regular organization candidate.

It was an exciting three days for me, and to add to all the other surprises I was seated in a room in the Grand Union Hotel when my second son, Arthur, then eleven years old, walked into the room. I inquired how he got there and he said that he had come up with Tom Campbell to give me a surprise and congratulate me. Tom Campbell was a neighbor from Oliver Street and, naturally, interested in the outcome of the conference. Arthur had persuaded his mother to let him come by saying that he was sure that if he went "he'd bring home the bacon." As soon as he knew the result he went to a telephone and called up his mother to tell her he had kept his word.

I was not unopposed in the primary. A group of independent Democrats filed a petition for William Church Osborn to run against me. The decision in my favor was overwhelming and on the night of primary day at twelve o'clock I started on the New York, Ontario & Western Railroad for Binghamton where, the next day, at a place called Whitney Point, I made the opening speech of my campaign at the Broome County Fair.

Notwithstanding my long service in the assembly and my record in the Constitutional Convention, I encountered considerable antagonism in the rural sections of the state. At one county fair I was introduced to a farmer who had just won a blue ribbon for his dairy herd, as the "Democratic candidate for governor." He was arrayed in a brand-new suit of overalls and he stepped back about six feet, looked me over from head to foot, and said, "Well, you look pretty good, but you can't get any comfort from me." At the various county fairs interest was centered on me and many of the visitors were more anxious to get a look at the Tammany candidate for governor than at the prize-winning exhibits.

During the 1918 campaign the war was on. The lists of American casualties in the daily papers were growing every day, and throughout the countryside the flags with stars hanging in the windows indicated that the minds of the occupants were on something other than politics. They were eagerly scanning newspapers, looking for something they were hoping they would not find.

In addition, we were in the midst of the influenza epidemic. In a great many upstate cities public gatherings were prohibited by action of the local Board of Health and some of the speeches reported in the papers and supposed to have been made by me to large audiences were

161

made in the dining rooms of hotels with the newspaper reporters who accompanied me as the only audience. Buffalo, Albany, and Ithaca were the only cities in which I had an opportunity to speak to large gatherings in places of public assemblage. I made a great many speeches in the open air. For three solid weeks I campaigned in the upper part of the state, devoting the fourth and last week to the counties of Greater New York and Long Island.

It will be remembered that 1918 was the first year that women voted in the state of New York, and my Republican opponents attempted to spread the story that the women of the state would be opposed to me on my "record of votes on bills affecting the liquor traffic." Having studied the charges and found them not to be the fact, the women displayed more intelligence than the Republican leaders were willing to give them credit for. They looked at the whole record and were impressed by what the women themselves called my interest in the human side of the government.

In addition to the regular political organization, a citizens' committee was organized in New York City, made up of Democrats not directly affiliated with the regular organization, some Republicans anxious for a change in Albany conditions, and a large number of independent voters and former members of the Progressive party. Its headquarters were at the Hotel Biltmore. The chairman was Abram I. Elkus, counsel for the Factory Investigation Commission, afterward United States Minister to Turkey, and by my appointment judge of the State Court of Appeals.

My loyal and devoted friend John F. Gilchrist acted as liaison officer between the Citizens' Committee and Tammany Hall. He also was responsible for all the financial transactions of the committee and the accounting for funds as required by law in the observance of the Corrupt Practices Act. Among the advisers who would sit in with the committee was the late William F. McCombs, who had directed Wilson's campaign.

While its activities were confined almost entirely to Greater New York, its personnel had a very beneficial effect on my candidacy in other parts of the state because of the character of men and women who made up the Citizens' Committee.

Another organization formed for the campaign gave wonderful help. It was called the Young Democratic Club. These were young men and women attracted by my record of service in Albany who worked hard for my election.

The story of my first election as governor and the forces operating against me would not be complete without a mention of the religious issue which found its way very strongly into that campaign. It was effective against me in certain sections of the state but was beneficial in others. The strong resentment in the city of Albany against the injection of the religious issue into the campaign reacted distinctly in my favor there. In the country sections, particularly outside of the city of Buffalo, it operated strongly against me. While the Ku-Klux Klan had not yet reared its head as actively as it did in subsequent years, there were other organizations equally ill-intentioned.

My mother, by the way, was violently opposed to woman suffrage and hoped, in the fall of 1917, when the question was submitted to the people, that it would be defeated. When she found that the men of the state voted the suffrage to the women, she openly declared that she would never vote. When she said that, though, she had no idea that I would be the candidate of the Democratic party for governor of the state the following November.

Immediately after my designation she inquired of my sister when and where she was to register. If my recollection serves me right she was among the first five who registered at the polling place of her election district. After election she realized that she had the distinction of being the first woman in the state to vote for her son for governor.

Election Day of 1918 was probably the longest day of my life up to that time. I was anxious from early morning for night to come to see the count of the ballots. All day long I thought of what a wonderful thing it would be for me to be able to bring my wife and children and my mother to the Executive Mansion.

Beginning at eight o'clock at night the Citizens' Committee assembled in the Hotel Biltmore. The first returns naturally were from the big cities and from sections of Greater New York, and they indicated a tidal wave of

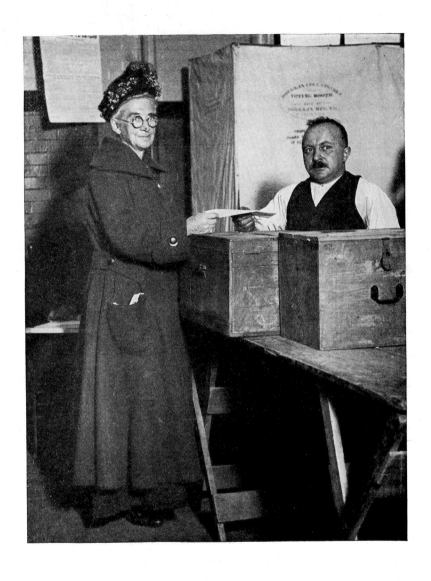

THE CANDIDATE'S MOTHER CASTS HER FIRST VOTE FOR HER SON
1918

VOTING FOR THE DEMOCRATIC GUBERNATORIAL NOMINEE

Mr. and Mrs. Smith at the polls.

Democratic victory, but toward midnight the enthusiasm was materially dampened by the returns, meager in themselves, but overwhelmingly the other way, coming from the rural sections and from some of the upstate cities. I took a hand myself in stemming the enthusiasm of the gathering. Some of my intimate and personal friends began calling me "Governor" at twelve o'clock and shaking hands with me and congratulating me, but I said, "Wait now. All the places so far heard from are favorable. Give the other fellow his day in court and we will see what the result will be. Wait till we hear from some of the small cities and villages upstate. They're probably voting yet."

That night was a great lesson in what strong friendship means. The hotel was packed all night long, and so great was the anxiety of my mother that she remained until after three o'clock in the morning, when I insisted that my sister take her home. My wife and several of the older children remained with me to the finish, as did thousands of my friends.

About two o'clock in the morning the ticker tape indicated an overwhelming majority for my opponent in the city of Jamestown. An old school-time chum of mine connected with one of the newspapers was in a café in Park Row that had remained open all night. When he read the returns from Jamestown he jumped into an automobile and, in company with three or four of his friends, came uptown to the Biltmore and insisted upon getting into the inside room where I was checking up on the missing counties. The immediate friends around me knew him well and allowed him in. He appeared heartbroken and simply wanted to know where Jamestown was. I never asked him his intention, but I had an idea that he wanted to go there at once. When I explained to him that it would take him about two days to get to Jamestown by automobile, he went back to Park Row.

As time wore on to six o'clock in the morning the returns were so slow from the central part of the state and the southern tier of counties that my friends were apprehensive that everything was not going right and that the returns were being held back. Messages from leaders in the central and northern part of the state spoke of possible fraud in the handling of the late returns.

A hurried conference was held and Alfred J. Johnson, then City Chamberlain, Senator Wagner, Judge Van Namee, Senator—now Mayor—Walker and myself left on the Empire State Express at 8:30 in the morning for Syracuse, the upstate headquarters of the Democratic State Committee. From there we could get direct communication with the parts of the state where the returns were missing. We all remained in Syracuse until Thursday, and I communicated by telephone with the various county headquarters in the northern, central and western parts of the state and the counties bordering on the Pennsylvania line.

I found the Democratic county leaders on the job, enthusiastic, and fighting for their rights. One Democratic commissioner of elections to whom I spoke at his home told me that his wife was over in the county clerk's office sitting on the ballot boxes while he was eating his dinner.

By Thursday night reports indicated my election by a majority of about seventy-five hundred. I returned to New York and was greeted at the Biltmore by my mother, my wife and family, and an army of friends who crowded the campaign rooms to the door. They were anxiously awaiting the word from me that everything was all right. Before I spoke to anyone, I had a whispered word with my wife, and her greeting indicated that everything was safe. It was one of the few occasions on which I had been separated from Mrs. Smith on November sixth, her birthday. She had had an anxious day, but her spirits were kept up by the enthusiasm of friends and their certainty that I was elected. The excitement in and around the Biltmore Hotel lasted for some days. The secretary of state's report of the soldier vote in the camps in the United States added seven thousand five hundred more votes to my majority, making it finally around fifteen thousand.

Governor Whitman, my opponent, did not concede my election at once. Instead, he instituted a court proceeding to open the ballot boxes in certain election districts in New York. A number of ballot boxes were taken to court and the records were reviewed.

Curiosity and suspicion about the election district in which I was born had been excited in the minds of the men around the Republican state headquarters because Governor Whitman received only two votes there, while

I received three hundred and eighty-seven. One attaché of the Republican headquarters not familiar with the law declared it to be an impossibility unless the appointed representatives of the Republican party at that particular polling place voted against their own candidate. They believed that to have been quite unlikely.

The Republican leader of the district was summoned to headquarters, and he cleared the atmosphere in a moment when he stated that it was impossible to find eight Republicans in that district willing to man the polls against me, and that all the Republican election officials in that district, in accordance with the law, were imported into it from other districts.

I sent for the Democratic captain of the district and spoke to him about the result in his district. His quick reply was: "They can take the ballot boxes, open them up and do anything they like to them. That result is honest and strictly on the level. I am not concerned about the ballot boxes, but I would like to know who the two people were that voted against you, and I will find it out in less than a week."

Three nights later he reported to me that one of the two was a man who believed that I could have assisted his son to a position in the Police Department and had refused to do so. He voted against me. The other ballot was cast against me by mistake. A woman in Cherry Street who went to school with me discovered, upon looking at a sample ballot, three nights after election, that she had put the crossmark in the wrong place and came up to explain it to the captain of the district. Far from fraud, I lost one vote through error, and if the man had been acquainted with the full facts with regard to his son the decision in that election district would have been unanimous.

The delay of the court proceedings prevented me from receiving my certificate of election from the secretary of state until the end of December.

CHAPTER XI

The First Year as Governor

AFTER the children had their Christmas tree in Oliver Street we started to pack for Albany, and on my birthday, the thirtieth of December, 1918, I started off with my wife, my children and my mother, and we celebrated my forty-fifth birthday at the Executive Mansion. It was a busy few days for the children, getting their affairs straightened out and selecting their rooms at the Executive Mansion.

Not waiting until the inauguration, I started during December to prepare my first message to the legislature and to lay out plans for carrying out the Democratic platform and the promises made during the campaign. It was during this period that Mrs. Belle Moskowitz, who had been chairman of the women's division of the Citizens' Committee for my election, laid before me the suggestion to create a Reconstruction Commission, whose work and accomplishments I will deal with later.

On the eve of the inauguration following an old custom in Albany I attended the charity ball at the Tenth Regiment Armory with the departing governor. The Sixty-Ninth Regiment escorted me to Albany and took part in the inaugural parade. The rooms at the various hotels in Albany were taken weeks in advance. State Street, Broadway and Eagle Street in Albany looked like the old Fourth Ward. Pretty nearly everybody who lived on Oliver Street and who could afford it was in Albany that year.

The inaugural ceremonies made a deep impression on all of my family. They had the deepest thrill of their lives when they heard the cannon booming on Capitol Hill, proclaiming the inauguration of the new governor.

It would be difficult for me to conceive of any man being inaugurated governor of New York with a deeper sense of responsibility than I had when I took my first oath of office as governor in the assembly chamber on the first of January, 1919. So much had been said about me and my record of usefulness to the state that I felt that much must be expected of me as governor. The enthusiasm of my friends, their hard and honest work for me, impressed further upon my mind and laid upon me the desire and the obligation to prove them right. I wanted to justify, if possible, to the last degree all the claims they made for me during the campaign. Again, there were my wife and children, my mother, my sister and all her children. I was deeply anxious for their sakes. I was eager to demonstrate that no mistake had been made by the people of the state of New York when they entrusted their government to a man who had come up from the lowest rung of the ladder to the highest position within their gift.

I approached the duties of the governorship with but one single thought in mind, and that was to make good for the state of New York, and not to think of seeking

171

higher political preferment. I was not urged even for a moment by the thought of a second term. For all these reasons, I surrounded myself with people of all political faiths as well as people of no political faith, and sought their counsel in order that I might be in a position to reap the full benefit of any ideas they would give me. I learned the lesson, during my legislative career, of looking for outside help from people personally disinterested, but very much interested from the standpoint of what is best for the state. The history of the last twenty-five years clearly indicates that the state has received at least as much help from disinterested citizens with no ax of their own to grind as she has from her public officials.

While I was president of the Board of Aldermen I discovered that there was a room in the City Hall in New York set aside for the use of the governor under an old-time provision of the charter. Right after my first election, I let it be known that I would use it as a New York office in order to give the people of the city an opportunity to talk with the governor. I undertook the same action at the mayor's office in Syracuse for the central part of the state, and in Buffalo for the far-western counties.

There is no doubt in my mind that I meant well, but the experiment was far from successful, because I found all kinds of people with all kinds of queer notions about things anxious to come and talk to me. It would have been bearable if the pressure had not been so strong to secure my attention for every kind of detail. I was entirely willing to meet the mother whose boy was in prison and to talk to her about him, because I felt that she, at least, ought to be given an opportunity to talk to the governor herself. I had always discouraged the idea of retaining attorneys to plead for pardons or commutations of sentences. I had a feeling that it was not strictly legal work.

Two employees of the Street Cleaning Department were overheard in conversation about that time, in a café in the lower end of New York City. Frank asked Jack where he had been that night, and he answered, "Down to the clubhouse to see the alderman. I'm dissatisfied with the stable I'm driving from and I want to be transferred."

Whereupon Frank said, "Never mind the alderman. Wait until Saturday and go down and see the governor."

Some people, apparently intelligent, had an idea that the governor could straighten out all court decisions not to their liking. Several women called upon me to increase the allowances the court had given them out of the husband's weekly salaries after they had separated. I need scarcely tell that a small army of men came to see me volunteering their services to the state in any position to which I could see my way fit to appoint them at salaries anywhere from two thousand dollars a year up.

Finally I was compelled to abandon these public receptions. Not that I did not think they were good, but I found that no man could stand up under the physical strain of them.

Curiously enough, it was at one of these sessions in

the City Hall that I met Colonel Frederick Stuart Greene. I had heard about him and his service to the country and his ability as an engineer in road construction. I asked him to meet me in the City Hall, and he appeared in full army uniform, having not yet been mustered out since the war. It was in that room I offered him the superintendency of the State Highways Department.

Every conscientious official who has appointing power is considerably concerned to secure people of caliber, standing, character and general fitness. Immediately after my first election, Judge Elkus, advising with me one day, cautioned care in the selection of my official cabinet. Whereupon I said to the judge, "All right. I am right-minded about it. I appreciate the importance of it. I am going to need help." I thereupon asked the judge what position he would accept and he promptly declared that his business was such that it was impossible for him to give attention to any public business at that time. I did persuade him to become president of the Reconstruction Commission, and he gave it time, money, and leadership.

A short time later, Supreme Court Judge D-Cady Herrick, of Albany, came to me with the same advice. I asked him to accept appointment in my cabinet and he assured me that his law business was such that it would be impossible for him to give his attention to any public business at that time.

Mr. George Foster Peabody, of Saratoga Springs, volunteered the same advice. I asked him to help me by naming his own place. He said he was sorry, but he had been made a state director in the Federal Reserve Bank and had promised President Wilson to remain there for several years, which, of course, made it impossible to accept any other political appointment. There were other similar instances.

In spite of these difficulties, it has been a source of pride to me that I secured for the state the best people who were available, considering the character of the work to be performed, the salary paid, the inconvenience of spending so much time in Albany, and the difficulties people expect to encounter in meeting the political problems which are bound to arise.

So embedded in the mind of the average man is the belief that politics is the only control over state appointments that the first thing Colonel Greene said to me when I offered him the Superintendency of Highways was that he did not know anything about politics, and I promptly said to him, "That's one of the reasons I want to appoint you. We have had a good many political superintendents of highways and now we want one who knows how to build roads. Probably the less he knows about politics the better it will be for the state."

I appointed the present Comptroller of New York, Charles W. Berry, adjutant general of the state. He had had twenty-five years experience in the Guard and at a late age in life went across with the 27th Division to France. When he appeared before the Senate Finance Committee to explain the needs of the Guard for the next fiscal year, Senator Sage, Republican Chairman of that committee, said to me, "Governor, where did you find General Berry?" I told him that I had found him in Brooklyn and asked the reason for the question. He replied, "I have been Chairman of the Senate Finance Committee for a good many years. General Berry is the first Adjutant General in all my time who is able to give a clear cut, clean and intelligent explanation of the needs of the National Guard."

In my early experiences I found many men appointed to public office relying entirely upon the chief clerk of a department or a deputy of long standing to do the work, with the department head acting as a sort of figurehead. I determined, at the beginning of my governorship, to hold the head of the department directly responsible for its operations. In order to do that it was necessary to find men trained either in professions suitable to the department or in business.

From the day I entered the governorship until I left it I was always impressed with the fact that the greatest contribution that a man can make to his own success in high elective office is to surround himself with men who understand their business, have intelligence and are interested in the subject but personally disinterested. Instead of trying to fit men into jobs I tried to find the man that fitted the job and taking into consideration natural human frailty I made as good a job of it as anyone should have reason to expect.

During 1919, as a natural outgrowth of the unrest throughout the country generally, there was much trouble in industry because of strikes. There was the strike for higher wages on the Brooklyn-Manhattan transit lines. There was a serious strike in the United States Steel Company at the Lackawanna Works. The hatters in the city of Beacon called a strike and there was a prolonged strike at the Rome Brass and Copper Company at Rome in Oneida County. The strike on the railroads in Brooklyn settled itself and I assisted as far as I was able in the settlement of the Lackawanna Steel strike.

The attorney for the Rome Brass and Copper Company was a former member of the legislature and he asked me to intervene in the disturbance there by ordering the state police into the city of Rome. I told him I was quite ready to do so for the preservation of law and order, but that I believed that the officials of the company in Rome should first be willing to sit around the table with a representative of the Department of Labor and talk terms of settlement. After communicating with his firm, he conveyed to me the information that they would.

Then I designated Miss Frances Perkins, whom I had appointed a member of the State Industrial Commission, as my representative. The heads of the business were shocked to find that I had selected a woman to negotiate a treaty of peace between the workers and their employers. They seemed to imply by their attitude the belief that any such undertaking was entirely outside the province of a woman. Afterward the attorney told me frankly that they wondered what was the matter with me that I would make any such suggestion; but after Frances Perkins had visited the city of Rome and called the warring sections into conference, one of the leading officials of the Rome Brass and Copper Company said to the attorney, "Do us a favor and ask the Governor where he found that woman."

The Beacon hat strike I settled myself in the Executive Chamber. Every strike lingers on some final point of contention. This strike, simple as it may appear, but nevertheless sufficient to paralyze the industry and stifle the business of that city, hinged upon the demand of the employers that apology be made to an individual woman worker who had been insulted on the streets of the city of Beacon by the men strikers who had gone out because of a series of grievances. After hours of conference and deliberation I succeeded in securing from the workers the apology exacted by the employers, and the industry of Beacon started up overnight and progressed without further interruption.

After a conference in Albany of employers, workers and representatives of the public from all parts of the state, I appointed a Labor Board representative of the three viewpoints. They enlisted other citizens from time to time who acted as mediators between strikers and employers. The Labor Board was particularly helpful in the Buffalo street-railway strike.

In less than a week after my inauguration a milk famine threatened New York because of a quarrel between the distributors and the producers of milk. I rode down from Albany to New York City, met representatives of the contending forces at the Biltmore Hotel and adjusted their differences so that the flow of milk so necessary to the life of New York was resumed immediately after the conference. Later the milk-wagon drivers threatened to strike. The decision was to be made on a Sunday. I was visiting my mother in Brooklyn that day and was out of reach for several hours. When word finally came to me that mothers and babies might have no milk on Monday morning, it was late and I had, at most, an hour to reach the meeting place at Manhattan Casino, far uptown in Manhattan, and make my plea to the men. I left my dinner on the table, rushed to the meeting and found a sullen group, held in leash only by the promise that I would speak to them. I came upon the stage, made an appeal in the name of human needs, and in a few minutes they were cheering and the strike danger was over.

When labor troubles were at their height, the civilized world had been treated to such an exhibition of military force and power that I determined to exhaust every bit of energy and ingenuity that could be mustered before there would be resort to force. For that reason, during the troublesome times of 1919 and 1920, I resisted every call for the use of the militia in a strike. I sent the state police into cities only when the local authorities certified that they were unable to cope with the disturbances. Whenever I sent the police, it was with the stern command that they were there only to preserve peace and to protect life and property, but never to show partisanship to any of the contending factions. They were only used twice for such a purpose.

During my incumbency of the office of sheriff, the state police were established by statute. Years ago an attempt had been made to have state policing of all cities under a bill introduced by Senator Raines. It gave rise to such widespread dissatisfaction in the various localities of the state, which suspected that the state police would usurp local functions, that it was abandoned.

I did not understand thoroughly the purpose or make-up of the state police and I regarded it as an attempt in a small way to resurrect the theory of centralized state control of all police functions, so I recommended in my first message to the legislature that the state police be abolished and the responsibility for carrying out their functions be placed on local authority.

Later I made a study of the state police under the then superintendent, Colonel George L. Chandler. When I saw for myself the effective work they were doing, I frankly and publicly acknowledged my error, and admitted the usefulness of the state police. Instead of abolishing them, I recommended that their forces be augmented.

Colonel Chandler had been appointed by Governor Whitman and remained during my first administration. I became personally attached to him because of his efficiency, honesty and ability. It was in 1923 after I returned to Albany for my second administration that he imparted to me his desire to resign in order to return to the practice

THE FAMILY GROUP IN 1917

The children standing are Emily, Alfred Jr., and Catherine;
seated are Arthur and Walter.

ALFRED E. SMITH IN THE MIDDLE YEARS
A favorite State campaign portrait.

of medicine. I was in a quandary as to whom I could appoint to succeed him who would maintain the high standard he had set. Needless to say I had thousands of applicants. I asked him to name his own successor from among the men of the department because I was convinced that he was the best judge of which of his lieutenants was best able to carry on his work. He suggested to me the name of John A. Warner, who was then captain of the troops lodged at the White Plains barracks.

Upon Colonel Chandler's recommendation and without even having seen Captain Warner, I appointed him and was introduced to him after he had been sworn in as chief of the state police.

I little dreamed the morning I met him that he would afterwards be a member of my family by marriage to my daughter Emily in June, 1926. Towards the latter part of 1925 and the early part of 1926 I realized that the chief of the state police was making quite a number of visits to the Executive Mansion. In the rush of business incident to the many duties placed upon me, I was probably the last one in the official family to discover a romance between the government and the household of the governor.

One of the strange chapters of the history of our state, when it is impartially written, will be the incomprehensible attitude of the Republican legislative leaders toward me during all my administrations as governor. They were all personal friends of mine. There was between myself and them an intimate and real friendship. They would exchange cigars and pleasantries with me at any time or place. They dined with me at the Executive Mansion. They met me in New York City. They visited the Executive Chamber and were as cordial in their greetings to me as I was in my reception of them. Yet throughout the whole period there seemed to be a feeling on their part that they must play what they evidently believed to be good politics, and try to make sure that nothing of a constructive nature was accomplished while I was governor.

It is the nature of politics that when a particular political party has a long lease of power, whether it be over the whole state or in any of its civil divisions, there grows up among its leaders a notion that they own the state or the civil division that they have controlled for years. The deliberate intention of the people, as expressed at the ballot boxes, when it goes against them is interpreted by them to be merely a temporary set-back or, as some of the most reactionary of them have expressed it, "a mistake."

The attitude of the Republican leaders toward me, although most friendly in our personal relations, was that my election as governor was some kind of an accident and that after two years I would never be heard of again. Therefore, it seemed to them, it was not necessary for them to do anything I recommended.

This was certainly the attitude of the legislative leaders toward me in my first term. Common sense, good judgment and any knowledge at all of the elementary principles of good politics would have suggested to them that they clean up early in my term those matters which had public appeal, so as to leave me nothing to campaign for.

Instead of that, they displayed an uncompromising opposition throughout the eight years of my several terms, only to be compelled again and again to accept as a matter of party expediency all the proposals for the betterment of the government that originated either in the Constitutional Convention of 1915, or in the report of the Reconstruction Commission, or in definite suggestions made by myself from time to time in messages to the legislature.

In the fall of 1918 the proposed Eighteenth Amendment was delivered to the secretary of state of New York and was pending for action by the legislature. The Republican conference, held at Saratoga Springs for the purpose of designating candidates and formulating a platform and declaration of political faith for the state campaign that year, had side-stepped and ducked the whole question of the party's attitude toward ratification. The Democratic party was honest about it and declared in its platform in favor of a state referendum submitting the question to the voters of the state.

In 1905 and through the years until prohibition ratification became imminent, the question of the regulation of the sale of liquor was always a live issue in New York State. I was very caustically criticized in the recent presidential campaign for my attitude on that question. It is readily explained by the fact that the whole liquor question during all these years was an issue between city and country. Standing side by side with me in opposition to some of the drastic excise bills coming from the country sections of the state were some of the leading members of the Republican party who came from the cities. I have no recollection that Governor Hughes, himself one-time presidential candidate of the Republican party, ever made any recommendation to the legislature in regard to liquor legislation.

The strange part about the whole thing is that no mention of prohibition was ever made in the Constitutional Convention—not a word, not even a whisper.

When both houses convened for the session of 1919, the prohibition forces of the state as represented by the Anti-Saloon League and its allied organizations began a drive on the Republican party to force ratification. They met with no trouble whatever in the assembly, because that body contains so many members from the small, strictly rural communities of the state; but when they reached the senate, the situation was quite different and the required number of votes for ratification by the upper house was lacking.

Republican Senator Henry M. Sage, of Albany County, was opposed to ratification, on the ground that it was for each individual legislator to choose for himself between his conscience and his allegiance to the people whom he represented. The majority leader of the senate, Henry M. Walters, of Syracuse, represented a wet constituency and was personally unalterably opposed to ratification. Senator Thompson, of Niagara County, a radical dry, succeeded in inducing his colleagues to caucus, although ratification was in no sense a party measure or even a party pledge. Senator Sage refused to go into the caucus for the reasons I have just mentioned. Senator Walters, however, being the majority leader, entered the caucus, and by the use of the party whip and as a result of pressure by the Anti-Saloon League and its allied organizations, the majority in the senate was whipped into line for ratification in spite of the expressed desires of some of their constituents who opposed it.

It was freely rumored in Albany that the political leaders in the counties suggested ratification upon the theory that the rural sections of the state containing the dry fanatics were the backbone of the Republican organization vote for years and that to abandon them might bring about complete destruction of the party throughout the state.

I am reasonably certain that had there been a referendum to the voters of New York State at that time, an overpowering majority would have voted against ratification. In 1926 a referendum as to what should be the attitude of the state regarding modification of the Volstead Act, was carried by more than a million majority for the wet side of the argument.

It was amusing to find that the identical legislature of 1919 which ratified the Prohibition Amendment also passed a bill attempting to legalize the manufacture, sale and distribution of light wines and beer of an alcoholic content of two and three-quarters per cent under severe state regulation, only to have such an amendment declared in violation to the Constitution of the United States by the Supreme Court. The same leadership which passed the so-called light wine and beer bill was the leadership which had forced through the ratification of the Eighteenth Amendment by party caucus.

Due in large part to the effects of the war upon the government the affairs of the state were in a chaotic condition. I was inaugurated only seven weeks after the signing of the Armistice. As might have been expected, the regular and orderly procedure of the state's business had been interrupted by the necessary war work and much routine work had been neglected. The state's plant was run down. Public construction of all kinds had ceased. War conditions and the high price of labor had bankrupted the contractors who had undertaken state work. The return of the state troops and their readjustment to a peacetime basis was causing much concern. War had shown neglect and carelessness in dealing with public health. The complicated problems of taxation needed special attention. There was an acute housing situation due to a let-down in building during the war period. Employment had to be found at home, in a decreasing market, for the four-hundred-odd thousand men and women who had gone to the war from New York State, and the rise in the cost of living presented another pressing difficulty.

With a feeling of personal responsibility that I had to do all I could to find a solution for these problems, I realized how impossible it would be to do it with the limited means at my disposal which could be found in the

186

regular departments of the government, let alone by myself. Therefore I appointed a body of representative men and women who had given freely of their time, energy, and ability toward the success of the war, and I asked them to aid me and form the Reconstruction Commission so that they might help the state to work out the post-war problems. Without regard to politics, I appointed as representative a commission as I could find in the state of New York. Labor, capital, agriculture, commerce, banking, insurance, social work, manufacturing, science, law, business, large and small, every known group was represented in the make-up of the commission. Abram I. Elkus was elected chairman and Mrs. Belle L. Moskowitz was elected secretary.

I asked the legislature to transfer an appropriation of seventy-five thousand dollars left over from some of the state's special funds for war activities to the financing of the Reconstruction Commission. This was denied by the Republican leaders of the legislature and in a spirit of civic duty the commission financed itself.

To the Reconstruction Commission I recommended the study of practically every problem of the after-war period caused by the economic and political changes taking place at that time. The achievements of my first term can best be told by dealing with these recommendations.

When the commission held its organization meeting on the evening of January 25, 1919, I addressed it at the City Hall in New York City. I told the members that while I would have special sympathy for their activities for the welfare of the state, it was necessary to emphasize that the commission ought to make a study of financial problems. The state had lost some twenty-six million dollars in revenue by the enactment of the Prohibition Amendment. It would be necessary to find some source of revenue to replace the excise tax or to develop a program of retrenchment which would make it possible to administer the state in such manner that none of its functions need suffer in spite of the curtailment of revenues. This was in addition to their main purpose of broadening the humanitarian activities of the state and pressing forward its public works.

I particularly committed to the Reconstruction Commission for solution the shortage of housing for the thousands of people cramped in small quarters because of the cessation of building during the period of the war.

Since the Republican leaders regarded me as an accidental governor and were satisfied that I would only be around for a few months, and while governors come and go, legislative leaders apparently seem to go on forever, they were entirely content to bide their time and wait for me to return to New York City, when they might go on with the business of the state to suit themselves. The year 1920 was a presidential year. The Republican machine felt sure of its ground. It had planted seeds of dissatisfaction throughout the United States and was reasonably certain of victory in November.

As a consequence, the legislature did not take the work

of the Reconstruction Commission very seriously. Not only did it refuse to make any appropriation for the commission, although funds were available, but it was referred to on the floor of the senate in debate as a "rump legislature" and an attempt to duplicate the lawmaking functions of that body.

The full and complete report of the Reconstruction Commission was presented to the 1920 legislature. Its major recommendations covered a permanent policy for unemployment which embraced the enlargement and strengthening of the state system of employment agencies and a more careful direction of employment; a program of public improvements to be so planned as to be undertaken or progressed whenever business depression and unemployment threatened. To further this policy the commission through its committee on business readjustment, made a study of public improvements in progress, not started, and contemplated, so as to be able to set up reserves of public improvements.

Through its committee on education the commission reported that compulsory military training of a technical character for boys of sixteen, seventeen and eighteen years of age was inadvisable. The committee recommended in place of military training the extension of health instruction and all-round physical development, and that generous appropriations be made for these purposes. The same committee recommended the establishment of compulsory continuation schools up to the eighteenth year, for boys and girls who are at work, and that a number of periods be set aside each week in such schools for physical training. They also recommended the extension of the Americanization program of the State Department of Education, recommending even some form of compulsion for adults to acquire a knowledge of the English language.

Together with a report on public health, food production and distribution, the commission made recommendations on many other subjects, including housing, which I have dealt with elsewhere.

All these reports, together with the important one on the reorganization of the State Government, laid down a program which for the ten years following was the background of political platforms, the program of civic organizations and the basis of much remedial legislation. The battle for the reorganization of the state government continued until just before I went out of office for the last time.

When the amendments for the reorganization for the government were introduced, I began an active campaign for them throughout the state. At a dinner given by the City Club of New York, former Governor Hughes and I both spoke in favor of them. I had addressed many Chambers of Commerce, the Merchants' Association of New York, and Boards of Trade and business organizations generally in all the large cities in the state. The reforms appealed to business men, and public opinion was sufficiently aroused to compel the legislature to accept the amendments even against the advice of their own leaders.

John Lord O'Brian and Martin Saxe were other Republicans who spoke from the same platform with me in support of the plan. The press favored it and under the pressure of strong public opinion the legislature of 1920 finally adopted the resolution to amend the constitution providing for the reorganization of the government, although the legislative leaders in the session at first declined to give it any consideration and at least two of them made public speeches against it. They refused to consider the executive budget or the four-year term for the governor which are really part of the complete plan.

Just after the close of the 1919 session the Nineteenth Amendment to the Federal Constitution enfranchising women was submitted to the state for ratification. New York having enfranchised women by amendment to her own constitution in 1917, I felt that the attitude of the state had been expressed by the result of that referendum. Therefore I was ready to submit the amendment for ratification by the legislature without further action by the people. I deemed the matter of sufficient importance to the other states of the union to call the legislature into extraordinary session at once and submit to them a request for the ratification of the Nineteenth Amendment.

Suffrage once a reality, some of the party leaders believed in it. Some did not. Some were very hesitant about it. Others maintained their old reactionary attitude toward it. Commissioner Murphy, then leader of Tammany Hall, advised equal representation of men and women on the county committees in New York City and insisted on equal representation in the executive committee of Tammany Hall. He was not concerned as to how this was to be accomplished, so long as each individual leader was willing to accept responsibility for the consequences. This worked out well, on the whole. Some of the Democratic women who had been active suffrage leaders now became party leaders, and where there were no active suffragists in a district, the leader was always sure to find someone who had the necessary qualifications.

All during my public life I recognized the value of the services of women. When I was sheriff and before women were entitled to vote, I appointed a woman as my secretary, and when I was elected president of the Board of Aldermen I reappointed her to the same position. While I was governor I appointed women where, in my opinion, they were as well, if not, as in some cases, better qualified than men. I appointed a woman to membership in the State Civil Service Commission and afterward elevated her to the chairmanship. I appointed a woman to the Industrial Commission and another to the State Hospital Commission.

Were I to be asked whether or not, in my opinion, equal suffrage for men and women was a step forward or a step backward, I would feel compelled to say that I believe it to have been a step forward. Women are just as much interested in the government of the country and the state as men are, and are just as intelligent. I uniformly favored all measures that gave women an equal voice in party affairs with that of men. Nevertheless, I do not believe that the principle of equality is carried out by doubling the party representation simply to permit women to participate in party affairs. I believe that, wherever the contestants for a party position are a man and a woman and the woman happens to be better qualified she should be elected.

Women interested in politics were among the strongest supporters of all reforms in government which I advocated, particularly those that were touched by the human appeal. As a new force in our public life, they had added strength because they were devoid of any element of selfishness. It was easy to discriminate between the unselfish woman and the practical lobbyist.

Comparatively few people show any lively or active interest in any variety of subjects. That is to say, the average farmer as an individual takes very little interest in anything that is going on in relation to government and relies for his information about public affairs entirely upon the officers of the agricultural societies. I cannot escape the conclusion that these are many times actuated by political motives. This is true of all other groups, and especially true of women. A small committee of women goes to Albany year after year with the slogan: "Equal opportunity for women." The average woman does not know what that means. I have been an advocate all along of equal opportunity before the law, but I am unable to subscribe to the theory of absolute equality between men and women. There are some positions in the service of the state which women are better equipped to handle than men, and some other positions that men are better equipped to handle than women.

I remember that after a public hearing along about 1923, I suggested certain amendments to the civil-service rules and regulations establishing the right of women to participate in civil-service examinations for every position that a woman could hold. The enthusiastic women advocates of equal opportunity, lacking understanding of the different kinds of work and service to be rendered for the state, sought to have women made eligible for all positions. I finally ironed the matter out and satisfied all concerned when I explained to them, as an instance, the impossibility of allowing a woman to take an examination for prison guard, and, on the other hand, the impossibility of allowing a man to take an examination for matron in a training school for girls. Aside from where the work was of a special nature or of a character absolutely requiring sex discrimination, I applied the principle of equal opportunity in all examinations for positions in civil service.

There is no question in my mind that women should be on an absolute equality with men as to the custody of children by law or the right of domicile by law. I have even gone so far as to say that women should be permitted to serve on juries if they desired to do so, but I did oppose and I am still opposed to compulsory jury service for women. They are excluded in New York State today by a law that requires the juror to be a male citizen. They are, therefore, disqualified. This puts them in the same class with idiots, insane people, aliens, illiterates and citizens not worth two hundred and fifty dollars in real or personal property. I have always expressed myself as being entirely willing to lift them from that class, but I have insisted that they be given the privilege of immunity extended to other groups of citizens—for instance, doctors, clergymen, lawyers, even undertakers—who, because of their callings in life, are entitled to exemption if they desire to claim it.

Women have always been particularly interested in legislation affecting social welfare and have frequently conducted intelligent and able campaigns to influence public opinion which were of great use to me in securing legislative action while I was governor. They certainly were of great assistance in obtaining the reorganization amendments, the child-welfare laws, the extension of maternity and infancy care, and many other public health and educational measures.

Six months after my inauguration, and for no reason that I was ever able to understand, the Hearst newspapers in New York City launched a violent attack upon me, endeavoring to put into the minds of gullible people the thought that I was in some way responsible for an extraordinary rise which had taken place in the price of milk. The most dastardly and infamous cartoons were widely circulated through the city, depicting me as the friend of the milk trust, willing to starve helpless women and children for the extra pennies wrung from the poor. In the early part of this attack I paid little or no attention to it, in the belief that it was so stupid and silly that nobody else would pay any attention to it.

Strange, though, if you keep saying a thing, keep pounding long enough at it, some people will believe it. I discovered in the late summer of 1919 that this foolish attack was making some impression on the minds of people who, from the very nature of things, would naturally be friendly to me. I called it to the attention of a number of my friends and they formed a citizens' committee headed by the late Col. Jefferson de Mont Thompson and offered me the opportunity to challenge Mr. Hearst, the owner of the newspapers, to come before the public and make good the statements he made about me. A public meeting was organized and held at Carnegie Hall, October 9, 1919.

Of course I never expected Mr. Hearst to come, and neither did anybody else who knew anything about his methods. On that memorable night I cleared up in the minds of the people of New York City and the rest of the country any misgivings they might have that these attacks might be true, and I taught Mr. Hearst and his cohorts a lesson. It was the first chime in the death knell of Hearst's political power in the eastern part of this country.

Our first Christmas in the Executive Mansion was in 1919. The large hall and the spacious reception room and grounds around the mansion presented a sharp contrast to the small, cramped apartment on Oliver Street, and Santa Claus had plenty of room for his operations. His endeavors to make the Smith children happy over

196

Arthur, Alfred Jr., Alfred, and Walter.

With adoring Scouts at Bear Mountain, New York.

JUST BOYS

A STATE CAMPAIGN CONFERENCE IN 1920

Norman E. Mack, Governor Smith, H. C. Pell, and Franklin D. Roosevelt.

Christmas-time were supplemented by admiring friends all over the state to so great an extent that, when the folding doors of the reception room were thrown open to the children, on Christmas morning before church, it resembled the toy department of one of the big department stores. Santa Claus, in his generosity to the family, did not overlook Cæsar, the Great Dane. He received a new shining brass collar that, when hanging on the Christmas tree, looked as though it could surround the smokestack of the *Leviathan*.

The local elections in New York City in the fall of 1919 disclosed a queer phenomenon in local politics. The Republican National Committee had begun to sow the seeds of hatred against the Democratic party within the ranks of her own people by an insidious well-planned propaganda looking to influence the election of 1920. Out of power in Washington for eight years, the Republican machine began to build its political fences for 1920 ahead of time.

The peace conference was going on in 1919 and the agitators were urging Murphy in Tammany Hall to use Democratic influence in Congress to force President Wilson to recognize the republic of Ireland. The German organizations wanted to do away with some of the harsh conditions of the Versailles Treaty and the Italians wanted the local Democrats to do something about the final disposition of Fiume on the Adriatic Sea.

Locally the 1919 campaign was a forerunner of 1920, and the regular Democratic organization was defeated in

197

New York County, the seat of its great power in the city and state. What might properly be called a Republican appeal to passion and prejudice lined up large numbers of people, friendly before that time, against Tammany Hall and the Democratic party.

The strangest thing of all about the 1919 election was that while on the surface the antagonism of the voters seemed to be directed toward Tammany Hall, the son-in-law of the leader, former State Senator James Foley, running for surrogate, and one of its most active members, was the only man elected on the ticket. Personally I always believed that to be due to strong Republican support of Surrogate Foley because of his outstanding brilliant record as a legislator in the assembly and in the senate. But the seed of racial antagonism was sown and the injection of foreign issues into the local situation had been begun, and 1920 saw their full fruition.

CHAPTER XII

Safeguarding Political and Personal Rights

ENCOURAGED by partial victory in the city of New York in the election of 1919, the new session of the legislature in 1920 came in full of hope for party success and thoroughly wedded to the reactionary opinions characterizing the session of 1919.

At this point I was halfway through my first administration and I had thoroughly convinced the legislative leaders of my intention to attempt the accomplishment of something of material and lasting benefit to the people of the state. With a national and a state campaign in view in 1920, they bent all their political energy toward an effort to frustrate it. They felt that I was perhaps gradually making an impression upon the voters of the state, and in the early part of the session of 1920, in order to smoke-screen the whole situation, a great alarm was set up as to the future security of the state and the nation because of what they called the activities of the Reds.

Five members of the Socialist party had been elected to the assembly in the fall of 1919, and suddenly, without warning, the assembly of 1920 refused to seat them, on the constitutional ground that the legislature shall be the judge of its own membership. That was undoubtedly put into the constitution for the purpose of permitting the legislature to deal with an elected member who may have done something reprehensible between the time of his election and the time of the convening of the legislature, or to deal with a member whose election to office had been proved to be fraudulent. It was never intended to give authority to exclude men duly and properly elected, because of disagreement with their political views.

No theory I can think of could be further from the views of Jefferson, who counseled, in the Declaration of Independence, that when the American people were dissatisfied with their form of government they could tear it down and put up the kind they wanted. That has been regarded throughout the years of our national history as being sound doctrine, provided the change is not attempted by force of arms.

This agitation against the Socialist members and what was called the activity of the Reds was really part of a false atmosphere created by the appointment, in 1919, of a joint legislative committee which came to be known as the Lusk Committee, named after Clayton R. Lusk of Cortland County, its chairman. When it was appointed its purpose, allegedly, was to inquire into the activities of what were designated as "enemies of the government," because they entertained radical opinions on the administration of the affairs of the state and nation. There never was any doubt in my mind that the decision to expel the Socialist members from the assembly was preconceived, and I regarded the trial during which the Republican leaders sought to establish the unfitness of these members as a mere formality intended to lend color and give virtue to the undemocratic and un-American performance of their expulsion from the body.

The day after the Socialists were expelled and after a conference with the leaders of my party, I decided to issue a statement. It was a busy Saturday, and it was not until late in the afternoon that I was able to meet with the Democratic leaders of the legislature. It is quite true that there was some objection on their part to opposing the action of the Republican group. But after presenting my point of view to them they were entirely in accord with the action which I took.

There was an Amen Corner dinner that evening. The Amen Corner was an organization of newspapermen and Republican politicians. It was the custom for everybody in public life to attend this dinner. Tad Sweet, the Speaker of the assembly, was there. I took from my pocket a copy of the statement which I had already handed to the newspapermen, showed it to him, and said, "This is what I have just told the newspapermen. It is the position which my party and I intend to maintain."

The statement read:

"Although I am unalterably opposed to the fundamental principles of the Socialist party, it is inconceivable that a minority party, duly constituted and legally organized, should be deprived of its right to expression so long as it has honestly, by lawful methods of education and propaganda, succeeded in securing representation, unless the chosen representatives are unfit as individuals.

"It is true that the assembly has arbitrary power to determine the qualifications of its members, but where arbitrary power exists it should be exercised with care and discretion, because from it there is no appeal.

"If the majority party at present in control of the assembly possesses information that leads them to believe that these men are hostile to our form of government and would overthrow it by processes subversive of law and order, these charges in due form should have been presented to the legislature and these men tried by orderly processes. Meanwhile, presumably innocent until proved guilty, they should have been allowed to retain their seats.

"Our faith in American democracy is confirmed not only by its results but by its methods and organs of free expression. They are the safeguards against revolution. To discard the method of representative government leads to misdeeds of the very extremists we denounce and serves to increase the number of enemies of orderly, free government."

Sweet protested that I was unfair in not having given him notice that that would be my point of view; to which I replied, "You gave me no notice of what you were going to do or that you were going to expel these men, and I therefore feel no responsibility to have notified you that I am going to oppose such action."

There followed then, for several months after the legislature convened, a trial of these five Socialists. The Bar Association of New York appointed Mr. Charles Evans Hughes, Morgan J. O'Brien, Louis Marshall, Joseph M. Proskauer, and Ogden L. Mills to defend them. Morris Hillquit was the attorney representing the expelled Socialists.

Coincident with the expulsion of the Socialists from the assembly the Lusk Committee reported. Among its recommendations was an amendment to the law to require teachers in our public schools to submit to a loyalty test in order that the educational authorities might determine whether or not they were right-minded toward our country. I never thought it possible, reasonable or sensible.

Private schools were also to be licensed after submitting to the Board of Regents their curriculum of study. This bill was aimed at schools where liberal or radical theories were taught, and its implications could hardly have been comprehended by the legislature or they would never have considerd, much less passed it.

They even went so far as to pass a bill which, if it had been enacted into law, would have given to the Appellate Division of the Supreme Court in the Third Department (Albany and vicinity) the right to strike any party column from the ballot if, in the judgment of that court, any part of the platform of that party smacked of sedition or, in the opinion of the court, was not in harmony or in keeping with the court's opinion of the Constitution and the principles upon which the country was founded.

There was tremendous public interest in these bills when they were submitted by the Lusk Committee. An enormous volume of correspondence reached my desk daily. Important public men and women in every party of the state urged me to veto the bills. Prof. Felix Adler, who was a member of the Reconstruction Commission, Raymond V. Ingersoll, and the many civic organizations, wrote me stating their reasons. On the other hand, there was a prejudiced group, hysterical and interested in the control of liberal thought, who urged me to approve the bills.

I finally vetoed all of these bills. In part I said of the one which would require a loyalty test of teachers:

"This bill must be judged by what can be done under its provisions. It permits one man to place upon any teacher the stigma of disloyalty, and this even without hearing or trial. No man is so omniscient or wise as to have intrusted to him such arbitrary and complete power not only to condemn any individual teacher but to decree what belief or opinion is opposed to what he deems to be the institutions of the country.

"The bill unjustly discriminates against teachers as a class. It deprives teachers of their right to freedom of thought, it limits the teaching staff of the public schools to those only who lack the courage or the mind to exercise their legal right to just criticism of existing institutions. The bill confers upon the Commissioner of Education a power of interference with freedom of opinion which strikes at the foundations of democratic education."

Of the bill to license schools I said:

"The mere statement of the provisions of this bill is sufficient to demonstrate that in details it is wholly impossible of just enforcement. I prefer, however, to rest my disapproval of it not solely nor chiefly on that ground, but on the broader ground that in fundamental principle the bill is vicious. Its avowed purpose is to safeguard the institutions and traditions of the country. In effect, it strikes at the very foundation of one of the most cardinal institutions of our nation—the fundamental right of the people to enjoy full liberty in the domain of idea and speech. To this fundamental right there is and can be under our system of government but one limitation—namely, that the law of the land shall not be transgressed, and there is abundant statute law prohibiting the abuse of free speech. It is unthinkable that in a representative democracy there should be delegated to any body of men the absolute power to prohibit the teaching of any subject of which it may disapprove. . . .

"The clash of conflicting opinions, from which progress arises more than from any other source, would be abolished by law; tolerance and intellectual freedom destroyed, and an intellectual autocracy imposed upon the people. . . . The safety of this government and its institutions rests upon the reasoned and devoted loyalty of its people. It does not need for its defense a system of intellectual tyranny which, in the endeavor to choke error by force, must of necessity crush truth as well. The profound sanity of the American people has been demonstrated in many a crisis, and I, for one, do not believe that governmental dictation of what may and may not be taught is necessary to achieve a continuance of the patriotism of our citizenship, and its loyal support of the government and its institutions."

Of the bill to permit the court to strike a party column from the ballot I said:

"This bill would place upon one particular appellate division of the Supreme Court of this state, and no other, the duty of deciding upon the validity of the political principles advocated by any party in the state. Its determination would be final and controlling. To its members would be permitted the despotic power to strike from the ballot the candidates of any party. The tests which it would be compelled to apply would, of necessity, be not legal but political tests. The bill would throw a high appellate court into the very midst of political controversy. This alone would require its disapproval, but to this objection must be added an even more vital and far-reaching one.

"The bill would confer upon this small body of men, perhaps

all of one political faith, the absolute power, in effect, to disfranchise hundreds of thousands of voters. . . . . A few judges, elected in one part of the state and assigned to the appellate division of their department, would have the power to keep from the ballot all candidates of whose party principles they disapproved. . . . Law, in a democracy, means the protection of the rights and liberties of the minority. Its rights, when properly exercised, and its liberties, when not abused, should be safeguarded. It is a confession of the weakness of our own faith in the righteousness of our cause, when we attempt to suppress by law those who do not agree with us. I cannot approve a bill which confers upon three judges, learned though they be, but nevertheless human, the power to disfranchise any body of our citizens."

CHAPTER XIII

Conventions, Platforms and Policies

AFTER the session we made preparations to attend the Democratic National Convention. That it was to be held in San Francisco delighted me, because it gave me my first opportunity to visit the Pacific Coast.

The first national convention I ever attended was in St. Louis in 1904, when Alton B. Parker was nominated for President on the Democratic ticket. It was quite an experience. I had never been so far away from home before. Strange to say, I never got into the convention itself, although I was deeply interested in its outcome.

In 1908 I attended the national convention at Denver, at which Bryan was nominated for the third time. In 1912 I attended the memorable convention at Baltimore, where Woodrow Wilson was nominated. Being by that time a leader of the assembly, I was in the inner circles of the party. The New York delegation under the leadership of the then governor, John A. Dix, on the first ballot cast its lot with Judson Harmon of Ohio. Champ Clark, former Speaker of the House of Representatives, was well in the lead and was supposed to have behind him the backing and influence of the Bryan forces. It was the consensus of opinion, however, among the leaders to whom I spoke during the progress of the convention, that Bryan was never really and sincerely in favor of Clark. He was

207

rather seeking to bring about a condition which would make possible his own nomination. Governor Dix asked the New York delegation to give Harmon a complimentary vote. Nobody in Tammany knew anything about Harmon. They merely followed the leadership of the governor of the state. After doing this they turned to Oscar W. Underwood. This caused Bryan to attack the New York delegation and Tammany most bitterly, charging that the Wall Street interests and reactionary elements of the country controlled the delegation. His bitter attack did not help Bryan or Clark with the New York delegation.

During the Baltimore convention it adjourned once on Saturday afternoon until the following Monday morning. Instead of remaining in Baltimore I came on a sleeper to the Pennsylvania Station in New York and went right out on a Long Island train to Far Rockaway, went to church, had a swim, had dinner with Mrs. Smith and the children and jumped back to Baltimore the same night.

I was again in St. Louis in 1916 when Wilson was renominated.

We went to the San Francisco convention in a private car. Mrs. Smith, my daughter Emily and my son Alfred, Mr. and Mrs. Charles F. Murphy, Judge and Mrs. James A. Foley, Gen. Charles W. Berry and William Humphreys, called the Chief, a friend from Albany, made up the party, which assembled at Chicago. The male members had spent the week before at French Lick Springs.

We went over the Overland Limited route. I saw the

Great Salt Lake and the snowsheds of the Sierra Nevadas for the first time. Until the convention closed I had very little opportunity to see anything of the far western country. I stole two hours out of one day to buy a pair of cowboy saddles for the two ponies that were at the Executive Mansion at Albany, the property of my two younger boys, Arthur and Walter.

The convention was very tame and there were few interesting characters in it. The leading personality of the convention was W. Bourke Cockran. To begin with, Cockran's debate with Bryan on the wet and dry plank was the one thing that livened up the convention. Cockran had the best of the argument. He overpowered Bryan both by reason and logic. He was an infinitely better orator than the Boy Orator of the Platte. Of course, Bryan won out as a matter of party expediency and because of the overpowering influence of the South and West on the dry question. All the congressmen and senators from the Democratic states had voted in favor of the Eighteenth Amendment to the Constitution.

Cockran's speech nominating me was in his best vein. He was just tuned up for it. I met him at the St. Francis Hotel the night before and, putting his arm around my shoulders, he pulled me to one side and said, "I am about to achieve the joy of my life. For as long back as I can remember, at national conventions I have been fanning the wind either against somebody or against something. At last I have an opportunity to be for somebody." He took Judge Morgan J. O'Brien into a side room and sat up with him until 3:30 in the morning, rehearsing what he was going to say.

His concluding remark was: "We offer him to you as President of the United States. We will accept no compromise in the convention. If you take him we will give you the state of New York and if you reject him, we will take him back and run him for governor!"

Cockran was at the height of his power, in the eventide of his life. He had been out of Tammany Hall for a long while on account of disagreements with Croker. He had come back under Murphy's leadership and had been elected to Congress. He was rejuvenated and went into the 1920 convention with great spirit, being there to accomplish something and not to oppose something, as he had been doing for so many years. He threw his whole heart into that speech for me and then the band struck up with—thinking they had a Harrigan and Hart melody— "East Side, West Side, all around the town." Since that day I have probably heard "The Sidewalks of New York" one million times, all over the Atlantic seaboard, through the South, the Middle West and in Butte, Montana.

It was not in the cards, of course, that I was to be nominated. I was not in the convention hall during the demonstration which followed Cockran's speech. At least I hid there—I was not actually in sight of the delegations. I was not so well known in 1920 throughout the country. I had accomplished comparatively little in the governor's office that would give me national prominence, and I always believed that most of the credit for the San Francisco demonstration was due to Bourke Cockran for his speech of nomination.

I never spoke to Bryan until 1924. I met him at the dinner held in the Hotel Commodore, given by the city administration to the visiting delegates to the national convention. I had paraded for him in 1896 and 1900, and was at the convention in 1908, when he was nominated, and had cheered for him, but had never met him. He was for years a powerful figure in the national Democratic party.

Bryan was an opportunist. Bryan did the thing that helped Bryan. When he found it convenient for his own purpose to assail Tammany Hall and Wall Street, he did so, but when he was a candidate himself no man ever cultivated the support of Tammany Hall more than he did. When returning from one of the conventions, he met the Tammany Hall delegation en route, and he said, "Great is Tammany and Croker is her prophet." When he was a candidate himself, he not only declared himself in favor of Tammany Hall, but he was for Richard Croker too. If he could not secure the nomination or did not get the support of Tammany in the convention, he immediately linked her up with big business, sordid politics and everything that was mean and rotten.

Bryan was a man who was never for anything new, except to help himself. In not one of his three campaigns for the presidency did he ever speak in favor of woman suffrage or about prohibition. It always seemed to me that

211

Bryan invented issues to get a nomination, but after getting it he never said anything about them.

One of the strangest things about him is that in his earlier years he advocated governmental reforms about which he said nothing when he was a candidate for the presidency. In fact, I have in my possession an old-time campaign badge from Nebraska showing him running at one time on the ticket opposed to prohibition.

The great difficulty with Bryan as a candidate, to my mind, was that he talked over the heads of the people. He referred to himself as the "Great Commoner," as a man of the common people; but his fluent oratory was too much for them and the very people to whom he appealed never definitely understood the major issues for which Bryan fought. I would be willing to venture the suggestion that not one in ten thousand voters, or maybe one in fifty thousand voters in New York understood what he meant by the coinage of silver at the ratio of sixteen to one.

His famous speech in the Chicago convention which won him the nomination in 1896 is a gem of English and oratory but it stops there. It is carefully pasted into my first scrapbook. Bryan claimed that he spoke for the hardy pioneers who "braved the dangers of the wilderness," who "make the desert to blossom as a rose," who "rear their children near to Nature's heart, where they can mingle their voices with the voices of the birds." But I could not find in the speech a specific place where he definitely promised what he was going to do to better their lot in life or where he even outlined what their complaint was. He stated simple and palpable truths. For instance, "Turn down the farmers and grass will grow on the streets of your principal cities." What that refers to would be difficult to tell from his speech.

There was nothing unusual about Bryan's form of political oratory. With the exception of Lincoln, Roosevelt and Wilson, most of our public orators have talked in such general terms that it is quite difficult for the ordinary man, after he leaves a political gathering, to remember for any length of time anything he has heard.

As a boy, I can remember the campaign orators. The Republican orator talked about "the immortal principles of Lincoln," but failed to say what application they had to present needs and necessities. The Democratic orator, like his opponent, talked about "the undying principles of Jefferson," but likewise without any application to present-day problems.

At the close of the 1920 convention we visited Los Angeles. I went out on the steamer to the Catalina Islands, where I had my first swim in the Pacific. While at Los Angeles we visited one of the movie studios. The party was photographed as we proceeded from one building to another. Our pictures and scenes from the different pictures then in process of being made were incorporated into a film and the reel was presented to me. I brought it back East for the amusement of my friends.

William Fox of the Fox Films Company, at Christmas of 1923, presented me with a moving-picture machine and a portable screen, which was in use in the Executive Mansion all the years that I was there. The moving pictures were the delight of the small children in the immediate vicinity of the Executive Mansion. Walter, my youngest son, was president of the Capital Athletic Club, and his club members had choice and preferred seats. The main stairway served as the gallery and was always filled to capacity. When the playmates of the different children assembled, there was a good-sized audience for each production.

We returned to New York over the Santa Fe system, stopping at Denver, Colorado. I made my second trip up Pike's Peak at that time, in an automobile. My first ascent had been in 1908, on the old cog railway that ran up the side of the mountain, when I made my first visit to Colorado.

Those who participated in the national campaign of 1920 will never forget it. Under shrewd and clever leadership the Republican party throughout the country for months before had been sowing the seeds they hoped would ripen into a harvest of votes.

Through their agents and through publications, and particularly through the foreign newspapers, they led the German element to believe that the election of a Republican President would mean the removal of some of the harsh terms of the Versailles treaty. They promised the Italians to give Fiume to the Italian Government. They started a successful agitation among the Irish people to blame President Wilson for not freeing Ireland while he was giving freedom to Jugo-Slavia, Czecho-Slovakia and Poland. They never at any time let the people to whom they appealed know that these were countries which had been under the domination of the fallen enemy. They went so far as to promise that a Republican President would recognize the republic of Ireland.

At the conference of leaders, which took place in Saratoga in 1920, to name the ticket to run in the primary for the governorship of the state, it was not difficult to convince the Democratic leaders to accept practically the entire report of the Reconstruction Commission as part of the party's definite declaration of policy, notwithstanding that the body which originated it was nonpartisan and contained representatives of all parties.

It has been a well-established policy for political parties to present a platform which is made up of the principles and promises of the party, and upon which the candidate bases his appeal for votes. The platform of a political party is really its declaration of fundamental principles and its promise to the voters of what it proposes to do constructively, if given the power to improve the government.

I have always regarded each plank of the Democratic platform as a definite.promise made by the party to the voters, for which the party, as such, assumes responsibility. Practically all the constructive reforms under my administration were parts of the Democratic platform or of the Democratic promises in the event of success at the polls. All the Democratic legislative leaders and, for that matter, all the Democratic members of both houses supported me vigorously in obedience to the platform declarations of the Democratic party.

It is a popular impression that platforms are hurriedly drafted during the excitement and tumult of a convention. So far as the Democratic party is concerned, that is not the fact. The important constructive planks and the definite promises are well studied out in advance. In 1922 in company with a number of advisers, I prepared practically the entire Democratic platform during the month of August. I followed the platform planks in the preparation of my messages to the legislature.

It is difficult to deny that the platform of the successful party represents the decision of the people themselves upon these questions. Of course, there are many voters who pay no attention to the platforms. They vote either the Democratic ticket or the Republican ticket year in and year out because they are convinced of the ultimate rectitude of the party to which they belong. On the other hand, a large number of independent voters study the party platforms and naturally expect, in the event of success, that the platform will be lived up to just as accurately as a man would live up to his promise.

In a big state like New York it is almost impossible to satisfy all groups and all sections of the state, and that makes platform drafting a difficult undertaking. If you apply the principle of what does the most good for the greatest number, which is a thoroughly Democratic precept, the road to successful platform drafting is made easier.

One fair criticism can usually be made of both party platforms. They contain too much destructive criticism and too little of definite promise. Sometimes a comparison of the party platforms will show that whole sections have been lifted from the year before and the same general promises made. The Republican party for years has used the stock phrase which runs as follows: "The Republican party has ever been solicitous of the welfare of working men, women and children." Once when I showed that plank to a prominent Republican legislator opposing some of the factory bills, he smiled and remarked to me, "Well, the working man had his day last November. We were all shaking hands with him and saying nice things about him. What do you want—have him on top all the time? Give somebody else a chance."

It is a matter of fact that definite promises in the platforms of both political parties have been deliberately ignored or compromised with. The ultimate effect of that attitude on the part of the parties, plus the very apparent neglect of so many of our voters to pay any attention to party platforms, will lead us in time to a contest between individuals rather than between parties, if, in fact, we have not already arrived at that. If party government is to be successful, the rank and file of the people themselves have the responsibility of paying some personal attention to party promises, the party declaration of political principles, and the party's reputation for making good its promises.

The party is essential to our form of government. Not all the men nominated have previous political records that permit the voters to study them as individuals. In state elections few people have personal acquaintance with many of the elected officials. They must take them on the faith of the party they represent. It is interesting, at times, to put even men in public life to the test of asking them for whom they voted for some prominent office as short a time as five years ago. If public men interested in government do not remember for whom they voted, what about the private citizens who, aside from performing their duty on Election Day, take little or no interest in the government of the state? For a number of years, in New York State, we were electing minor officials, and not one in a thousand people could tell whom he voted for at the last general election for some of these special offices.

At a joint meeting of the Men's City Club and the Women's City Club, of New York, when I was urging the short ballot, I made the statement that I could stand on the corner of Broadway and Forty-Second Street in the city of New York and stop the first thousand people who passed me and ask for whom they had voted for state engineer and surveyor, and I hazarded the guess that not one of the thousand could tell. That remark impressed the audience, because I could see from the way they were looking at one another that I did not need to go to Broadway and Forty-Second Street to find the thousand. I could find them in the audience before me.

Preparation of the platform is essentially the duty of the leaders of the party, as it is usually drawn before the candidate is named. I frequently had the advantage of sitting in with the party leaders prior to nominations and assisting in the preparation of the platform.

The preparation of the governor's message is an entirely different matter. For years the party leaders assisted in the preparation of the governor's message. I prepared all my own messages and showed them to nobody until they were in print. The only people familiar with them were my immediate advisers and the secretaries and stenographers who assisted me, and they were under instructions to talk about them to no one. I owe it to the leaders of my party, both in and out of the legislature, to say that they made no attempt to have anything to say about any of my messages and followed my policies in everything that I suggested.

Every definite promise made in the Democratic platform in all the years that I was a candidate found its way into the constructive recommendations which I sent to the legislature by message. At the close of my term the bulk of these found their way on to the statute books, and the people of the state enjoyed the reforms in government that came as a result of carrying out these promises.

It has always been my belief that the term of the governor of New York should be extended from two years to four, and I have always believed even more strongly that he should be elected in a year when there is no national election.

It was impossible, during the campaign of 1920, to debate the issues confronting the state—the executive budget, the rehabilitation of the hospitals, reorganization of the government, permanent relief for housing, and many other less important, but, nevertheless, pressing problems of the state. They were all disregarded and entirely pushed aside. No mention of them was made during the long campaign, and the chief things discussed by Nathan L. Miller, the Republican candidate for governor, were Article X of the Covenant of the League of Nations, and the threat of some of the interior states to force through the canalization of the St. Lawrence River. The governor of the state of New York had absolutely nothing to do with the former and could do no more than express his opinion of the latter.

The upheaval caused by this campaign can best be understood by the returns from the city of New York. What is called the gas-house district—the home of Tammany leader Murphy himself—was carried by President Harding. Out of the sixty-two assembly districts in the city of New York, President Harding carried sixty-one. He failed only in the district I came from. He carried every county in the state of New York and rolled up a plurality of more than one million, eighty-eight thousand votes, and nobody remembers anything that was said during the whole campaign except the subtle propaganda spread throughout the country. Every home which had sent a boy to the war was led to believe that under Article X American boys were to be used for gun fodder to settle the disputes of foreign nations and preserve the peace of the world.

In spite of the Republican landslide, I came within 75,000 votes of being elected. William Church Osborn sent me a telegram saying, "Even in defeat you came nearer to swimming up Niagara Falls than any man I have ever seen." Although he had opposed me in the primaries in 1918, he was greatly interested in the 1920 campaign and accompanied me around the state, speaking in all the principal cities.

Senator Joe T. Robinson of Arkansas also accompanied me on this trip, and later when I knew he was to be my running mate on the national ticket, I telegraphed him, reminding him of our pleasant association in 1920:

"When we campaigned together through the state of New York in 1920 I little thought at that time that I would have the great honor bestowed upon me by the convention, and I little thought that when we would campaign together again, it would be for the Presidency and Vice Presidency of the United States."

CHAPTER XIV

Public Service and Politics Again

AFTER the 1920 election I went to French Lick Springs for a vacation and while there became acquainted with the late Fred Upham, then treasurer of the Republican National Committee, and George F. Getz, his personal friend and business associate. George Getz owns the only private zoo which I will acknowledge to be superior to mine in Albany. In the course of a conversation at the Southern Indiana resort, they spoke to me about the United States Trucking Corporation, in New York City. It was made up in large part of a number of old-time friends whom I had known back in the old days of my own trucking ventures. They offered me the position of chairman of the board of directors of the company with a salary of fifty thousand dollars a year.

Upon my return to Albany I closed up the affairs of the state and after consulting with my close personal friends and advisers I reached the decision that I would become a trucking boss again. Accordingly, on the second day of January, 1921, I appeared at the office of the company at Canal and Thompson Streets and took up its active management. Practically the only man in the company with whom I did not have a previous acquaintance, although I knew of him, was the president, James J. Riordan. He has been one of my close friends ever since and is now president of the County Trust Company of New York, of which I am a director.

When I went to the trucking company it was losing money at the rate of sixty thousand dollars a year, due to natural causes largely growing out of the slump in business in 1921 and 1922. I made a close study of its operations and in the fall of 1921 brought about its complete reorganization, decentralizing its control and holding the vice president in charge of each branch responsible for its operation in every detail. The company was brought to a paying basis, where it has remained ever since, although I have no further interest in it.

The years 1921 and 1922 found me in business for the first time in my life since I sold newspapers. I thoroughly enjoyed the experience. It was exciting, took all of my time, and gave me Sundays and evenings with my family as free as it was possible for me to be from the political cares I had carried around with me ever since I 'entered active public life.

When we returned from Albany we refurnished the old house in Oliver Street. Of course it wasn't as comfortable as the Executive Mansion, but it meant much to me because of all its old associations. I was back among my neighbors and oldest friends. The house itself was large enough to accommodate itself to our needs. I spent the summers of 1921 and 1922 at Sea Gate, Coney Island, where I could indulge in my favorite summer sport of swimming.

President Wilson appointed me a member of the National Board of Indian Commissioners when I left office, and in my spare moments from the trucking business I found myself discussing problems of Indian tribes, wards of the government on reservations throughout the United States.

I regarded the first administration of President Wilson as the most constructive national administration during my time, and in the campaign of 1916 I worked hard for his re-election. When on election night and on the Wednesday following it looked as though he had been defeated I suffered keen disappointment. The election returns from the northern section of California were late in being tabulated and the whole country up to Thursday night believed him to have been defeated. On that Thursday night I attended a performance by Willie Collier. Governor Hughes was in a box with his wife and some friends. With me was Mrs. Smith and the then under-sheriff John F. Gilchrist and his wife. The plot of the play made Collier the custodian of some property left in trust for an infant and when he saw Governor Hughes in the box he added some lines not in the play. He walked to the footlights and said that he would hold the money box until the returns came in from California. Whereupon the audience rose and cheered Governor Hughes.

After the play was over we stopped at the Knickerbocker Hotel, then at Forty-Second Street and Broadway, for a little supper. I suggested that we walk across Forty-Second Street to the Third Avenue "L" passing the Democratic National headquarters on the corner of Madison Avenue and Forty-Second Street. We dropped in to see if there was any news from California. We found the place in a complete state of disorder: newspapers thrown around, furniture heaped up in the corner, and every sign that a cyclone had hit the headquarters. Inquiring what it all meant a man shouted to me, "Wilson is elected!"

When I was leaving Governor Miller on January first after his inauguration, I told him that if at any time he thought I could be of assistance I hoped he would feel free to call upon me. In April of 1921 he took me at my word, called me on the telephone and asked me to accept appointment as a member of the Port of New York Authority, set up that year by a treaty between the states of New York and New Jersey.

This commission dealt with a subject with which I had considerable acquaintance. Although I was in a line of business which might be adversely affected by the adoption of a unified plan for freight distribution incidental to port development, I accepted an appointment on the commission, feeling that I owed it to the state not to decline any opportunity given me to serve it.

Following the Reconstruction Commission which perfected and reported the proposals to reorganize the state government, many people interested in this program formed an organization called the New York State Association. These prominent Democrats, Republicans and Independents led the fight for the amendments to the

Constitution and organized the pressure of individuals and groups all over the state. Adelbert Moot, leading Republican of Erie County, was its president. One of the vice presidents was former U. S. Attorney General George W. Wickersham, now chairman of President Hoover's Law Inquiry Committee. Dwight Marvin, publisher of the influential and powerful Republican newspaper, the Troy *Record*, was the chairman of the board of directors. The secretary was Robert Moses. Frank Gannett, newspaper owner, John G. Agar, and Addison B. Colvin of Glens Falls, were among the directors.

It was my firm intention, publicly expressed, when I left Albany, not to return there unless on some public business. Since I had not lost interest in the matters begun under my administration, it was only natural that the New York State Association should ask me to attend the joint hearing of the legislative committee appointed to consider constitutional amendments for the reorganization of the government. I journeyed to Albany, hoping that I might be successful in persuading the legislature to pass for the second time the amendment consolidating the state departments, which had been passed once in 1920, and for the first time the amendment creating an executive budget. Constitutional amendments in New York before being voted on by the people, must pass two legislatures not having the same senate.

The legislative leaders made my appearance before them a sort of field day. They enjoyed heckling me as a private citizen appearing before them without the power of the governorship.

This hearing was part of a running fight to put over these amendments, and I was satisfied to answer questions at the hearing in the senate chamber, because it was apparent, from their tone, that if the amendment was defeated it would be because of political antagonism to it, and not because the proposal was unsound in any respect. The attitude of the legislature was well expressed by one of the Republican leaders who met me in the corridor of the Capitol on the day of the hearing and said, "Al, you attend to the horses and trucks and we will run the government."

Undoubtedly the largest hurdle I had to overcome was the unalterable opposition to these amendments of the Speaker of the assembly, H. Edmund Machold. He disregarded the advice of his own leaders in the assembly and also the counsel of the most distinguished leaders of his party, permitted the consolidation proposal to go down to defeat, and would not permit the executive budget or the four-year term to be voted on at all.

It was well known that this attitude of the Speaker had the full sympathy of the governor. At a private gathering just prior to the legislative session, Governor Miller had declared that there was no necessity for a constitutional amendment to reorganize the government. He declared it could be done just as well by statute. The whole fight that we were making to secure constitutional amendments had for its purpose the permanency of the change and the prevention of the creation of new departments of government in the same haphazard fashion in which it had been done up to that time.

I made another appearance before a joint session of legislative committees in 1922, when I addressed them, as a member of the Port of New York Authority, in favor of the comprehensive plan for port development which that body had drawn up.

During my brief two years in the business world, while I was chairman of the board of directors of the United States Trucking Corporation, I was a director of the Morris Plan and a member of the board of directors of Pattison & Bowns, wholesale coal dealers. I was also a director in the National Surety Company. As I sat around the table with the other directors in these companies, listening to business problems and attempting to find a solution for them, I was impressed with how much government is like business if a man is minded to put business principles into government. My experience in the governorship, in the legislature and with the Port Authority was of benefit to me in the solution of business problems, and the businesslike attitude of the men I was associated with during those two years was likewise helpful to me in the adoption of business principles to be applied to government.

During the first eighteen months that I was in the trucking business I had no idea that I would ever return to Albany. It was definitely fixed in my mind that my political career, so far as public office holding was concerned, had come to an end.

In the late spring and the early summer of 1922, leaders from all over the state began gathering at the office of the United States Trucking Corporation, then located in the Cunard Building at 25 Broadway. They brought stories of an organized movement to bring about the nomination of William Randolph Hearst for governor. Mayor Hylan—re-elected for a second term—was his chief spokesman in New York City and was very anxious to bring about Hearst's nomination.

In control of the patronage of Greater New York, Hylan was regarded by the upstate leaders as a formidable figure in the state convention. Upstate feared the nomination of Hearst and came to me in an effort to have me lead the forces against him in the convention.

They were all unanimous that the fight would not be effective unless I was willing to become a candidate myself. This I was reluctant to do. Having had a long and stormy political career, I was content to stay in business. The children were growing up and I felt I could make better provision for them by remaining in business than by going back into public office. I discouraged all suggestions until Norman E. Mack of Buffalo called upon me one day with the plain statement that unless I consented to head the opposition, a full Hearst delegation would be elected from Erie County.

Franklin D. Roosevelt, the present governor, urged me

to accept the nomination and in an open letter he called upon me to become a candidate.

HYDE PARK, DUTCHESS COUNTY,
NEW YORK,
AUGUST 13, 1922.

HON. ALFRED E. SMITH,
25 OLIVER STREET,
NEW YORK CITY.

Dear Al: Over a month ago I wrote to the conference of Democrats in Syracuse, urging that the Democratic party of this state must put its best foot foremost in the selection of candidates this year. It appeared to me then that the sentiment of the overwhelming majority of Democrats was for your nomination again for the office of governor.

Today, a week before the filing of designating petitions for delegates to the state convention, I am of the same opinion. I have been in touch with men and women voters from almost every upstate county and there is no question that the rank and file of Democrats want you to run.

Many candidates for office are strong by virtue of promises of what they will some day do. You are strong by virtue of what you have done. People everywhere know that in 1920, while you lost by a narrow margin in the landslide, you received a million more votes in this state than the presidential ticket.

More than that, your support came not only from Democrats but literally hundreds of thousands of Republicans and independent men and women who knew that you had given to this State an honest, clean and economical government, and had consistently opposed the privilege seekers and the reactionaries.

These voters are not satisfied with the present conduct of affairs by Republican leaders in Washington and Albany. To them will be added many more who are now sorry that they voted the Republican ticket in 1920. You represent the hope of what may be called "the average citizen."

Something must be done, and done now. In every county the chief topic of political conversation is: "Will Al Smith accept if he is nominated?" Already unauthorized agents are saying that you will not accept, and many are being deceived and beginning to lose interest as a result. It would surprise you to know what enthusiasm would spring up overnight if we knew you would accept the nomination.

Frankly, I don't want to see things go by default in this most hopeful year, and that is why I am writing you before the primary petitions are filed. I am taking it upon myself to appeal to you in the name of countless citizens of upstate New York, Democrats, Republicans, Independents, men and women, to ask you to say now, not later, that if nominated for governor, you will accept.

We realize that years of public service make it most desirable that you think now for a while of your family's needs. I am in the same boat myself—yet this call to further service must come first. Some day your children will be even prouder of you for making this sacrifice than they are now.

You represent the type of citizen the voters of this state want to vote for for governor, and you can be elected. The decision must be made now, as I have tried to point out. That is why— reluctantly to be sure, for I know what unselfishness it will call for on your part—I am asking you personally and publicly to accede to the wishes of so many of your fellow citizens.

Very truly yours,

FRANKLIN D. ROOSEVELT.

Feeling that I could no longer stem the tide of pressure, I answered him and said:

Dear Frank: I have your letter of August 13th and I have carefully read it. I appreciate your kindly sentiments, and they compel me to talk to you from my heart. I would not be entirely frank with you if I did not admit that evidence has been presented to me which would indicate a desire on the part of the Democratic rank and file that I again take the post of leadership. It has been and still is my desire to remain in business life for the reason you state in your letter—for my family's sake—but during the past twenty years I have been so honored by my party that even the members of my family would be dissatisfied if I did not answer the call.

Therefore, considering the facts as I know them, and answering your letter, I feel myself that I would be ungrateful if I were to say that I would be unwilling to assume the leadership. The state convention will be composed of elected representatives of the rank and file of the Democratic party throughout the state. They will undoubtedly come to the convention alive to the sentiment in their respective districts. If a majority of them desire me to accept the nomination for governor and lead the party in this state to what seems to me to be a certain victory, I am entirely willing to accept this honor from their hands and to battle for them with all the energy and vigor that I possess.

With kind regards to your mother and Mrs. Roosevelt and all the children, I am

Sincerely yours,

AL.

That seemed to settle the question of the nomination for governor, but the Hearst forces still had their eye on the senatorship.

In the late summer of 1922 I suffered from an attack of neuritis and for several weeks I was unable to walk. With great difficulty I got to Syracuse and was housed in a suite of rooms on the eighth floor of the Onondaga Hotel. I was unable to leave the rooms throughout the period of the convention.

Every conceivable form of pressure was put on me through personal friends to consent to the nomination of William Randolph Hearst for United States Senator. This, of course, I could not do, and I frankly served notice on the leaders that if his nomination was brought about I would have to decline the nomination for governor. In view of our past relations, in view of his bitter attacks upon me as well as upon the Democratic party for so many years, I was unable to reconcile myself to both of us being put on the same ticket by the Democratic party.

Tom Foley was there, and he would bring me bulletins now and again from the meeting rooms of the leaders. Once, when I was alone for a minute, he put his head in at the door and said "Stick." That meant that he knew I was right, and, being so, would win out.

When the Hearst strength was tested here and there in the convention, his lieutenants soon grasped the fact that he was in no position to secure the nomination. Upon the receipt of a telegram from Hearst, his forces suddenly capitulated, and the word passed through the hotel lobby—in any convention always swayed by hundreds of rumors—that Mayor Hylan and all his aides had departed for New York on the afternoon train.

There remained nothing then but the actual ratification of my nomination by the convention, and then the usual afterthought came to the leaders. Every four years a United States Senator must be nominated, and this was the year. There had been so much excitement centering about my own nomination that no discussion was held concerning the senatorship until the Hearst menace was out of the way. Then Dr. Royal S. Copeland, Health Commissioner of New York City, was suggested, because he was known to be agreeable to the city administration. There is always a tendency to cement peace after a political battle, because a united front toward the enemy is essential.

CHAPTER XV

Back to Albany

So I was launched on another campaign for the governorship. A long experience in campaigning gives a man the power to sense the general feeling of the community. Particularly in country districts with sparsely settled population, there are always some indications on the surface as to how the public mind is running.

In 1920, I left Syracuse and motored through the Chenango Valley into Binghamton. We were riding for two hours and I never saw a single picture of James M. Cox, the Democratic candidate for President, but just as I made up my mind that there were none in that section, I spied one in a window. I called to the chauffeur to pull up to the curb, because I wanted to get a look at the first man in that section who had the courage to speak out for the Democratic party. Whereupon, my secretary, Jerry Connor, said: "It's all right. He is the Democratic postmaster."

Things were quite different in 1922. Running for governor against the same opponent, I saw an entirely different attitude in the small cities and villages in the upper part of the state. The heat, dust and excitement of the great national campaign had died down and the people had turned their attention to the questions affecting the state. In many respects the campaign of 1922 was novel.

One of the candidates was then governor, Nathan L. Miller, and one was myself, the former governor, defeated in 1920 by the same opponent. There was a sharp division between our political policies and the things which each of us represented.

This campaign differed very much from the previous ones in which I had taken part, because it was more a debate on definite subjects rather than a campaign of general speech-making. In my first two years in Albany, I had taken a position on many public questions and given my reasons. Over a period of three weeks during the campaign, each candidate summed up his cause before a jury which was the people of the state of New York.

One of the principal differences between Governor Miller and myself was the question of reorganizing the state government by constitutional amendment. Though he did not oppose the principle of reorganization, he declared that it did not require an amendment to the constitution. That argument he was unable to sustain, and he was compelled, in the campaign of 1922, to bear the brunt of having advised against its adoption during his administration as governor.

He was also opposed to an executive budget made permanent by constitutional amendment. He likewise held to his belief in the principle of centralized state control over what I considered were local problems of control of public utilities. He was unwilling to debate the laws curbing freedom of thought and speech and compelling teachers to submit to a loyalty test, which he had signed after I had vetoed them.

He based his campaign on what was heralded by his campaign managers as a great achievement of economy in government. I was prepared for this issue, and before the campaign had even begun I had made a study of the claim he was likely to make, of savings amounting to twenty millions of dollars in one year.

My familiarity with appropriation bills soon disclosed that the reputed savings had been made in three ways. The appropriations for the Department of Labor had been cut arbitrarily, so that three principal bureaus of the department could not function. Inspection of factories, the Workmen's Compensation Bureau and the Bureau of Women in Industry were completely crippled. It was easy to prove that this was false economy.

No appropriation whatever had been made in 1922 for indemnities for tubercular cattle slaughtered by the state. The sum, amounting to more than five millions of dollars, was just allowed to accumulate, drawing interest. It was not difficult to explain to voters that the mere nonpayment of bills was not economy. Something of the same procedure had been followed in curtailing appropriations for the care of the insane in state hospitals.

Governor Miller and I differed on water-power control and development, although he had signed bills to permit the state to develop and operate two power plants on the Erie Canal. On the basic principle affecting the power site on the St. Lawrence River he opposed me.

Senator Seymour Lowman, afterward lieutenant governor and a prominent dry, now Federal prohibition administrator, sought to embarrass me on the wet-and-dry issue on my visit to his home city of Elmira in the course of the campaign. Before reaching the city I was informed that he had personally paid for a half-page advertisement in the local newspapers asking me a number of questions about prohibition. It must be borne in mind that during the term of Governor Miller the Mullan-Gage Act had been passed which brought violators of the Volstead Act into the state courts for trial.

When I began my speech that evening at the Opera House in Elmira, I carried a copy of the evening paper onto the stage. Holding it up to the audience, I answered Senator Lowman's questions in detail and succeeded in turning the tables against him. Then I advised him to ask Governor Miller the same questions. Needless for me to say, he did not dare ask them of Governor Miller, because so far as prohibition was concerned the Republican party that year was again engaged in its old trick of trying to be dry among the drys and wet when among the wets.

Men who ask questions in a political campaign must be prepared to state their own position. No Republican candidate has ever done that in the state of New York so far as prohibition is concerned when he desired the votes of the big cities.

In dealing with the Lowman questions I followed a policy to which I have adhered throughout my public life. I have always been willing to answer frankly questions put by responsible people, and I have enjoyed particularly those intended to embarrass me. In the city of Omaha, in the recent campaign, I had an experience similar to the Lowman one, when some of that city's leading citizens were induced by the local Republican committee to allow their names to be signed to a series of questions addressed to me. I answered these and one of my Democratic friends in Omaha, who had talked to a prominent Republican citizen who had allowed his name to be used, told me that the citizen there whispered in his ear that he'd see that that would never happen to his name again.

Strangely enough, in 1922 the newspaper reporters strongly favored me, but the editorial writers and all the owners of the big metropolitan dailies, except the Hearst newspapers and the New York *World*, morning and evening, either because they believed the economy claims or because they thought Governor Miller ought to have the advantage of a second term, were outspoken editorially for Governor Miller. The climax of the enthusiasm of the newspaper reporters came during one of our press conferences at the Biltmore Hotel when they undertook to estimate the size of the plurality by which I would be elected. Some had it up to half a million. I offered a suit of clothes to the newspaper reporter who made the best guess. One reporter's guess was accepted on newspaper tabulations the day after election and he received my order for the suit. But the official canvass brought another man nearer the correct figure and I paid twice for being in too much of a hurry to make good my promise.

My dear old friend, Frank Munsey, who ever after that time supported me in everything I tried to do, took sharp issue with me in his paper, the *Herald*, which he then owned. In the morning *Herald* on the day before Election, he printed in large black-faced type the editorial which follows. It sums up the issues for and against me.

To the Voters of New York:

You have had the arguments on both sides set clearly before you in the campaign just closed. You are the judges of the merits of their arguments.

If the statements of Governor Miller concerning the achievements of his administration will stand the acid test; if they cannot be discounted or disputed in fairness; if they hold against any and all assaults on them, then you must conclude and acknowledge that he has shown rare ability in his conduct of the State's business; that he has demonstrated that he is a great leader and a great business executive.

The argument and statements of Al Smith should have the same fair consideration. They differ widely from those of Governor Miller. It is for you to decide if they are as convincing as the arguments of Governor Miller; if they carry the same weight as the arguments of Governor Miller; if they check up as soundly as the arguments of Governor Miller.

This is a piece of work that in all honesty you must do seriously, do thoughtfully, do thoroughly. To pass it over without digging into the facts, to pass it over with indifference is to write yourselves down as indifferent to the interests of your state, is to write yourselves down as unwilling to carry and to perform the single, plain responsibilities of citizenship, and clearly the man who isn't willing to do this isn't entitled to the privileges of citizenship.

Citizenship in a democracy, citizenship in this country, is a great endowment which carries with it a sacred responsibility. Make no mistake about this.

While the big issue in this campaign is Miller against Smith, the heart and soul of the issue is business against politics or to put it in another way the issue is, shall the business of the great state of New York now involving the expenditure of a hundred and forty million dollars a year, be handled in a business way or be handled in a political way; shall it be handled by a business man or by a man born and bred and wedded to politics?

And there is another very big matter involved in this election. It is this: If Miller with his matchless record as an executive, his matchless record as a business Governor, his matchless record in cutting expenses and in cutting taxes, his matchless record in efficiency, is turned down tomorrow by you, the voters of New York, you will at the same time serve notice on the able men of the state—the sound, clear headed business men of the state—that you do not want and do not propose to have them in the public service, do not want them in the management of the State's business, that you are content to have these affairs handled by politicians with the inevitable graft and leakage attached to such handling.

So this election goes further, very much further than the mere choice of Miller and Smith—between Al Smith, the acceptable Governor as Governors go, or Nathan L. Miller, the very great Governor.

If, then, Miller should be defeated at your hands tomorrow what incentive will there be for men of ability, men of brains and leadership and honesty and courage to have anything to do with politics in this State?

(Signed) FRANK A. MUNSEY

I was somewhat puzzled as to just how to deal with this editorial coming so late in the campaign. After thinking it over I decided that Mr. Munsey was undoubtedly fair and that he would be sure to print a reply which I might make to his editorial in his evening paper, the *Sun*, and probably in the *Herald* of the next day. I promptly wrote my answer and gave it to George Van Slyke, political reporter to the New York *Sun*, and asked him to take it at once to Mr. Munsey. He did so and it appeared on the front page of the *Sun* that same evening with Mr. Munsey's editorial reprinted alongside of it:

MY DEAR MR. MUNSEY:

I read your letter in the *Herald* of Monday, November 6, addressed to the voters of New York. I agree with you that the big issue in this campaign is "business against politics" and I have by far the best of that argument.

I gave the State a thorough-going business administration. Governor Miller substituted politics and I will show it to you.

I appointed to office people with particular qualifications for the places they were to fill. Governor Miller, in the matter of appointments, was led by the Republican State machine. The four large patronage offices of the State were divided by Governor Miller between the leaders of the party, commonly known as "The Big Four."

"Boss" Ward of Westchester got the Tax Department with a lump sum appropriation in the hands of his commissioners to hire and fire at will; the result was increases in salary to the commissioners and to the holders of all positions exempt from the provisions of the Civil Service law.

Barnes of Albany got the Conservation Department. The able and competent Commissioner Pratt himself a Republican failed of reappointment to make room for the chairman of the Albany Republican County Committee.

Rochester got the Department of Public Works.

Greiner of Erie got the Department of Highways. The competent, able engineer, the best Superintendent of Highways the State has ever had, Col. Frederick Stuart Greene, was removed by Governor Miller and that important engineering department was placed under the direction of an Erie County politician who was formerly Excise Commissioner.

The same story runs all along the line in the minor appointments.

It was good business to reorganize the government of the State. Nobody favored it any stronger than you did. It had the approval of Senator Root, Attorney-General Wickersham, Secretary of War Stimson, Charles E. Hughes, Adelbert Moot of Buffalo and leading citizens, men and women, throughout the State. During my time as Governor I forced the constitutional amendments to accomplish this through the Senate by the weight of their own merit and when the Assembly destroyed them Governor Miller openly said that he would take the responsibility.

I, therefore, stood for a good, practical, common sense business plan for the reorganization of the government and Governor Miller stood for politics.

You know, as well as I do, that the State needs to change its system of making appropriations. I urged an executive budget to the end that the appropriation bills may be scientifically drawn and responsibility for them definitely fixed on the Governor. This is good business and it is what I advocated. Gov. Miller insisted upon the present system, which you know has nothing to commend it but politics and the strong desire for pap and patronage for the machine.

It is strange that forward looking Republicans like yourself desired an executive budget at Washington in the interest of economy and then you stand with the man who has denied

243

it to this State. The budget, during Governor Miller's time, far from being placed on a business basis, was drawn and passed along the same lines that have been in vogue for half a century. Pork barrels were inserted in the interest of certain communities and certain individuals and they have become law. Governor Miller made no record in cutting either expenses or taxes. As far as taxes are concerned, he increased them.

If that record by Governor Miller is to receive the approval of the people no man in the Governor's office, upon the theory that the machine wins after all, will ever again attempt an effective reorganization of the State Government or the adoption of an executive budget.

Sincerely yours,

(Signed) ALFRED E. SMITH

The opening paragraph bears out my statement that the arguments on both sides were set clearly before the people. Mr. Munsey, with characteristic astuteness, put in a saving clause and said, "if the statements of Governor Miller will stand the acid test"—"if they cannot be discounted or discredited in fairness" and "if they hold against any and all assaults on them," Miller should be re-elected. But that is exactly what his statements could not do.

After that campaign Mr. Munsey, although his papers leaned strongly to the Republican party, was always a warm friend and advocate of my major policies. I frequently dined with him at the Ritz Carlton where he lived. I remember having been invited to dinner with him one Friday night and he had ordered chicken. I told him I was sorry but that I could not eat chicken. He asked me why and I said that my church prohibited eating meat on Friday. He wanted to know why it was prohibited and I told him that I could not answer that but that if it made no difference to him I would prefer to have fish. He said he wouldn't mind having fish himself for that matter.

No man displayed greater interest in the passage of the constitutional amendments and the bond issues advocated by me than did Mr. Munsey. He called me from his apartment on election night after twelve o'clock the year that the reorganization amendments were voted on, to know if I had any news for him.

On Election Day the people went to the polling booths and rendered the verdict. I was victorious by 387,000 plurality—the largest ever given to a governor in the history of the state. Not only did I win but the whole Democratic state ticket was elected with me. Strange to say, because of our unfair and discriminating apportionment, the assembly was Republican and the senate was Democratic by one vote. This presented to the people of the state the unique situation of having approved of my policies, a great majority of which required legislative enactment, and having the Republican assembly, following the ideas and principles of their leaders, proceed forthwith to annihilate every proposal which I offered.

The situation was summed up in a few words when I said: "I won office, but the people of the state, temporarily at least, lost the opportunity to get the benefit of the things I promised in the campaign." I remember an argument with Fred Hammond, the clerk of the assembly. He had been a member of the assembly with me. When the legislature of 1923 made known its determination to defeat our program, I called his attention to the different planks and promises of the Democratic platform, and he replied, "That wasn't in our"—Republican—"platform." I said: "Your party didn't win. You were overwhelmingly defeated." But the leaders of the assembly clung to the theory that they must oppose everything I advocated during the campaign and adhere to the principles and policies of their own lost cause.

Tripping back and forth between Albany and New York disorganized the family. The day after election, I was at the Biltmore with Mrs. Smith. The children were at Sea Gate. No. 25 Oliver Street was closed for the summer and we were at a loss what to do about it. We decided to leave the old house on Oliver Street as it stood. We stayed at Sea Gate until the weather, the opening of school and constant trips back and forth made it impossible to stay longer. Then the whole family moved into the Biltmore.

During this period the schooling of my children suffered seriously. They were taken out of school in New York in December, 1918, and had to begin in the middle of the term in Albany in January, 1919. They were again taken out of school in December, 1920, and had to start in the middle of the term in New York in January, 1921. And again in December, 1922, they were taken away from New York and obliged to begin in the middle of another term in Albany. Because of the differences in curriculum and the requirements in Albany and New York they lost much time and had to begin some of the studies they had abandoned or changed all over again, to meet the requirements of the new school and the Board of Regents.

During Governor Miller's term in 1921 and 1922 a board of water-power control had been set up and given the right by law to lease to private operators the available water powers of the state. Immediately after election in 1922 it was brought to my attention that this board proposed to act before leaving office and intended to grant one of the applicants the right to develop hydro-electric energy for private profit from the water that was the property of the people of the state.

Inasmuch as I believed state ownership and control of water to have been an issue in the 1922 campaign, and feeling that the people had resolved the policy with respect to it in favor of the argument made by me, I telegraphed to the board:

Nov. 22, 1922.

Hon. Charles D. Newton,
Attorney-General, Albany, New York.

My Dear General: It has been called to my attention that the State Water Power Commission is to meet in Albany tomorrow morning at ten o'clock. I have been further informed by a newspaper article that it is the intention of the commission to act upon some applications for licenses to develop electrical energy by private corporations. The paper that I read says that there is a possibility that a license may be granted to some company to develop energy from the waters of Niagara below the falls.

Before and during the campaign I took a decided position with regard to the development of electrical energy from water power owned by the state. I have held that it should not be given to private companies for private development, but should, on the other hand, be developed by the state itself under state ownership and state control for the benefit of all the people of the state.

I would therefore ask you, in view of the decision of the people at the polls following the campaign in which this subject was a distinct issue, not to grant any license or permits to private corporations for development of electrical energy from water-power resources that belong to the state, and permit that subject to be dealt with by the incoming administration in accordance with the explicit promises made during the course of the campaign.

(Signed)   A<small>LFRED</small> E. S<small>MITH</small>

This effectively stopped the granting of power leases at that time.

In order to bring about reforms in the conditions of which I had complained during the campaign, there was a great responsibility placed on me to begin my labors before the first of January. Accordingly, after a very short vacation—less than two weeks—I started on my annual message for 1923 and on the preparation of the financial statements, the budget and the appropriation bills to make my recommendations effective.

We had a small Christmas tree in the Biltmore Hotel— the smallest in our experience because of the limited quarters. A friend gave Mrs. Smith a Pekingese dog for Christmas and a policeman gave me a monkey. All hands, including the animals, boarded the train for Albany, on the thirtieth of December, 1922, serenaded by the police band. Arrived at Albany, a large delegation of towns-people were at the depot awaiting us. I marched on foot through the slush and snow—it was alternately raining and snowing—to the Executive Mansion, where Gover-nor Miller and the out-going Republican state officials gave us a cordial welcome.

To the children it seemed like returning home after being on a vacation. As they entered the main entrance, each shot as fast as possible to the room left two years before. It took less than fifteen minutes to settle everybody except the monkey. He was in a small cage, and after the long ride I took a chance and let him out in one of the cloakrooms. He surveyed the entire mansion and looked everything over carefully, before he was induced to go back to the cage by the odor of an overripe banana. Cap-tain, the police dog, was the prize animal of the house-hold at that time. Great was our grief when he was run over by a truck and killed.

Throughout four terms in Albany one of the attrac-tions of the Executive Mansion was animals. In my first term I confined the menagerie entirely to ponies, dogs and birds, but when I returned in 1923 I used the large space at the back of the mansion for housing animals native to New York State. I gathered them with the assistance of the Conservation Commission and by dona-tions of other animals not native to New York State from friends who heard about the Executive Mansion Zoo.

I left it open to visitors to the city of Albany and to the children and residents of the city. At various times I had raccoons, bears, elk, deer, monkeys, rabbits, pheasants, a red fox, barn owls, and for a while the goat which had appeared in the motion picture entitled *Homeward Bound*. The goat's name was Heliotrope. At the time that the picture was being shown in the Executive Mansion, Heliotrope was in the menagerie in the rear. Live alligators, turtles and terrapin were sent to me from the tropics. An elk was a present from the Boy Scouts of America and was captured when young in Bear Mountain Park. It was presented to me on one of my summer visits to the boy-scout camp. When he arrived at the Executive Mansion he was wild. In a very short time the boys of the family, with the staff at the Executive Mansion and with me, were able to go into his inclosure and play with him as you would with a horse or a pony.

All the deer, fawns, raccoons or bears that were brought to me were young and were found by the game protectors in the Adirondack Mountains, the mothers having been killed or lost. An Adirondack deer that was brought up on a nursing bottle in the kitchen became familiar enough with the mansion to come in and out of the house himself.

One small Adirondack black bear which afterward grew to weigh 350 pounds was so young when it arrived at the Executive Mansion that one of my boys fed it with a nursing bottle. After he had attained full growth, in some way or other he got off his chain one day, climbed an electric-light pole and went over into the yard of an orphan asylum, just back of the mansion. He went in at a window where more than a hundred small girls were at play and was in there for some time before any grown person knew anything about it. He was so tame and so accustomed to being handled by children that he rolled around on the floor with the youngsters for a solid hour. One little girl went upstairs and brought him down the sugar off a cake, and that inspired him to take a walk upstairs himself. One of the sisters in charge became frightened and telephoned to the Executive Mansion. The superintendent and another man went in after him. He was very ugly to the men because he was quite unwilling to leave the asylum. He had to be roped and walked through the street to get him back into his den. The bear is now in Bronx Park with a sign over the cage saying: "Presented to the New York Zoölogical Society by Governor Smith."

All my dogs were well known in Albany, particularly to the police, and when they strayed away from the mansion, it was a regular thing to have a police sergeant or captain call the mansion and give the name of the dog and state where he was. My Great Dane, Cæsar, was succeeded by another one called Thomas Jefferson and nicknamed Jeff. He attached himself to me personally and I am eagerly waiting to have him back with me again. He is temporarily a house guest of Congressman Parker Corning in Albany.

Great excitement occurred in the mansion one night when it was discovered that a careless attendant had left a monkey cage open and that four monkeys were at large in some part of the city of Albany. My youngest son promptly telephoned to me to come over from the executive chamber. I left the State's business as soon as I could and tried to tempt the monkeys down out of the trees with ripe bananas, but without success. Finally, at eleven o'clock at night, we gave it up and contented ourselves with leaving the cage door open. An early arrival at the cage in the morning looked in and found all four monkeys fast asleep after having had a wonderful night abroad in Albany.

CHAPTER XVI

Remaking a State

WHEN I was inaugurated governor for my second term, on the first of January, 1923, I had absolutely no idea that I was to spend six consecutive years in the office of the governor. It had grown to be a fixed custom in the state to give a governor only two terms, and the history of the six years compels the conclusion that many of the reforms accomplished would have been impossible had it not been that I remained so long in the governor's office.

The senate was in the control of the Democratic party and the assembly in the control of the Republican party when I returned to Albany in 1923. The legislature became wholly Republican again in 1924 and remained so through to 1928.

Throughout the three terms which followed, I divided my recommendations for legislative action into three groups: First, the reorganization of the state government; second, the preservation of political, individual, state and legal rights; and third, welfare legislation.

In the first group I centered attention on the proposal to amend the constitution to establish the short ballot and reduce the one hundred and eighty-seven agencies of the state government into nineteen distinct departments to be named in the constitution. The legislature was to be prohibited from adding any more. To this program the executive budget and the four-year term for the governor were the necessary complement.

The senate promptly passed the constitutional amendment to consolidate the departments. The assembly began to tinker with it, but the arguments of the campaign were fresh in the minds of people all over the state, and the assembly was unable to withstand the public pressure. With some minor amendments to indicate active interest and to claim credit for perfecting it, the amendment finally passed and was sent to the office of the Secretary of State to await repassage by the legislature of 1925, as required in the constitution.

While awaiting the referendum on the constitutional amendment, which could not come before the people for two years, it would have been possible to undertake some departmental consolidations by statute. If this were done it would simplify consolidation when the constitutional amendment would finally pass. The legislature was agreed on the general policy of consolidating agencies, but when I made some specific proposals in a special message, all of them passed the senate but were defeated in the assembly. By not passing the statutory consolidations, the assembly compelled the state to lumber along for two more years under the burdensome machinery of one hundred and eighty-odd departments of government.

Evidently the assembly leaders were biding their time to see what position they would be in to defeat the required second passage of the amendment. They were taking a chance that when my term would be over I might either not run for governor or the amendments might be overlooked in the excitement of a national campaign due in 1924. They had a theory that it would be impossible to elect a Democratic governor in the fall of 1924 and, therefore, the approval by the legislature of 1925 might not be necessary. That would give to the amendment the same treatment it received from the legislature of 1921.

Fate was against them, and though the entire Democratic ticket was overwhelmingly defeated in the presidential campaign of 1924, I was reëlected, and in the session of 1925 fireworks started. Immediately after election I resumed the battle for the constitutional amendments.

By this time thinking people throughout the state had discovered the attempt to defeat this proposal and were more insistent than ever that it receive legislative approval, and it did.

The constitutional amendment embodying departmental consolidation and the short ballot was adopted by the people at the election of 1925. Passage of the amendment was only the first step. There were literally dozens of statutes affecting the various agencies and departments which would need to be reconciled and amended. When it became apparent during the session of 1925 that the amendment would pass, I recommended to the legislature the setting up of a joint commission consisting of appointees by the governor and by members of the legislature to prepare a program of consolidation for report to the 1926 legislature. Their recommendations could then be promptly enacted into law and the consolidation completed. This the legislature refused to do, but after adjournment it set up a committee of its own appointment without warrant by law, and, of course, without appropriation. After some public protest the legislative leaders permitted me to name a few members of the committee, and accepted from the list I submitted Addison B. Colvin and Robert Moses. They refused to name Raymond V. Ingersoll and Mrs. Moskowitz, who were also on my list.

At the close of the session, and while on a vacation at Absecon, New Jersey, my attention was directed to an attempt by the Republican legislative leaders to have Mr. Machold, former Speaker of the assembly, selected as chairman of this committee. Inasmuch as Mr. Machold had been the most persistent and most outspoken foe of reorganization of the government, I naturally objected to his selection as chairman of the committee to prepare a plan to carry out the mandate of the new amendment. Through the medium of the newspapers I suggested the name of Charles Evans Hughes. This took root immediately and in response to popular demand throughout the state Mr. Hughes agreed to take the responsibility. The committee became known as the Hughes Committee and reported to the 1926 legislature a series of recommendations which were adopted.

To complete the details, a legislative committee was then named. The Republican leaders, although the con-

solidations were ready for the beginning of the fiscal year
—July 1, 1926—insisted on making them effective as of
the first of January, 1927. Again they were probably relying upon their belief that they would certainly capture
the governorship in 1926, upon the theory that four terms
would never be given to any individual. Indeed they made
their hardest fight for the office that year. With consolidation effective, a Republican governor would have a large
batch of appointments to make and whole departments to
reorganize, with the accumulated patronage that a change
of administration would bring.

It is scarcely necessary to point out that because of the
persistent and aggressive opposition by the legislative
leaders and the small party bosses to these great constitutional reforms, the benefits of consolidation of state departments, the short ballot and the executive budget were
held back from 1922 to 1927, or five full years.

Demand for budget reform had originated in the Constitutional Convention. Under the old system the budget
originated in the assembly and was prepared by the chairman of the Committee on Ways and Means. It went to
the senate after passage in the assembly, and from that
time on represented nothing but compromise. Each assemblyman used his influence to put what he wanted into
the appropriation bill before it left the assembly, and
when it reached the senate the same thing happened. In
fact, there was a story prevalent in Albany in 1915 that
one of the clerks of the assembly amended the appropriation bill himself by inserting an item in it while

carrying it from the assembly to the senate chamber.

While the attempt to create an executive budget by constitutional law had apparently died with the death of the proposed 1915 constitution, both Governor Whitman and Governor Miller attempted to reform budgetary methods by statutory law. Both were doomed to find that it would never work that way, and these failures gave me a convincing argument in all the debates and campaigns for the executive budget which followed.

When I returned to Albany in 1923 I had again urged the executive budget upon the legislature. I appealed to the people and campaigned for it throughout the state, and soon found that when I would address the Rochester Chamber of Commerce in favor of the budget on a Tuesday night, Speaker Machold would address it in opposition on the Thursday night following.

The Republican leaders of the state were outspoken in their opposition to this reform. It passed the senate promptly, but Speaker Machold accomplished its defeat in the assembly. Nothing daunted, I urged it again in 1924, when it was again defeated in both houses of the legislature. Once again I urged it in 1925, but it again suffered defeat in both houses of the legislature.

In the course of its deliberations on consolidation of the government, the Hughes Committee saw the necessity for the companion measure of an executive budget and made a strong recommendation in its favor to the legislature of 1926. Mr. Machold, its enemy for four years and a member of the committee, but no longer

Speaker of the assembly, signed the report. Unable to escape the logic and the pressure, both houses of the legislature passed it in 1926 for the first time.

At the annual dinners of the newspaper correspondents in Albany it is often said that there are many true words spoken in jest. One year a sketch was written around Governor Whitman and his form of executive budget which consisted of the submission to the legislature of a budget prepared by the Governor but which had no recognition in law. This particular dinner was held a very short time after a chef in a Chicago Hotel had been accused of putting poison in the soup and arrested. One of the members of the association dressed as a policeman rushed into the dining hall just as the diners were about to eat the soup and shouted "Stop! Wait a moment! something terrible has happened! Don't eat the soup." He rushed out to the kitchen and brought forth another member dressed up as a chef. They had a hurried consultation and the chef was cross-questioned about the soup that the diners were about to drink. In the course of the examination he was asked what it was he had put in the soup and he said: "Senator Sage [then chairman of the Senate finance committee] told me to put the Governor's budget in the soup."

It created quite a laugh because that, in vulgar parlance, is exactly what happened to all governor's budgets attempted under statute law.

Some of the debates in opposition to the executive budget were carried to a ridiculous point. Lieutenant

Governor Lowman, debating the subject with me before the Women's City Club in New York, made the declaration that I was seeking to make a king of myself. Its absurdity was quickly apparent when I arose to speak in reply. I began my speech with the words—"Behold the King! The King from Oliver Street."

Assemblyman Jenks of Broome County, Chairman of the Judiciary Committee who attended the assassination of the amendment, came to confer with me as a member of the legislative committee on the subject of the executive budget and I noted that while I was developing my points, instead of listening to me, he was giving all of his attention to the antics of a couple of dogs on the lawn in front of the Capitol. I told the reporters about it and it was printed in the newspapers.

On the day the assembly assassinated the executive budget, my dear old friend Jenks arose and relieved himself of the following: "The Governor is right. I was interested in the antics of the dogs because the dogs are what God Almighty intended them to be: just dogs. But the Governor wants to be a King."

Of course this kind of argument was helpful to the executive budget because thinking people throughout the state regarded that as sheer nonsense.

The executive budget places the responsibility for expenditures, in the first instance, on the governor, after consultation with his department heads. He must certify to the legislature what, in his opinion, is required for the maintenance of the government for the next fiscal year.

The legislature retains the power thereafter to reduce items, strike them out altogether or insert a new item with the proviso that it be so inserted that it may be subject to the veto of the governor. That makes for greater responsibility and it compels the members of the legislature to operate in the open.

Upon my return for my fourth term in 1927, I urged the final legislative passage of the constitutional amendment setting up the executive budget. It passed and was submitted to the people in the fall of 1927. It was adopted and it is now part of our constitution and makes a very important and drastic change from the old method of appropriating public funds. Although the executive budget is functioning, the battle is now on to weaken its effectiveness. The Court of Appeals will have to make the final decision as to whether it can function as now constituted or must be further amended.

Related to these two great reforms is the proposal to extend the term of the governor from two to four years. Every man who has ever held the governorship, every disinterested student of our government, every man not trying to help himself by the practical operation of political manipulation, is in accord with what I regard an indisputable fact—the term of the governor of New York is entirely too short.

By amendment to the Greater New York charter, in 1904, the term of the mayor of the city of New York was extended from two to four years. The arguments that local issues alone should determine the election, made by the Republican leaders in extending the term of the mayor of New York and placing the election in years when neither a governor nor a President is up for election, apply with even greater force to the governorship of the state. No man has a chance to see any of his policies bear fruit if he continues every two years to submit himself to the electorate, and unless he has a strong constitution and a strong determination he will be unable to stand the strain of it.

What happens? A man is nominated for governor. He goes through a hard, vigorous campaign. The state of New York is big. Its interests are diversified. Its large cities are far apart. It means work, night and day, for a month and a half at least. After election he is physically worn out and must rest. That finished, he must prepare for the inauguration on the first of the following January. The Christmas holidays intervene. He owes a duty to his family at that season of the year. He must prepare his annual message to the legislature by the first of January. He soon finds himself reduced to the condition he was in the day after election. Then, for the months while the legislature is in session, every minute of his time not devoted to sleeping is absorbed by the questions coming before the legislature.

After adjournment the legislature leaves from seven hundred to a thousand bills lying on his desk, and under the constitution he has thirty days in which to dispose of them. At the end of the thirty-day-bill period he needs another rest.

True, some people believe that the governor has nothing to do in the summertime. There isn't a day or a week in the year that the executive business at Albany is not sufficient to take up every minute of the governor's time, even in July and August. And if he wants to acquaint himself firsthand with the business of the state he will feel the necessity, during the summer and early fall, of visiting some of the state institutions. During my first two terms I visited practically every one of them.

The summer over, the governor immediately plunges into the preparation of his executive budget. With the state spending $250,000,000 a year, that is no small job and extends over several months. That finished, he is preparing to meet the legislature for the second time. His annual message is again to be written during the period of the Christmas holidays, when he should have some time for himself and his family.

Before he realizes it the legislature is back on his hands for another three and one-half months and the thirty-day-bill period follows after it. Before he really catches his breath he finds himself running again for governor, with the burden placed upon him of again traveling around through the state.

What would happen to a great business corporation if it went through an upheaval of all its executive heads every two years? All this was impressed upon the legislature and some of the leaders were in favor of the change. I recommended it year in and year out.

Republican legislative leaders and the little bosslets

around the state were unequivocal in their opposition to the four-year term. Speaker Machold made a declaration before the Buffalo Chamber of Commerce that if a governor made a good governor, he would be reëlected. This was in 1923. I shot back at him, "According to that theory neither Governor Miller nor myself was any good." It was finally agreed to submit the proposition to the people, but before doing so, its effectiveness was completely killed by providing that the election must occur in a presidential year. With all of the experience, with all of the lessons that were taught in this state about the absurdity of trying to center public opinion upon state issues during a great national campaign, the opponents of the four-year term stubbornly persisted in putting that provision into it. When it came before the people in 1927 in that form, the people rejected it on the the same day they adopted six other amendments to the constitution by substantial pluralities. I have no doubt that it would have received the majority vote had its provisions been otherwise.

Recommended again this year by Governor Roosevelt, the legislature defeated it with the assertion that it had been rejected by the people. The answer is that the Republican leaders want the election of a governor to happen every two years. One of them said, "It's a chance to discipline him if he isn't all right."

In the treatment of amendments to our constitution by the people themselves, one decided step has been made in advance. Of recent years the people of the state as a whole have taken a lively interest in amending their fundamental law. Something that happened in 1911 indicates how little attention it received years ago. Several constitutional amendments were submitted to the people that year and among the amendments a proposition to bond the state for $22,000,000 for construction of canal terminals. Several of the amendments were to safeguard the expenditure of this money. The amendments went down to defeat, but the proposal to spend the money was adopted.

The former lack of interest I hold to have been due to two things: First, the carelessness of a great many people with respect to their state constitution. Second, to a reactionary spirit, particularly in the rural sections of the state, against constitutional amendments. I remember, when the new constitution of 1915 was pending, I asked an upstate legislator what he thought about the chance of its passing, and he said he did not think it had much of a chance. He had been speaking to the village oracle, and he asked him, "Are you going to vote for the new state constitution?" Whereupon his friend immediately replied, "What's the matter with the old one?"

CHAPTER XVII

Some Social Problems

IT would require a large volume to tell the full story of all that happened in the field of legislation in those six years. I can only group it inadequately and touch the more outstanding and significant efforts. In dealing with the preservation of political, individual, state and local rights, I recommended that the legislation enacted under the administration of Governor Miller taking away from localities their rights with respect to their agreements with public-utility corporations be repealed. I also recommended legislation giving New York City the right to construct, operate and regulate its own transit facilities. All this legislation passed the senate but was defeated in the assembly.

I recommended the repeal of the law requiring school teachers to submit to a loyalty test. Strange to say, the repeal bill passed both houses and I signed it, although the men who assisted in its repeal in the assembly were the very ones who had been responsible for its passage the year before. The same thing happened to the bill requiring a license and supervision for private schools.

In this period also the censorship of motion pictures had been established while I was out of office. In my annual message to the legislature, January, 1923, I began the struggle to repeal this un-American measure. The whole field of individual liberty seemed to me to be threatened with invasion. I wrote:

Censorship is not in keeping with our ideas of liberty and of freedom of worship or freedom of speech. The people of the state themselves have declared that every citizen may freely speak, write and publish his sentiments on all subjects, being responsible for the abuse of the right, and no law shall be passed to restrain or abridge liberty of speech or of the press. This fundamental principle has equal application to all methods of expression. . . .

Carrying this policy to its logical conclusion, everything written or spoken or taught might be subject to a censorship by public authority. We have abundant law in the state to jail the man who outrages public decency. If we have not, enact it. And we have jails enough to hold him after his conviction. I believe that the enactment of a statute providing for censorship of the moving pictures was a step away from the liberty which the Constitution guaranteed, and it should be repealed.

Despite the fact that the Republican administration fastened the Volstead Act into the state law, they agreed in 1924 to a petition to Congress to liberalize the Volstead Act. It looked like smart politics to the small-minded to amend the resolution in the assembly so as to provide that I personally transmit the resolution to the various congressmen and senators. I forthwith did so and had quite a correspondence with senators and representatives of both parties, some of whom agreed with New York State and others, like Senator Fess of Ohio, sharply took issue.

That same year a bill to repeal the state enforcement

act passed both houses and came to me. Here again we had the identical men in the assembly who, two years before, had passed the Mullan-Gage bill for state enforcement, now voting for its repeal.

Prohibition and its enforcement had grown to such prominence not only in the state of New York but everywhere else, that New York's final determination on the question of enforcement by state statute became an acute issue and was watched with interest throughout the country.

For probably the first time in my governorship the newspaper representatives from practically every city in the country came to Albany. My hearing on the bill, after it had passed both houses, occurred in the Assembly Chamber, no other room being sufficiently large to hold the great crowd of people who came to listen to the proceedings. Literally thousands of letters poured into the executive chamber on both sides of the question. It was quite apparent that here was a sharp division of opinion, and after the hearing I definitely determined in my mind that I would have to resolve the question according to my own conscience.

Friendly warnings and sometimes threats were made as to the effect upon my political future if I signed the repeal act. I signed it with the simple statement that I never allowed any future political consequences to myself to influence my action on any legislative or executive proposal or any definite principle.

In every year while I was governor I sponsored improvements to the labor laws and extensions of the workmen's compensation act. Public health and child welfare laws received much of my attention.

Among the social issues which came up during my various terms, housing gave me great concern. In August, 1920, housing conditions had become acute in New York and other large cities. Recommendations on housing made by the Reconstruction Commission had been ignored at the regular session of the legislature and a legislative commission had been appointed to study housing and rent profiteering. In September of that year the members of the legislative committee were prepared to join with the Reconstruction Commission in recommending an extraordinary session of the legislature to meet the emergency.

Every governor has hesitated to call the legislature into extraordinary session unless he is prepared to point to a real emergency. I called three extraordinary sessions of the legislature, and each time I felt that the public welfare required it. The first was called to ratify the suffrage amendment in 1919, the second to act on the housing shortage in 1920, and the third came in 1925, to secure action on the state park bond issue appropriation.

Before calling the 1920 session, I conferred with a group of advisers on the advisability of holding a special session of the legislature. Most of them were against it, being influenced by the consideration of what might happen to the Socialist assemblymen who had been expelled that year and whose seats were vacant in case of a special session. When I reached the decision that the session must

269

be held because of the housing shortage, I decided also to call a special election to fill the vacancies in the assembly districts not represented. These were five of the largest assembly districts of the state, where the housing problem was most pressing, and I could not reconcile myself to leaving them unrepresented in the extraordinary session called for the express purpose of relieving distress in these neighborhoods. Thereupon the electorate sent back to the assembly the same five men who had previously been dismissed for their political views. This time the leaders changed their procedure. After permitting the Socialists to take their seats a resolution was introduced to expel three of the five. This was debated all night and all five were permitted to participate in the debate. The next day the resolution expelling three out of the five was adopted. The two who were to have been permitted to remain resigned on the open floor.

The legislative commission on housing, of which Senator Charles C. Lockwood was chairman and to which Mr. Samuel Untermyer had been special counsel, was prepared to recommend legislation to amend various provisions of the law covering the method by which people are ejected from their homes for nonpayment of rent, known as summary proceedings.

New York's moving season has come to be October first. The method pursued by landlords had been to refuse to renew leases at the same rentals which people had been paying. Landlords made a practice of refusing to renew leases, and families were unable to find homes at the rentals which they had been paying. Mothers became panicky with the fear that there would be no place for them to live, since new construction had not kept pace with the growth of population, and all building had fallen off during the war. The courts were crowded with cases which the judges were attempting to adjudicate under the laws which had been passed at the special session of the legislature in 1919. Nearly a hundred thousand families faced eviction. I was convinced that the shortage of new housing and the importance of solving the housing problem as a whole was just as important as meeting the emergency created by attempts to profiteer in rents. I sent a message to the legislature asking for consideration of the bills presented by the special legislative committee and also requested the creation of a bureau of housing in the State Architect's office, as recommended by the Reconstruction Commission.

It must be borne in mind that the so-called rent laws enacted at the extraordinary session of September, 1920, were nothing more or less than temporary expedients to carry people over a period of stress. They were, in fact, temporary in their nature, because they were predicated on the state's police power and would have to fall to the ground when it could no longer be shown that a condition existed which menaced the health and welfare of the people.

The legislature refused to create the bureau of housing or to do anything toward the permanent solution of the housing problem. They only passed bills curbing rent profiteering and in order to stimulate building, a bill permitting cities to grant tax exemption on new construction. Absolutely nothing was said or done by the legislature to encourage the replacement of the old, dilapidated tenement houses in New York City and elsewhere. They had been deemed detrimental to the public health a quarter of a century before.

At the time of the passage of the original tenement-house law, it was believed that additional means of transportation and the construction of bridges over the East River would so distribute the city population as to change the character of certain of the old-fashioned neighborhoods of Manhattan Island. Experience taught us that you cannot move people by law. If a considerable number of people insist upon living in a given neighborhood, nothing done by law will change their ideas. Dilapidated old tenements are still being used for dwelling purposes. Children are still being brought up in dark, ill-ventilated, overcrowded, unsafe tenement houses not only in New York City but in all of the cities and even in some of the smaller communities of the state.

In order that some permanent policy might be established, I recommended, in 1920, the creation of a bureau of housing to make the necessary studies to encourage low-cost housing undertakings on a large scale and to study plans for tenement replacement. Nothing came of it in 1920, but in 1923 both houses of the legislature passed an act setting up such a bureau within the office of the state architect. This body was also charged with the duty of studying the situation from the standpoint of the short-age of housing, so that the legislature might be intelligently informed as to the necessity for prolonging the rent laws.

My personal experience assisted me in my studies on this subject. A survey made twenty-five years ago of tenement houses personally known to me on the lower East Side declared them to be unfit for human habitation. One block in my own assembly district was called, in the report, the Lung Block. It got its name from the number of deaths there in a given period from tuberculosis. That block is still in existence and the houses are still inhabited.

Nothing has been done toward tenement replacement for many years. For a time I shared the belief of many people that the northward growth of business would eventually wipe out the tenement sections, but experience has shown that that was a miscalculation. In fact, it has jumped over these old sections and moved farther uptown and left the tenement houses declared unfit for human habitation twenty-five years ago still being used. It was with that though in mind that I proceeded with my study of how to replace them with modern, sanitary, fireproof buildings. As a result of the studies of the bureau of housing a plan was evolved which was presented to me and which in turn I sent to the legislature in my annual message for 1926.

Upon the theory that better housing was essential for the protection of the public health, I advocated the creation of limited-dividend corporations which would undertake the construction of modern multiple dwellings at rentals not to exceed a certain limit per room per month. In order to encourage the establishment of such limited-dividend corporations, the state offered to them the power of condemnation in order that large sites which are essential for such undertakings could be readily and reasonably secured. I had discussed this plan with Mr. Frank Munsey shortly before his death, and his newspaper strongly advocated it. The localities, in turn, were empowered to lend their aid by the passage of local ordinances restricting tax assessments to the original value of the property without regard to the new improvement. The state was empowered to exempt the securities of the limited-dividend corporation from state taxation.

One of the chief difficulties in financing large-scale cheap housing is the cost of the financing. In order to meet that the creation of a state housing bank was suggested. Organized much like the Federal Farm Loan banks, they would have had power to borrow large sums of money at low rates of interest and lend it to limited-dividend companies engaging in cheap housing.

This scheme of a state housing bank did not meet with favor at the hands of the Republican legislators, and once again the old cry of socialism echoed through the halls of the Capitol. During the course of a conference on the proposed bill with the Republican leaders, their representatives and members of the State Housing Bureau, one young Republican leader accidentally let the cat out of the bag. He frankly told the conference that he had been talking to the leader of the Republican party the night before at a dinner and the leader told him that under no circumstances was he to stand for the housing bank.

Whereupon I said, "Gentlemen, what's the use of coming into conference with me about a subject which had been settled by the leaders of your party before you came here?"

As a result, I was compelled to accept the legislation minus the important part of it dealing with the finances. Incidentally, let me say that the trouble today in getting limited-dividend corporations under way to replace tenements is the difficulty of financing the cost of housing for really poor people.

Some few operations have taken place under the law which are gradually lending encouragement to people in a position to form limited-dividend corporations for better housing. The Amalgamated Clothing Workers, a trade union, was the first to avail itself of the opportunity to secure better housing in co-operation with the city and the state, and has built a group of multiple dwellings in the Bronx, modern in every respect.

Another limited-dividend corporation was started in Brooklyn, and the Sunshine Apartments are now ready for occupancy at Fourth Avenue and Twenty-fifth Street. The same corporation is about to build more. The recent purchase of two square blocks on Grand Street in New York City by a limited-dividend corporation headed by Lieutenant Governor Herbert H. Lehman, and Mr. Aaron Rabinowitz, member of the State Housing Board, is paving the way for modern dwellings on the lower East Side where they are sorely needed.

Naturally enough, I took a deep interest in the Department of Education. Since according to the constitution of the state the legislature "shall provide for a system of free common schools in which all of the children of the state are to be educated" I wanted to do everything I could to aid the department to function in accordance with that mandate. I lived in a neighborhood and was brought up in an environment where, because of conditions outside of the control of parents, I saw many deprived of that opportunity. While they may have been successful in after-life, I always realized their handicap when they entered the struggle that comes in after years. I might add that I brought my own personal experience to my study of the subject. I have often said that without great injury to the state we may postpone or delay some of our obligations, but the processes of education must always be kept at one hundred per cent of efficiency, if that is possible, because time lost cannot be regained by the children who are injured by the state's failure to make adequate provision for their education.

It was gradually borne in upon the state that the increasing cost of education would have to be met and that the problem of financing it was a most difficult one for both localities and state to solve. In 1919 and 1920, it became apparent that if we were to maintain a competent corp of school teachers and find new recruits for the teaching service, it was necessary for the state to increase its contributions to the localities for teachers' salaries. They were entitled to receive at least as much as is paid to a bricklayer, a carpenter or a painter, for the important function they were performing for the state.

To do it required two things—money and nerve. In 1920, although I was about to enter a campaign for reelection and was warned that one of the issues against me would be the increased cost of government, I recommended and signed a bill increasing the state's quota for teachers' salaries by twenty-two million dollars.

Throughout my governorship there was contention between myself and the leaders of the legislature on the consolidation of rural school districts. I have always held that there are entirely too many small school districts in the state. They were set up years and years ago, before the advent of the bus and the automobile as modern means of transportation. New York still has today many of the old-time, one-room schoolhouses where the school teacher devotes a short part of each day to the different grades from primary to highest grammar grades. Certainly the children in the country sections of the state are entitled to the same advantages of education as are given to the children in the cities. By persistent efforts we finally managed to get increased appropriations for rural districts amounting eventually to eleven million dollars.

When the pressure for increased state appropriations to localities for subsidies for teachers' salaries became so strong as to be undeniable and I had failed in all attempts to convince the reactionary element of the legislature,

I called a conference at the Executive Chamber consisting of leaders in the educational world, men and women interested in the promotion of public education, and economists. As an outcome of the conference I appointed an unofficial commission whose members represented educational thought and leadership in every part of the state. Needless to say, the legislature refused funds for any study of education which the Commission planned to undertake. After a meeting for organization, they elected Michael Friedsam, president of B. Altman and Company, chairman of the commission. So deep was his interest in the subject that he provided the finances for the operations of the commission.

This commission found that there was an uneven distribution of the state's share of teachers' salaries. They recommended a definite basis upon which state aid ought to be increased and submitted such a report with bills to carry it into effect at the legislative session of 1926. Their chief recommendation was increased state aid to localities.

In what I might call a stupid effort to embarrass me, the legislature declined to enact the statute giving additional state aid to the localities, but in the dying moments of the legislative session education and school teachers' salaries became the football of politics, and at the behest of the local New York City Republican leaders, a bill was passed making a special law for mandatory salary increases for teachers in New York City. The budget of the city had already been made up and there was no way that the city of New York could comply with the provisions of such a statute, except by the issuance of short-term revenue bonds in anticipation of the following year's taxes.

While it left me much to explain, I took the only position I could under the circumstances and I vetoed the proposed school teachers' salary increases for the city of New York. The political hope was that were I to be a candidate for governor again in 1926 the opposition might be able to enlist the antagonism of 23,000 school teachers in New York City, with all of their relatives and friends, not to speak of the influence this might have upon the school teachers and their families throughout the state.

When we entered the campaign in 1926, I was well able to explain to school authorities that a salary increase bill was offered at the same time that the Friedsam proposal that the state increase its quotas to localities was denied.

In 1927, after a full year of foolish opposition, the same leaders in the legislature accepted the recommendations of the Friedsam Commission in toto. The result of this has been an increase in the state subsidy for localities which has been spread over a number of years. It increased the annual appropriation bill of the state in the ten years covered by my period as governor from seven millions of dollars when I first began to seventy millions when I left. You cannot serve the cause of education without spending money to do it.

CHAPTER XVIII

An Eventful Year

THE year 1924 was an eventful one for me. Early in that year I was greatly shocked by the sudden death of Charles F. Murphy. He was stricken down when he appeared to be in possession of very good health. He left Tammany Hall around five o'clock in the afternoon of the day before he died. Employees at the hall remarked that they had never seen him looking better or stepping out more lively in his life.

My intimate acquaintance and association with Charles F. Murphy bore out what thousands of people have said of him, that "to know him was to love him." Outwardly he had a rather cold appearance. He was a man of great dignity and of very few words. But under the surface he had a heart of gold. He knew all about the struggle of life. He had risen from humble surroundings and was unquestionably one of the great political leaders of recent years.

When a triumvirate succeeded Richard Croker as leader of Tammany Hall, ex-Police Chief William Devery in nicknaming them called Mr. Murphy "a sport." Nothing could be further from the truth. Murphy was a plain, simple-living, straightforward man. He had no use for sport in the usual sense of the word. He never went to the race track. He never gambled. He played

ALFRED E. SMITH AND CHARLES F. MURPHY
On an Atlantic City holiday, Palm Sunday, 1916.

FACING THE MICROPHONES

The Notification Ceremonies at Albany, 1928. Seated on the platform with Governor Smith is Senator Joe T. Robinson, the vice-presidential candidate.

cards for amusement only. He was a regular attendant at church and frequently displayed a great admiration for young men who lead clean lives. He gave liberally to charitable causes but never talked about it and never permitted any publicity about it.

He never turned his back on any of the friends who started up the ladder with him. In his later years he often remarked to me that he would like to retire from the leadership of the Tammany organization but was unable to see his way clear to do so because of the assistance that he felt he could be to his friends.

His devotion to the men around him was well known. It took him several weeks to get over the shock of the sudden death of Tom Smith. Smith himself was one of the leading characters of Tammany Hall, for years its secretary. He was astute and able and a close adviser of Mr. Murphy. He was accidentally killed by a taxicab at the corner of Fourteenth Street and Broadway just after leaving Mr. Murphy at Tammany Hall.

Charles F. Murphy always exhibited a fatherly interest in the young men who advised with him. I will never forget my first meeting with him after the election of 1918 had been definitely decided. He said to me, "Al, it is a great thing for you, Mrs. Smith and the children and your mother. The organization will stand behind you like one man so that you may make good in the office of governor. I am anxious to see you make good so that we can show the people that a young man who has come from the lower east side and has been closely associated with all the phases of party activity, can make good." What he undoubtedly had in his mind was that I was the first man actively identified with the organization to be elected governor in the last half century.

Leadership, when you try to estimate it, is the survival of the fittest. Murphy was a great leader because he was a man of strong determination. It took him some time to make up his mind. He listened to all sides of a question, and a more patient listener I never met in my life. He finally made a decision and when he made it, he stood by it. He had an intimate knowledge of men. He could separate the selfish ones from the devoted with rare discrimination.

Upon the death of Mr. Murphy, for the first time in twenty years there arose the question of a new leader for Tammany Hall. The overwhelming consensus of opinion favored his son-in-law, Surrogate James A. Foley, whose ability and integrity had never been questioned. I tried to prevail upon Judge Foley to accept the leadership, and thought that I was meeting with some success, but his desire to continue in the work he was doing and to avoid as far as possible the labor and conflict incident to party leadership won out. The executive committee finally selected Judge Olvany, then judge of the Court of General Sessions.

In May of 1924 my mother died. She had never fully recovered from two attacks of pneumonia she had suffered, and though it was not apparent to my sister, who was with her all the time, I had begun to notice her fail-

ing gradually on my week-end journeys to Brooklyn to
see her. When she had her third attack of pneumonia
early in May, I felt that her resistance was so weakened
that it would be difficult for her to survive. She appeared
to be rallying, but finally, on Sunday afternoon, the
eighteenth of May, she passed away. It was the first real
sorrow I had ever suffered. I was looking forward to
making plans for her for the summer, and irrespective of
what might ultimately happen, I knew that she would
have been pleased with the reception given to my name
in the national convention, scheduled to occur at Madison Square Garden the following June. She was the old-
fashioned type, and all of her amusements and recreations
consisted of her life with her children and her grand-
children. She had no desire to go anywhere. She had not
been fifty miles away from the city of New York until I
took her to Albany.

After her death and after the labors of the legislative
session of 1924, I took a short vacation. The New York
World conducted a campaign, directed by Herbert
Bayard Swope, to bring the national Democratic convention of that year to New York City. The National Committee met and finally selected the big city. Appropriate
committees were formed and the city officials joined in
the welcome to the delegates and in June the national convention took place. Prior to the convention I had headquarters in the Prudence Building that had been opened
by a number of my friends, and there I met delegates from
all over the country.

In many respects the convention was unique in the history of the party. The religious issue used against me in my first campaign for the governorship in 1918 was reawakened by the activity of the Ku-Klux Klan. It was freely mentioned in the newspapers that in certain of the Southern and Western States the Ku-Klux Klan took an active part in the primary election for the selection of delegates. The influence of the Klan in the 1924 convention was so apparent that a large body of delegates insisted upon the passage of a resolution denouncing the Klan and voicing the Jeffersonian Democratic theory of freedom of religious belief.

Having kept personally in close touch with what was going on for weeks before the convention, I did not feel that anything would be gained by the passage of a resolution denouncing any large group of delegates or finding fault with their theories. Delegates from several of the larger states explained to me the unalterable opposition to the Klan of their people at home. They said that action denouncing the Klan was demanded of them. I saw then that it was a hopeless task to try to stop the passage of some resolution to set these delegates right with their people, as they expressed it, "back home."

After the convention was in progress for several days I became convinced that the united action of the Klan interests could not be overcome and I personally entertained very little hope of securing the nomination. It was apparent to me that I would receive no support in the convention from certain sections of the country no matter how long it lasted. Only one man south of the Mason and Dixon Line ever voted for me in all of the one hundred and three ballots that were taken. He was an elderly man named Applegate, from Tallahassee, Florida, who, after he had talked to me, decided to vote for me. When he returned to his seat after doing so, the Florida delegation pushed him off his chair and would not let him sit with them until he returned to the McAdoo camp.

The fears of the Klan delegations that the Tammany organization would take unfair advantage because the convention was held in New York City were very apparent. They came as though to the enemy's country. This gave the managers of the convention considerable concern. Though it was impossible to stem noisy demonstrations, I think it can be said that the convention was as ably managed as any in the history of the party. Admission was by ticket only, and the convention officials, aided by the police, were so alert that it was difficult even for leaders of the party not in possession of their credentials to enter the convention hall.

It was during the 1924 convention that the publication known as the *Fellowship Forum* which played such a large part in the recent presidential campaign made its first appearance in New York. Thousands of copies were sent to New York for distribution to the convention delegates. These papers contained a deliberate appeal to religious prejudice and bigotry.

It is known that the Anti-Saloon League spent large

sums of money telegraphing from a local telegraph station near the Madison Square Garden to the leaders of the Anti-Saloon League throughout the country. The purpose of their telegrams was to get large forces of people to keep in constant communication with the delegates from their own and other states, urging them to vote against me. Some of the telegrams received by the delegates were in the nature of threats of reprisal at the polls unless they did so. In fact, the late Wayne Wheeler, general counsel of the Anti-Saloon League, told me himself at the Manhattan Club that he was at the convention for the purpose of keeping alive and active the forces of the Anti-Saloon League against my nomination.

His friendly personal attitude to me in conversation prompted me to ask him some questions about the definition of an intoxicant as contained in the Volstead Law. I asked him why the Eighteenth Amendment was worded as we find it today and why he did not attempt the definition of an intoxicant in the amendment itself. He was frank enough to say to me that the Anti-Saloon League forces were afraid that it could not pass Congress in that form. I had quite an argument with him about the definition of an intoxicant as contained in the Volstead Law. He told me that they took the definition from the New York State excise law. I replied to him that New York State had at no time attempted to define an intoxicant by law for anything but taxation purposes. The state excise law, in order to prevent anybody dealing in beverages from escaping taxation, defined beverages subject to tax as those containing one-half of one per cent of alcohol.

Unable to maintain his side of the argument, he finally smiled and said "Well, we were in the saddle and we drove through." By that he meant that the Anti-Saloon League forces were in control of Congress and they wrote the Volstead Law and declared that any beverage containing more than one-half of one per cent of alcohol is intoxicating.

The Klan and the anti-saloon forces in the convention were practically identical. The force and power of the Anti-Saloon League was kept working all the time in the event that any of the Klan delegates should happen to weaken and come over and join my forces in the convention.

During the convention I made my headquarters in one of the small rooms on the top floor of the Manhattan Club directly across the street from Madison Square Garden. Here I received reports of what was taking place in the convention. While one of the sessions was under way, former Senator Owen of Oklahoma came to see me to solicit my help in securing for him the vote of the New York delegation for his nomination for the presidency.

As he approached me, he said, "Governor, how did this religious issue get into this convention?"

I replied to him, "I do not know, Senator. It certainly was not introduced by the New York delegation, because on that delegation there are men of all religions and men of no religion. I could probably secure their votes for you in the convention and there would be no question asked about your religion. The same would apply to a great many more of the Eastern States. How many votes can you get for me, Senator, in the Oklahoma delegation? You know, and I know, that you cannot secure one vote for me from your state, and you know why."

I was satisfied that Senator Owen did know why. I knew that I knew why, because two days before, the governor of Oklahoma had come to see me and asked me if anybody had promised me any votes from his state. I told him I wasn't sure, that I couldn't tell offhand, but I could find out.

The governor replied, "It's immaterial anyway. I'm simply here to tell you that you will get no votes from the state of Oklahoma. I am the Democratic governor of that state and I had all I could do to get on this delegation myself because I married a Catholic woman."

The speech putting me in nomination in 1924 was made by Governor Franklin D. Roosevelt, who was probably the most impressive figure in that convention. His speech was well received and excited much favorable comment. Its concluding line, with the quotation from "The Happy Warrior," has given me that title ever since.

When it became apparent to me and a goodly number of my followers that I could not be nominated and that the constant struggle, day in and day out, was working to the disadvantage of the party throughout the country, a conference between Mr. McAdoo and myself at the

Ritz Carlton apartment of former Ambassador Wallace was arranged by mutual friends. Here I met Mr. McAdoo face to face for the first time since the campaign opened. Herbert Bayard Swope, Thomas L. Chadbourne, Ambassador Wallace, and, I think, Stuart Gibboney, were the only others present. I suggested to Mr. McAdoo that we both withdraw our candidacies. I admitted that I did not believe I could be nominated and I was satisfied that he could not be. In the interest of party harmony, I suggested that we both remove our names from consideration, throw the convention into the hands of the delegates themselves and let them make the choice.

It was quite apparent from his attitude that he wanted to have something to say about the choice, and he suggested E. T. Meredith of Iowa, Secretary of Agriculture in the Wilson administration. I told him frankly that I did not have the control of the delegates who were for me. I was satisfied that they were for me, but after they left me I did not feel I could have anything to say about where they went, and consequently I could not accede to his suggestion. Whereupon we parted and shook hands like two old-time friends.

The next day I carried out my own suggestion and withdrew my name from further consideration by the convention. Mr. McAdoo did not do the same. Immediately after my withdrawal the convention started to drift to John W. Davis, former Solicitor General of the United States and United States Ambassador to the Court of St. James's. The drift gathered momentum as the days went by, and on the one hundred and third ballot the required two-thirds declared in favor of Davis and he was nominated.

Recess was immediately taken and a hurried conference was called, in which I was invited to take part, to decide the nomination for the vice presidency. We met in the large dining room of the Manhattan Club. The late Tom Taggart of Indiana suggested Vice President Marshall. I suggested Governor George S. Silzer of New Jersey, but when it was discovered that John W. Davis had changed his residence to New York City and had voted from his Park Avenue apartment, it was deemed inexpedient to take the vice-presidential candidate from the eastern part of the country, and accordingly names were suggested from the Middle West. Among them was former Governor Charles Bryan of Nebraska. I spoke at that time of the danger of nominating the brother of William Jennings Bryan because of the very apparent hostility of delegates from the northeastern part of the country to Mr. Bryan. The responsibility for the decision belonged to Mr. Davis, who was the newly selected national leader of the party, and he decided it.

Immediately following the nominations, and in order to remove any doubt that might have lingered in the minds of the delegates as to my attitude, I appeared before the convention and made a speech. I promised the delegates in no uncertain terms that I would take off my coat and vest and work for the ticket as hard as I knew how.

Running again for governor was not in my program for that year. I had had four years of it and I had made three state-wide campaigns. The work was beginning to tell upon me and I was anxious to retire to private life. My children were all young, and I wanted to get back to work so that I could establish a business I could leave to them. But the party leaders, headed by John W. Davis himself, made a strong demand upon me that I accept renomination. I asked Mr. Davis point-blank what he thought I could do for him that would make the biggest contribution to his success and he promptly replied, "Run for governor again." I at once pointed out to him the possibility that I might carry the state and he might not. I was afraid that under such circumstances my followers would be left open to the charge of disloyalty, but it made no impression upon him, and he insisted that I run for governor.

The nomination of Bryan for Vice President worked out afterward as I had expected. During the course of the campaign, not hundreds but probably thousands of people, particularly women, asked me if there was any way that they could vote for Davis and not for Bryan. It would be unreasonable to expect that the feeling injected in that convention would die out immediately. It was the first national convention that was on the radio, and in all parts of the United States people were listening to the proceedings. Shortly after the convention I went on a trip through the state to inspect some of our institutions and look over some public works, and I became convinced that the feeling had not died out. Every place I went I heard of the dissatisfaction over the proceedings of the convention. John W. Davis himself, as a man and as a candidate, was highly thought of. His great ability, his clean record, caused him to stand out in the minds of the people, but the feeling against Bryan and the feeling against the delegates from the Klan-ridden states was so strong that it seemed to me to be beyond the power of human accomplishment to wipe it out entirely.

In an effort to help the national ticket, I consented to renomination, and in September of that year was nominated for the fourth time by the Democratic party, in convention at Syracuse. The Republican nominee was Theodore Roosevelt, Jr. Probably there was no election that I ever entered that I felt so sure of winning as that of 1924. I did not believe that young Roosevelt, speaking with due respect for him and all his family, measured up to the proportions required for the governorship of New York. I was encouraged in that belief by the large number of Republicans who so expressed themselves.

Following the campaign of 1922, I had appointed Joseph M. Proskauer, who was chairman of the citizens' committee for that election, to the Supreme Court to fill a vacancy. He was afterward elected to the court and therefore, for campaign manager in 1924, I selected a distinguished New York citizen, Raymond V. Ingersoll, as chairman of the citizens' committee for my re-election. As usual, the headquarters were opened at the Hotel Biltmore. People interested in political campaigns unconsciously find themselves superstitious, and because of successes in the past, selection of places of meeting, methods of campaigning and personnel, selection of duties for the different people concerned, are followed out in practically the same way from year to year.

The citizens' committee for my election was always an independent body and contained numerous people not directly affiliated with the regular Democratic organization and, in fact, always had on it a goodly number of Republicans. After my first term we had an increasing number of applicants from the Republican ranks for membership on the citizens' committee. All the details of the campaign were attended to by this committee, John F. Gilchrist being always the point of contact between the committee and the regular organization in the different counties of New York City. George R. Van Namee and James A. Parsons were in control upstate outside of the limits of Greater New York. Both men were extremely valuable as upstate campaign managers because of long association and friendship with the party leaders.

Before the state campaign opened I made a trip to New England for the national ticket. I spoke at Manchester, New Hampshire, and at Boston, dealing in both places with the national issues. While in Boston I was taken with an attack of neuritis. It disabled me for a few days. I was unable to complete the New England engagement and came on to New York, and one week later plunged into the state campaign.

One advantage that I had over Colonel Roosevelt in

the campaign was that I spoke only once a day for an hour and a half at a time. Moreover, I took one subject a day and discussed it thoroughly. Colonel Roosevelt followed the old-time method of campaigning, making sixteen speeches a day from the rear platform of a railroad car. It was not long before it became apparent that I was making an impression on the voters of the state by dealing in detail with the big issues.

The figures of the result of that campaign gave me some concern. Calvin Coolidge had carried the state of New York by more than 850,000 plurality. I carried it for governor by 108,561. I was anxious to know the reason for the spread between John W. Davis and myself in New York City. I sent for one of the employees of the trucking company with which I was formerly identified, and asked him to talk to his men and sound them out and see why, in a particular section where a number of them lived, there was such a difference in the presidential and gubernatorial vote. He informed me that part of it was due to the feeling that grew up in the 1924 national convention and part of it was due to the "prosperity issue."

The 1924 election had furnished additional argument against the selection of a governor in a year that a President is running. Absolutely no attention was paid to the Democratic state ticket, and as a result the heavy vote for the presidential candidate dragged in the whole Republican state ticket aside from the candidate for governor. Had I not been so prominent in advancing constructive reforms for the state and able to make a vigorous campaign, the history of 1920 would have repeated itself and the whole Republican state ticket would have ben elected on national issues. I have always claimed that that is not in the best interests of the state.

Seymour Lowman of Chemung County was elected lieutenant governor. He was the same man who had represented the dry forces and sought to embarrass me in the campaign of 1922. The confusion of the issues brought about a peculiar situation in a state that declared for a modification of prohibition by more than a million votes in a popular referendum and then selected one of the prohibition leaders for lieutenant governor.

The campaign over, I promptly plunged into the business of preparing the budget and the annual message to the legislature of 1925.

None of my inaugural speeches was ever prepared. I delivered them extemporaneously. I never regarded Inauguration Day as the right time to deliver a long speech on policy. I would rather deliver that to the legislature in joint session, relying upon the newspapers and radio to carry it throughout the state, and in my inauguration on January 1, 1925, I simply said:

"History tells me that today I am the recipient at the hands of the people of the state of New York of the signal and most distinguished honor of being the first man in exactly one hundred years to be inaugurated as governor for a third term.

"I approach the reception of this honor with a heart full of gratitude. I am unable to make myself believe that there is anything in any small accomplishment of mine in the past to justify so great an honor.

"I come to my great office with no partisan mission. I feel as if I were standing alone amidst the wreckage and disaster that overtook the Democratic party on November fourth. All that I can say is that I shall continue to give to the state the best service of which I am capable.

"This is the sixteenth time that I have taken the oath of allegiance to the state in this room. I have a deep and abiding affection for the assembly chamber. It has been my high school and my college; in fact, the very foundation of everything that I have attained was laid here. I approach this term only with a desire to do what is best for the great state of New York and keep her in the forefront of the commonwealths of the Union, where she rightfully belongs. I have the desire and disposition, the heart and the courage, and thanks to God Almighty, the health to work hard, and I promise in this chamber and in his divine presence to give the people of the state the very best that is in me."

CHAPTER XIX

Some Responsibilities of Being Governor

AT a public dinner I once said, jokingly, that the constitution of our state should be amended to provide for the election of two governors—one to attend to the business of the state and the other to attend public and social functions not directly connected with the business of the state. I was prompted to make that remark by the enormous volume of invitations, supplemented by personal requests, that come to public men to attend all kinds of functions. Even a slight acquaintance at times leads people to believe that the governor should attend a wedding in the family or a christening. Invitations to attend the laying of cornerstones for private buildings, private charitable enterprises, meetings of trade bodies, anniversary celebrations of all kinds, testimonial dinners, requests for the use of the governor's name for drives for charitable and religious purposes or for donations, all pour into the governor's office.

Explaining to personal friends how impossible it was for me to attend any considerable part of the affairs to which I had been invited took much time. To convince them of the impossibility of what they asked, I had my secretary compile a list of the invitations I received at the executive chamber in the course of a given month. In many instances five different affairs took place on one night. For my own protection and to enable me to carry on the business of the state, I had a fixed and definite rule not to attend any public gathering unless, by going, I could in some way serve the state or the city of New York.

Sometimes an invitation to a quasi-public gathering affords the governor an opportunity to give a personal message not only to the people at the function but to all the people of the state. I have taken advantage of such gatherings to speak about water power, reorganization of the government and the various subjects in which I was interested.

Holding office over a number of years, the invitation difficulty is a great deal like a snowball rolling downhill. It gathers size, weight and momentum as it travels. In the early years of my governorship these invitations were limited to a few large cities of the state. In the later years I received them from all parts of the country. If I had accepted ten per cent of the invitations I would have traveled by rail a distance equivalent to four times around the world.

When all is said and done, it seems impossible to divorce the personal equation from politics. It makes no difference whether you are running for office in a small civil division of one county in a certain state or whether you are running for the presidency of the United States. If you have been active in politics you will find it exactly the same thing.

When I began holding elective office demands upon

my time and requests for my services in different lines came from one assembly district. When I was elected sheriff of New York County they came from the whole county. When I was elected president of the Board of Aldermen, they came from the city. When I became governor, it broadened out to the state of New York and, finally, to the United States. The man in the Far West writes to me about his son in New York just exactly as the woman on Cherry Street used to come to see me at the clubhouse about her son. Advice and suggestion in the form of letters that at first came only from the city of New York now come from the state of Washington or California. This is easy to understand when you take into consideration the fact that people remember most easily a man for whom they voted.

These letters and communications concern men who seek employment, business connections, care of the sick, requests for donations to various charitable endeavors, or the use of one's name in connection with enterprises that, in the opinion of the writers, require advertising they might not get in any other way. Added to these, of course, is the great army of people who desire to see a prominent man, if only to talk to him. My experience teaches me to make the definite assertion that politics is politics, whether you are an alderman or whether you are President of the United States, unless a man happens to be of the type who allows secretaries to dispose of all of his business—and that is something I never could do. I have probably read more personal letters and answered more personal letters than any man in the governorship in the history of the state.

All of this, of course, exposes a man, without his own knowledge, to certain dangers in political office. There is a familiar expression: "Save me from my friends; I can take care of my enemies." Under the guise of friendship a favor may at times be sought from a man in public life, which, in turn, may be used or sold to benefit the so-called friend. It is necessary to keep a sharp lookout, particularly on pardons or commutations of sentence, where the action must be taken by the governor himself, to say nothing of the operation of departments under him where special favors may be bought and sold by an individual who plays upon the friendship of the governor.

After I left the office of governor in 1920, two men were indicted in New York County for having secured money from a woman for the pardon of her husband, on the plea that part of it had to go to a brother-in-law of mine. Neither of these men knew his name. They simply knew that I had a brother-in-law. The fact of the matter is that neither of them had anything at all to do with the release of the prisoner. The commutation had been granted upon the express recommendation of the judge who sentenced him, after a review of all the facts; but having had access to the executive chamber for the purpose of shaking hands with me, these men convinced the woman that it was through their friendship for me and their desire to help my brother-in-law that her husband had secured his freedom. I was a witness against these men at their trial.

Years ago it was a common practice among foreigners to exploit their countrymen by stating that the favor they sought had to be paid for. One man of whom I know served two years in Sing Sing prison for extorting $200 from an alien on the promise that he was to secure for him some shares in the Brooklyn Bridge. To convince him of his ability to do so, he walked down to the bridge one day with the alien and left him standing on the curb. He walked up to a policeman and asked him a question, to which the policeman nodded his head "Yes." He went back to the foreigner and said, "Did you see that? It's all right. He is working for us." Thereafter he and his confederates gave the alien some stock certificates decorated with seals and blue ribbons to give them the appearance of genuineness.

Another man sold to one of his newly arrived countrymen the right to erect a fruit stand at the Staten Island ferry station, forging the permit from the Department of Public Works. He was able to make this impression because the foreigner knew that he was acquainted with the superintendent of the Bureau of Encumbrances. The foreigner discovered the fraud only when a policeman arrested him the day that he drove a wagonload of lumber to South Ferry in order to erect his fruit stand.

Comparatively few people out of the eleven million who make up the state know the social side of the duties

301

of the governor of New York. In the course of a year thousands of people from all over the country visit Albany and while in the Capitol express a desire to shake hands with the governor. It is difficult, if not impossible, to deny them that small privilege as visitors from other states. After the interview with the newspapermen, which occurs every morning at eleven o'clock, the governor goes to the outer Executive Chamber while the line forms in front of him to shake hands and in some instances to speak to him.

Sometimes other states and foreign countries appoint committees to visit the governor to discuss with him various phases of the government of the state. Courtesy to neighboring states and foreign countries requires that the governor at least meet the delegates although he may be compelled to turn them over afterward to the head of the proper department. A delegation from Japan came to Albany to study our educational system. None of the delegates could speak English, and so, by the time every one of the delegates said something to me and the interpreter interpreted it, and I answered back to the interpreter, and he, in turn, interpreted for the representatives, one whole hour was taken up in the exchange of cordial greetings, whereupon the Commissioner of Education took over seriously the task of giving them the information which was the object of their visit.

Likewise foreign countries came to study the road-building processes and program of the state. Other committees came to Albany to talk about the operation of the

Erie Canal. Agricultural societies, boards of trade, women's clubs which come to Albany for their annual meetings, all call on the governor.

Young couples visiting Albany on their honeymoon always find their way up to the governor's office, and at this critical moment in the young man's life he is anxious to show the young girl that not only has he entrée to the the Capitol but he proposes to introduce her to the governor. No governor could be found guilty of dampening the ardor of that young man at that particular time. I found myself devoting a good part of a week to congratulating young couples on their honeymoons and in many instances autographing photographs for them.

During the Easter holidays and at Christmas time many schoolchildren journey en masse under the direction of their teachers to the Capitol, where they get a practical lesson in government. They are lectured to in the state museum, in the halls of the legislature, and in the executive department. As one schoolteacher said to me in the inner office one day, "These children have seen everything in Albany except the thing they want to see most."

I said, "What's that?"

She replied, "That's you."

In the summertime, when one would imagine that the governor would have some leisure, he is going through one of the busiest seasons of the year. There is no deputy governor. The lieutenant governor rarely appears in Albany after the adjournment of the legislature. There is nobody except the governor to whom you can refer people who desire to talk to the head of the government. In a great many instances they talked about subjects not related to any departments of the government. Then again there are countless thousands of people who never hear of anybody else in connection with the government of their state except the governor himself, and when they have anything to talk about or any business to transact, they start at the head.

As a result, the daytime of the governor is completely taken up with matters that really have nothing to do with the routine business of running the executive department. The natural result of that is night work. In my eight years as governor I probably did as much real work at night in the Executive Mansion when there was nobody around as I did in the Executive Department.

One of the largest single drains upon the time of the governor is his necessary attention to extradition proceedings. Every fugitive from justice from any state of the Union apprehended within the state of New York can only be returned under arrest to his own state after the governor signs three sets of papers. Similarly, fugitives from justice from our own state can only be extradited after the governor signs a similar number of papers.

When residents of the state of New York are wanted for crimes in other states and they make a request for a hearing before the governor before he signs the order to extradite, it is difficult, if not impossible, to deny it to them. Much time is taken up in listening to arguments by counsel of both sides as to whether or not the extradition papers should be signed. In extradition proceedings the governor is both judge and jury. He passes, in the first instance, upon the law, and then upon the facts. It must be determined whether the prisoner was in the state on or about the time the crime was committed, whether he is the man named in the papers, and then the facts must be studied. In some of the cases there are indications of grave miscarriages of justice. One example was the case of a man charged with assault in Paterson, New Jersey, at a time and hour when it was definitely proved that he was in the city of Albany.

Many extradition proceedings are for non-support, where a disagreement has arisen between man and wife. The power of extradition in the hands of the governor can be used to effect a reconciliation. Sometimes the grievances of these parties are largely imaginary and, when brought before the governor, it is possible to patch up their differences, save the necessity of extradition and give them a new start in life in a happy frame of mind. A common form of extradition growing out of family disagreements is for kidnaping. I remember a recent case where the child was in the custody of the father in the state of California and the mother was a resident of New York City. She went out to California to see the child and found it in an institution where, according to the evidence laid before me, it was not receiving the proper care and attention. The look on the child's face, when I suggested that she go back to California to her father, was sufficient to lead me to the belief that the mother was the proper one to have custody of the child and I made an arbitrary decision and dismissed the request for extradition, leaving the child in New York with its mother.

Nothing in this world comes easy. The governorship gives a man great distinction, great honor, great glory, great happiness for himself and his family, but he has to pay. And at no time during his term of office does he pay harder than when confronted by the unfortunate parents, wives and children of the young men who find their way into the state's prisons or are condemned to death for capital crime. While, theoretically, this burden is supposed to fall upon the governor's counsel, the fact of the matter is that the largest part of it falls directly upon the governor himself, unless he wants to be hardhearted and cold-blooded about it and refuse to see the people. That I was never able to do.

Consequently, I gave a great deal of my time to talking to the relatives of the men in our state prisons. The power of pardon under our constitution is plenary, and it rests with the governor alone and can be exercised by him upon any terms or conditions he sees fit to impose.

Nothing is so distressing as the attention the governor is compelled to give to applications for executive clemency when the prisoner is to be put to death. It is impossible for a man to escape the thought that no power in the world except himself can prevent a human being from going over the brink of eternity after the Court of Appeals has sustained the verdict of the lower courts. I had very many unhappy nights when executions took place.

Some Responsibilities of Being Governor

The governor is constantly haunted by the terrible question that if anything should develop after the execution to indicate that the prisoner was not guilty, how much of the responsibility would he be compelled to carry personally for the ending of that man's life? I studied and worked very hard, sometimes into the small hours of the morning, on the record and papers, facts and arguments in capital cases.

When dealing with parents, the most difficult situation arises out of what is called statutory murder. In New York State that means murder which has been committed while another felony is in progress. Under our law, it is not necessary that the defendant take any part in the actual murder. If he takes part in the other felony and murder results from it, he is guilty of murder in the first degree under the law, and the judges invariably charge the jury that the verdict must be either murder in the first degree or not guilty.

I have particularly in mind the trying time I had with four men who were put to death for the murder of a ticket taker on the subway at Intervale Avenue Station in the Bronx. Two of the four men never saw the deceased, but they took part in the felony of highway robbery and were judged guilty of murder in the first degree and their conviction was unanimously affirmed by the Court of Appeals. The mother of one of the young men was never able to understand how her son could be convicted of the murder of a man he never saw.

In their despair the relatives of the condemned appeal to everybody to speak a word to the governor for them. In the Bronx murder case the lawyers resorted to writs of habeas corpus and battled every inch of the way right up to the night of the execution.

For fear of accident, it has been customary for the governor to be in touch with the prison on the night of an execution. By custom it occurs at eleven o'clock on Thursday night of the week which the Court of Appeals fixed for the execution. In order that I might know exactly to whom I was talking on the telephone, I had arranged a code with the Superintendent of Prisons, who was always at Sing Sing prison on the Thursday night when anybody was to be put to death. In the code I used two names from the cast of the play *The Shaughraun*, and when the superintendent called me on the phone from Ossining, he would say "Harvey Duff," and I answered back "Corry Kinchella." I then knew that I was talking to the Superintendent of Prisons and he knew that he was talking to the governor. Intriguing, sharp individuals might easily impersonate the Superintendent of Prisons, if for no other purpose than to delay the execution.

At such times there is a certain amount of hysteria and people who are not of well-balanced mind are affected by it. One night when a prisoner was to be electrocuted at eleven o'clock at Sing Sing prison, a man walked into the West Fifty-Seventh Street police station, asked to see the police captain, and informed him that he was guilty of the murder for which this man was about to be put to death, and asked the captain to stay the execution. The man was respectable in appearance and gave no indication of an unbalanced mental condition. The captain of the police actually called the Sing Sing prison, only to find that the man had already been executed. The story leaked out and an Albany newspaper blazed forth the next morning with a headline: "Innocent Man Electrocuted at Sing Sing."

When the newspaper was shown to me, I was incensed beyond power of expression to think that a newspaper, without any further investigation or knowledge of the facts, would put out that particular headline. The case was one of a young man who had committed murder in Rochester. He made no defense and his mother had admitted to me that he committed the crime. The man who brought the false information to the station house was the next day committed to the psychopathic ward of Bellevue Hospital and found to be insane.

While the governor is in this disturbed state of mind, clever lawyers can add to his state of confusion by statements so well put and so plausible upon their face as to start doubt in his mind. I had a very clear example of this in a hearing in the case of a young man who shot another man to death in a clubhouse on Sixth Avenue and Forty-Third Street, New York City. The doubt in the testimony raised by the attorney hinged around the fact that it would be a physical impossibility for the defendant to be back in the room where the murder occurred so shortly after he was seen at another place. I made a memorandum of all the facts, and the following week-end, when in New York, accompanied by my secretary and two detectives from Police Headquarters, I went to the premises myself, re-enacted the contradiction of the evidence and made a personal survey in order to satisfy myself that the testimony as given by the policeman was such as to be entirely possible. It disproved the assertions made on behalf of the defendant.

Probably the hardest time a governor has had in recent years came to me in the period of two weeks before and the night of the execution of Mrs. Snyder. I doubt if I ever felt for anybody as I did for her mother. Her helplessness in the whole situation was so apparent that anybody with a heart at all would have had to feel for her, but the crime was such an atrocious one, the evidence so overwhelming and the decision of the Court of Appeals being unanimous, nothing remained but to leave Mrs. Snyder to her fate unless, because of sentiment, the governor was prepared to set aside the laws of the state.

The volume of correspondence on both sides of the Snyder case that poured into the Executive Chamber was amazing. People wrote not only to me but to all the members of my family. A great part of the hysteria was, no doubt, promoted by the sensational press. So tense was the situation that for an hour before the execution and until it was all over I sat at an open telephone wire between Sing Sing prison and the place where I was in New York City on that night.

More people were executed during my time as governor than in the term of any other governor in the state's history. This is in part due to the length of time I was in office and also to the wave of crime following the war.

I gave public hearings on every capital case, and in only one instance did I find a man about to go to the electric chair for whom nobody spoke a word, whom nobody seemed to know. The cases come directly to the governor from the Court of Appeals with the notice of the week of execution. In every instance a request for a hearing was made except in this one.

I went over this case with the same amount of care that I devoted to all the others where a hearing was requested and given. I summoned my own counsel, a judge of the Court of Claims, and several other men to my private office in the Executive Chamber. I argued the case with them, and finally commuted the sentence of the man because I became convinced that he should have been found guilty of a lesser degree of homicide. I was urged to my position by the repeated statements of the district attorney that the woman with whom the defendant had been living was not his wife and that therefore there was no reason why he should have killed a man whom he found with her merely on the impulse of the moment. The fact, nevertheless, was that this man and woman had lived together for sixteen years, during all of which time he made ample provision for her support. I came to the conclusion that she was in his eyes his wife, and that the repeated statement of the district attorney had had a prejudicial effect upon the jury. I became convinced that had it not been for that repeated assertion the verdict in this case would probably have been second-degree murder.

It is hard to have an attitude on the question of capital punishment and have it sensibly. Most people who have one have it sentimentally. I would like some indication whether anything less than death in capital cases provides a sufficient deterrent against the commission of the crime of murder in the first degree. It might be well for the state to try an alternative, but before doing so the constitution should be amended so as to take away from the governor the power of pardon in capital cases and provide that no person convicted of murder in the first degree will ever get out of prison, except by decree of the court based upon newly discovered evidence tending to establish innocence of the crime.

Nobody can prove that capital punishment has not been a deterrent. The only way to prove it is to find out whether there are no more deliberate murders committed when the deterrent is less than death. All our murder cases in recent years have been committed when the murderer was engaged in another felony. The only deliberately planned murder of all of them was the Mrs. Snyder case. Years ago there were a great many deliberate murders. The murder of Harry Cornish, the murder of Mrs. Fleming, the murder of Mrs. Harris, and the Rosenthal murder were all prompted by and executed for profit to the participants.

The great question is: if the deterrent is less than death, will it encourage that form of murder? Nobody can answer that question without giving it a trial. My reason for suggesting that the pardoning power be taken away from the governor if capital punishment is abolished grows out of the experience that no prisoner dies in prison. Twenty or twenty-five years being a generation, the prisoner is old, the crime is forgotten, and if nobody else does it, the prison authorities themselves will begin to urge the governor to let the prisoner out. Therefore the person who sits down to plan a murder in cold blood can at least cling to the straw that while there is life there is hope, that as long as he is not going to be electrocuted for the crime, he has a chance to get out some day or other unless the constitution is amended.

The power of pardon is so great that it carries a corresponding responsibility. The fact of the matter is that few men are actually released from prison by pardon from the governor. The public mind is more or less confused on the question of executive clemency, because all pardons are regarded as alike in all circumstances. This is not the case.

Pardons are issued for various reasons and differ in their effects. Taking the year 1927 as a typical year during my governorship, I pardoned only five prisoners in that year, when the pardon meant their actual release from prison. In three of the five cases the pardon was extended because of the physical condition of the prisoners. They were suffering from advanced tuberculosis, and, unless pardoned, would, in all human probability, have died in prison. A fourth man I released from the Suffolk County jail in order that he might attend the funeral of his wife. He had but eight days more of his sentence to serve. The fifth one was pardoned on the recommendation of the district attorney and the sheriff of Onondaga County, who certified to me that the prisoner aided the state in preventing a jail delivery after several of the prisoners of the jail had overcome the keepers by throwing red pepper in their eyes.

A good many pardons are issued to permit aliens, convicted before they became citizens, to attain citizenship. In many cases these are minor crimes, and the judges in the courts of naturalization made a rule and regulation that they would recognize the applicant's right to citizenship after conviction of a crime, provided he had a pardon from the governor.

Another form is issued to prevent deportation. In many instances these are young men living in this country with their parents. All these pardons, however, are predicated on the further consideration that the conduct of the applicant while in prison was good and that he gave promise of reform. This particular form of pardon requires very little of the governor's time personally, as the facts about conduct are all prepared by the prison authorities and the information about his family is supplied from the same source. Both these forms of pardon are extended only after the full sentence has been served.

Some pardons are granted to remove disability after the prisoner has completed his sentence and paid his debt to society in full for his transgression of the law. A license, for instance, will not be issued to a man to practice the business of chauffeur after having committed a crime. The pardon of the governor removes such a disability. In some instances the men had been convicted only once and after their release from prison had given a good account of themselves.

Another form of pardon is for the purpose of restoring citizenship and giving to the pardoned man the right to exercise his franchise. In these instances the state requires that he furnish references as to his good character and good conduct for a reasonable time after he has completed his prison term.

The governor has not only the power of pardon but he has the power of commutation. That is to say, he can take off as much time from the given sentence of any man in the state institutions as, in his judgment, he thinks best. There is no fixed or definite rule with regard to commutations. They are extended by the governor for numerous reasons. In many cases commutation of sentence is directly recommended by the judge who sentenced the man and the district attorney who prosecuted him. These officials are moved to their request by knowledge which comes to them after the trial.

Frequently commutations are issued by the governor because of the physical condition of the prisoners. I remember commuting the sentence of a man in Sing Sing who was suffering from advanced heart trouble. While changing his clothes to leave the prison the excitement of the commutation brought about his death.

Practically all of these commutations were given to men sentenced under the indeterminate-sentence law, and the governor only commutes the minimum sentence to time served. The maximum sentence imposed by the court still remains. That means that the prisoner is out on parole and reports monthly to the Board of Parole. Unless he gives a satisfactory account of himself, he can, under the law, be brought back to prison under the direction of the Board of Parole and made to serve any part of his maximum sentence they may see fit to impose. Commutation of sentence is also extended to men in order that they may be sent home to their own countries.

Pardon and commutation are matters which rest with the governor and his own conscience. There can be no hard and fast rule governing them. The interest of the state must, of course, be the governor's first consideration. The governor is the spokesman for society. What is best to do in a given case must be dictated to the governor by his own conscience.

I pardoned a number of political prisoners and I frankly said in pardoning them that I did not agree with their political views, but I pardoned them in spite of my disagreement with them. In the case of James J. Larkin, convicted of criminal anarchy, one of the judges of the Court of Appeals, sustaining the conviction of the lower court, stated that "the sentence may have been too heavy for the offense." Larkin's prison record was of the best, and many highly respected citizens, including the assistant district attorney who conducted the prosecution, petitioned me for his pardon.

Executive clemency is a human thing. There are no two cases alike. I commuted the sentence of a man who was blind. He was an accidental murderer. He killed a woman with whom he had been living when he was well past middle age. His conduct toward society prior to the commission of that crime was beyond reproach. I was never able to see why the state, in his case, demanded the full penalty of the law. His impaired physical condition came upon him while he was awaiting the decision of the court of last resort and was the direct result of an attempt to take his own life. Once I had to pardon a man because of the attempts that were made on his life by the other inmates of the prison.

My long experience with applications for pardons and commutations of sentence led me quite naturally to the belief that there is a fundamental weakness in our whole method of dealing with criminals. So many district attorneys have certified to me that new facts developed after trial; so many judges have written to me saying that they afterward regretted the severity of some sentence, even to the point of admitting that when it was imposed it was in response to what seemed to be public clamor in their particular locality to put down crime, that I came to the definite conclusion that the modern state, with advanced ideas along other lines, might well take a step forward and change its method of dealing with criminals.

It is not so many years ago in the life of the state when the whole theory was punishment of the individual. We then found people being put to death for what we regard today as minor offenses. We look back on the ducking stool, the stocks and the thumbscrews as being part of the barbarity of an age that is past. Material progress in worldly things and in government in the last half century strongly suggests that we take advantage of modern psychiatry and modern social science, modern ideas and concepts in our handling of prisoners.

In the rush and bustle of our criminal courts, particularly in our large cities, it is physically impossible for a judge or a district attorney to make the proper study of an individual. Not what he did and what sentence the law allows the judge to impose for that act, but all the contributing factors, the things that led the man to the crime, the things that drove him to it, in some instances, should be before the court. It is because so much of this is found out afterward that judges and district attorneys constantly petition the governor to commute sentences. Time and again I have had a judge write to me stating that he had sentenced a man, but that he himself felt that the sentence was a little bit heavy. "There was a great hue and cry in our neighborhood because of the crime wave and I did it to scare off the others." A sentence coming from the courts that afterward has to be interfered with by the governor cannot be said to have been well considered.

Many of the young men committed to prison, if all the

facts about their physical and mental condition had been properly before the court, might have been sent to an institution for mental defectives. My study of many of the cases showed young boys with criminal intent starting off early in life by going to the juvenile society, the reformatory, the state penitentiary, and finally prison. Such punishment had no effect upon that prisoner. The state should also take into consideration the enormous cost of putting a man through all these institutions, the cost to business, and the expense of judges and courts, in trying and finding him guilty, and of transporting the prisoner around the state. Probably a little more scientific treatment after his first offense might have saved that man to the state and might have saved society from the crimes he finally committed. I would regard such treatment as not only a humane move on the part of the state but as a good business move also. In other words, I am afraid that, because of the pressure of cases in the large centers of population, our criminal courts become mechanical.

After conviction for a felony a prisoner should become the property of the people of the state. Why not let the state, through a competent board of doctors, psychiatrists and students of criminology, make the proper disposition of him? It would make for even-handed justice on the part of the state. Prior to the consolidation of the courts of special sessions in New York, a legislative committee of which I was a member found a man in one borough of the city sentenced to one term and another man in another borough sentenced to an entirely different term for exactly the same offense, with all the circumstances as alike as they could possibly be, taking the human equation into consideration.

Sensible, sound, even-handed judgment based upon expert knowledge is possible by the creation of a board to make disposition of the prisoner after conviction. It is not reasonable to expect that it can be done by numerous judges sitting in various parts of the state, with widely varying ideas on the subject. The function of such a board as I suggest will be to dispose of the prisoner after the verdict of guilty has been rendered by the jury. The judge would then simply preside over the trial, give the jury the law, and see that the prisoner gets a fair trial.

To the average man and woman the apprehension and conviction of the criminal are the beginning and end of their interest in him. Because of that the state has been exceedingly lax in what I believe it should do to fit the man for useful occupation after he has paid his penalty. At Sing Sing prison the state is supposed to teach a man to make a pair of shoes by machinery. Not that the state needs the shoes so much as it needs to train that man for gainful occupation. The fact is that the shoemaking machinery at Sing Sing is so obsolete that, if the man wanted to be a shoemaker after he came out of prison, he couldn't do it.

Industries in our prisons have not been modernized. I attempted some reform during my terms and had valuable assistance from Mr. Adolph Lewisohn, a prominent citizen of New York interested in prison reform, who personally financed a thorough and constructive investigation. The whole question is one of properly financing the industries of the prison to get them started. This the legislature seems to be unwilling to do, for the very simple reason that there is no public interest in it. No reform in government which costs money is possible until public interest is aroused to a point where it makes a demand for it.

Modernization of the workshops in the prisons must be accompanied by a reform in the general construction of the prisons themselves. The dungeons of a hundred years ago do not suit today. There is no reason in the world why society, after depriving a man of his liberty for an offense against it, should break down his health, rendering him useless after he serves his term, and probably driving him to further crime, if not in a spirit of revolt, at least through what he believes has become the only way he is able to maintain himself.

CHAPTER XX

Putting Business Methods into Government

USUALLY when the governor's annual message was being read by the clerk of either house, the members adjourned to the smoking room and the clerk skipped whole pages of it in order to get it out of the way. Large numbers of legislators often admitted that they never read the governor's annual message. In 1923 I read my annual message in person to the senate and assembly in joint session for the first time in the history of the state. In 1925, I again read my message in person to the legislature and began all over again the battle for the progressive reforms started in my first and second terms. My first annual message that year was in the form of a report to the stockholders by the president of a company. I dealt with the state as a business corporation.

In public speeches and in written memoranda I have often said that no private business could last very long if it was compelled to transact its business the way the state does. The policies of the government should be decided by law, as that is the expression of the direct representatives of the people themselves. The business side of the government ought to be in the hands of the executive, so that he may, without being tied down with red tape and restrictive statutes of all kinds, be prepared to put all his energy and ingenuity into the business of caring for the affairs of government, just as the president of a great corporation like the United States Steel, General Motors or the New York Central Railroad, can, without recourse to the directors for every little detail, transact the business side of the company's affairs.

In January, 1923, a fire occurred in Manhattan State Hospital. At that time it was overcrowded by some twenty per cent, and twenty-five persons lost their lives—some inmates and some employees. Needless to say that this shocked the state. The old building that was burned was used as a home for immigrant girls as far back as 1853. The interior was of wooden construction and the means of escape was cut off by a falling water tank that came through the burned timbers of the ceiling on the top floor. This happened less than two weeks after I was inaugurated for my second term, and I seized upon it as an opportunity to awaken the public mind to the obligation of the state to get rid of these dilapidated old fire traps as well as to provide new construction to meet the ever growing population in the hospitals.

I set myself then to make a concentrated effort to improve the state hospitals, and with the approval by the people of a fifty-million-dollar bond issue, we were able to see ahead clearly enough to enter on a building program for these particular institutions.

For many years legislative leaders had realized that the state's method of carrying on its construction of public works by piecemeal appropriation out of current funds was unbusinesslike and actually wasteful. The more I looked into it the more deeply I was impressed with the necessity for a thorough investigation of the state's method of conducting its construction of public improvements.

We needed an office building for the state in Albany, one in New York and one in Buffalo. We needed new prisons. We needed to complete the old prisons. New evidence of this has just been adduced by the revelation of conditions at two of our big prisons. Like the fire at Manhattan State Hospital, the public always has to be shocked into action. We had undertaken the construction of the Poughkeepsie bridge. All such public improvements far outlive the generation which pays for them if they are paid for out of current revenues. I proposed that the state should amend its constitution so as to permit the legislature to issue bonds for ten million dollars a year for a period of ten years to cover this necessary work. I discussed the proposal first with the two Republican leaders of the legislature. They agreed to it and it passed the legislature for the first time in 1924. It encountered no opposition worth speaking about in the session of 1925, and was passed for the second time although both houses were then Republican. Strange to say, immediately after the close of the legislature the whole proposition was challenged by Congressman Ogden L. Mills, who debated it with me at a dinner of the Economic Club in New York. The congressman did not have the facts on his side and was not successful in the debate.

Shortly after the dinner an open challenge was issued

to me by former Governor Miller and by Congressman Mills to debate the bond issue with both of them.

I accepted this challenge and at Carnegie Hall, in the middle of July, 1925, the debate with Governor Miller took place. Charles E. Hughes acted as chairman. One of the leading New York newspapers said that while we had a referee, no decision was rendered, inasmuch as that was up to the people themselves; but the editor awarded me the decision upon the ground that there was need for action and I had a plan and Governor Miller had none. He simply opposed mine.

Later, in Buffalo, I debated the question with Congressman Mills. I have always liked the method of discussing questions by public debate. I have never been unwilling to meet a challenge from an opponent and have always gladly mounted the platform for public discussion of both sides of a question. Going to the people by means of public debate has a strong appeal for me.

The proposal for the one-hundred-million-dollar bond issue was submitted to the electorate in 1925 and was carried, although it is a known fact that the Republican organization leaders throughout the state opposed it. Following its adoption and in 1926 state work began to progress.

Sing Sing Prison has been completed; the state office buildings in Albany and New York City will soon be ready for occupancy. Many other projects all over the state, including the State Health Laboratory, the Teachers' College at Albany, the Poughkeepsie bridge, and schools, hospitals, and parks, have gone forward and are nearing completion. But we have had only four allotments of this bond issue and some of the largest undertakings are yet to come. Another bond issue for which I assumed responsibility was $15,000,000 for a state park system reaching from Montauk Point at the outer end of Long Island all the way to Niagara Falls.

Believing strongly in public recreation and realizing the difficulty of making land purchases at reasonable prices, I was ready to accept from the New York State Association the suggestion of co-ordinating the park system of the state. There were at least thirty-five separate boards and commissions, each in charge of some separate park project or in charge of the preservation of some historic site. Appropriations were made, each of them without regard to any of the needs of the others. These appropriations were usually dictated by political influence.

In 1923 and 1924, at my suggestion, the Council of Parks, composed of the chairmen of the various park regions, was set up by law and a proposal was submitted to the people to bond the state for $15,000,000 for additional purchase of land for parks and the construction of parkways. This made such a popular appeal to the electorate that the proposal was carried even in the presidential year of 1924 by more than a million plurality. Democrats and Republicans alike shared in the achievement. The proposal was supported by the leading members of both parties.

One of the most striking illustrations of the increase

in land values is the story of Deer Range Park on Long Island. The Long Island Park Commission attempted to acquire some sixteen hundred acres on the south shore of Long Island in Islip for a state park. This attempt led to one of the most important and interesting political fights that has occurred in this state in twenty-five years. Influential Republicans on Long Island opposed the purchase of this park by the state and it was afterward discovered that they desired to acquire it for themselves for private uses. The price at which it was offered to the state was so tempting that they formed a company of their own and attempted to prevent the state from getting possession.

Under the Conservation Law for the acquirement of property for state parks or parkways two methods are outlined—either purchase or what we call "entry and appropriation." In this instance the opponents of the park, through social connections, induced the people to withdraw their offer of sale and left to the state only its other course of entry and appropriation.

I devoted much of my personal time to this particular park. I held a public hearing at my apartment in the Hotel Biltmore for the interested people on both sides, and made my decision, but not until after all kinds of political and social influences were exercised in an attempt to persuade me not to sign the papers.

The first week in December of 1924 I signed the necessary papers that made Deer Range Park the property of the state of New York. It was contended that when the state seized the property no appropriation had been made to pay for it, and the first entry by the state was invalid. Having in mind what this enormous tract of land meant to the women and children of the big city so close to it, I went where I knew I would find a sympathetic ear. I spoke to Mr. August Hecksher, whose philanthropy in the interest of children is known throughout the nation. He heeded my appeal and immediately deposited in a local bank $260,000 to cover the purchase of the property.

The state immediately entered and appropriated the land again and this time, the money having been made available by deed and gift, the title of the property actually passed to the state of New York.

The situation gave rise to a serious lawsuit and the matter was litigated back and forth until January of this year, when the Court of Appeals finally decided in favor of the state. In the course of the litigation, for the first time as far as my knowledge is concerned, the governor himself was a witness in favor of the state.

So influential were the opponents of acquiring this tract of Long Island that they were able to enlist the sympathy and active co-operation of the Republican leaders in the legislature. Incensed by the fact that they were defeated in the preliminary steps, they sought, in 1925, to amend the law so that when appropriations were to be made out of the park bond-issue funds for purchase of land for parks and parkways, these would have to have the approval of the Land Board then in existence, although they had previously voted for a constitutional amendment abolishing that body. I refused to accept the appropriation with the rider in it giving power to the Land Board to pass upon purchases.

Practically no reply was made to my appeal to the leaders and they adjourned the legislative session without making any appropriation from the bond issue for the purchase of parks or parkways, although they themselves, when seeking credit for the passage of the original proposal, said that it was necessary that action be taken at once, before the prices went up too high.

On the State Park Council there were a number of prominent and well-known Republicans. After consultation with the Council of Parks, I decided to call the legislature into extraordinary session and submit the proposal to them again, using an argument of their own that park lands should be purchased at once, before the prices went too high. Long before the legislature convened, and subsequent to my call, party pressure was being exerted upon the legislative leaders and the individual members of the senate and assembly. They met pursuant to the call. I addressed them and had the speech radioed in order to get the pressure of public opinion. They passed the same bill over again, with the joker in it giving power to the Land Board. I again vetoed it and the whole park program was held up during the year 1925.

The constitutional amendment reorganizing the government having been adopted by the people in the fall of 1925, there was no Land Board to which park purchases could be referred after January, 1926, and the legislators were compelled to make the direct appropriation to the Park Council the next year. From that time on we had smooth sailing with the park program. One prominent leader of the opposition said: "We may not have gained anything substantial by it, but at least we got one year nearer to the end of Smith."

The strange thing about this whole proceeding is that politics got into it in only one part of the state, and that a very small part. The rest of the park program was practically unopposed. The legislative leaders seemed to have no interest in any other park project except on Long Island, although not one of them lives within two hundred and fifty miles of the place.

I feel fully compensated for all the work and anxiety when I see breathing spaces in beautifully wooded countrysides and on lakes and beaches for the women and children of today and for countless generations to come.

There was a fourth bond issue which I sponsored. While campaigning through the state by automobile I was impressed over and over again by the menace of railroad crossings at grade and I determined that I would do what I could to get rid of them.

Collecting the data and statistics of grade-crossing deaths and accidents, I came to the conclusion that if the state is to eliminate dangerous grade crossings in the lifetime of a single individual, it would require complete change in policy and drastic measures to raise money. The cost of grade-crossing elimination is assessed, one-half on the railroads, one-fourth on the state, and one-fourth on the localities benefited. Accordingly I recommended an amendment to the constitution to permit the legislature to bond the state to the extent of $300,000,000 for the purpose, in the first instance of paying the state's share, and in the second instance of lending the state's credit to the railroad or locality where they were unable to meet their share.

Although the amendment was passed at the 1924 session, there was an undercurrent of rumor at the opening of the 1925 session indicating that the Republican leaders would like to reverse their action of the year before. They were reluctant to pass the proposed amendment to the Constitution for the required second time. That made it necessary for me to take the public platform in favor of this proposal and, as a matter of self-protection, individual Republican members of the Legislature decided to vote in favor of the proposal for the second time.

In the fall of 1925, the grade-crossing amendment to the Constitution was offered together with the amendment for the reorganization of the government and the proposal inaugurated by the legislature itself, for the revision of the judiciary system of the state, and also the proposed constitutional amendment with relation to bond issues for state public works, commonly referred to as the Ten Million Dollar a Year Public Works Bond Issue. All four were accepted by the people in spite of whispering campaigns and all sorts of propaganda against them.

Adoption of the grade-crossing amendment has developed comprehensive plans for eliminating dangerous crossings throughout the state, and a program for the expenditure of thirty million dollars is now being carried forward on Long Island alone.

After the close of the 1925 legislative session a new battle over the mayoralty in New York City arose. John F. Hylan had been mayor for eight years, and while he always seemed to think that I had some personal feeling against him, there was no basis for that in fact. I opposed his renomination, in the first instance, because I became convinced that the rank and file of the party were anxious for a change at the City Hall.

Countless thousands of people, during the winter and in the spring of 1925, came to me seeking this change. That I was right in my summation of the party attitude was borne out by the result of the primary. Mayor Hylan was defeated in his home borough of Brooklyn even after the leaders in that borough had declared in favor of him.

The primary campaign was marked by great bitterness and the real 1925 mayoralty fight took place before the nomination had been made. Mayor Walker had a long and creditable record at Albany. He sponsored personally many of the reforms suggested by me, being the Democratic leader of the senate from 1923 to 1925.

The rank and file of the party had become definitely convinced that Hylan was under the domination of Hearst and that Hearst was in reality the leader after the death of Mr. Murphy. They feared that a re-election of Hylan for a third term would give Hearst too great an influence in the government of the city of New York. That was my own attitude in the primary campaign, and, with a few exceptions, it was the attitude of the powerful leaders of the organization.

As usual, in New York City the Republican Party defeated itself. It nominated a man not known to the rank and file of the people and having no public record of any kind.

As the primary result had practically settled the election, I was free during the campaign to throw all my energy into the pending constitutional amendments.

In enumerating in the course of my story the high spots of those issues which provoked great public discussion and debate, I have a distinct purpose. I can, with perfect safety, say that innumerable smaller but very important subjects and principles of government received the same treatment as the others did at the hands of the legislature, and all for political reasons. To sum it all up, the opposition legislative leaders used their power to obstruct and stand in the way of progressive, forward-looking reforms in order that the credit for instituting them and seeing them to fruition might not be accorded to a Democratic governor.

Figures and Finances

FINANCIAL problems of the state have always had a deep and particular interest for me. Probably my own experience in the legislature and my feeling that the state must be brought to conduct its affairs in a businesslike manner account for this. Naturally, my advocacy of the four great bond issues for state hospitals, public works improvements, grade crossing elimination and public parks gave my enemies an opportunity to call me "Smith, the Spender." But I felt that I was treading on no uncertain ground. I was sure that the people of the Empire State wanted their business conducted with vision and provision for the future.

Both political parties for many years attempted to make political capital by misrepresentation of public finances whether it be in the city, the state or even in the nation itself. In the recent national campaign misstatements were made about federal finances. The temptation to do this is intensified by the knowledge which men in public life have, that comparatively few people have any understanding of government finances. To add to this, the fiscal reports prepared by accountants look to the average layman like a Chinese puzzle.

In the state of New York, the government gets its money in three ways—first, by direct tax upon real property; second, by direct taxation such as the personal income tax, the tax on corporations, the inheritance tax, stock transfer tax, the motor vehicle tax and similar forms; third, by the sale of its bonds. The first two classes represent income. The third class represents borrowed money. The proceeds of bonds are used only to finance capital improvements or to construct such public works as have a longer life than the life of the bonds themselves, the underlying theory being to spread the cost over more than one generation of tax payers.

Government financial statements present a difficulty in that they are dealing with futures when they list income and surplus. Surplus is the amount left in the treasury after all costs of government have been met by appropriation. Therefore, when the governor of New York State, as required by the constitution, certifies the income of the state he is accepting the estimate of the comptroller as to what is expected from the various forms of taxation during the fiscal year for which appropriation is being made. That is to say, in January the governor takes the comptroller's estimate of the income of the state from the first of the following July and for twelve months thereafter. Given that figure he then must estimate the cost of maintaining the government during that same period and add to that the appropriations which have been made immediately available and which will be paid out at once. He must deduct both sums from the estimated revenues. He has then an estimated surplus.

Inasmuch as this is all guess-work, that surplus may be

much larger or it may even be smaller in accordance with the number of transactions from which the state derives a revenue occurring within that fiscal year. The comptroller may estimate a six-million-dollar surplus based on the experience in taxation of the year before. Many more automobiles may be licensed during the year. Many more transactions may be recorded on the stock exchange. There may be a very marked increase in personal income, or three or four very wealthy men may die and increase the inheritance tax receipts and the estimated six millions may become an actual twenty-six millions. There is no way in the world that a surplus can be definitely fixed a year ahead of time. It can only be guessed at.

In its fiscal transactions the state does not differ from a business corporation. During good times the state's revenue is large. Periods of business depression are reflected in the state's income. Unlike a business concern, it is not easy for the state to retrench in its expenditures unless and until the state and her people are ready to stop some of the state's activities. When as a result of a good business year the surplus income will warrant it, either relief is extended to tax payers or additional appropriations may be made for state needs. In this year of 1929 the direct tax against real property was materially reduced.

Frequently I recommended reductions in both income tax and real property tax upon the theory that the state should not take more money from its tax payers than is actually required for the operation of the government in a single fiscal year. The underlying theory of all taxation is that its cost should be so regulated as not to carry over into another year the sums paid by the tax payers of this year. We frequently hear of the necessity for storing up a surplus for emergencies. I spent eight years in the governor's office and no emergency ever arose in all of that period that the state was not able to meet from a reasonable surplus which was never estimated much in excess of eight million dollars. Of course in case of catastrophe or disaster the legislature can always be brought into extraordinary session and special revenue measures applied.

Much political capital has been made out of the increased cost of the government in recent years. In my opinion the people are beginning to understand that these arguments are made only for political effect. The average man and woman thoroughly appreciate that since the World War the cost of everything has gone up. The state is really no different from the housewife. The state is obliged to pay more rent for the property it leases. It has certain fixed, definite overhead charges which it cannot get away from any more than the housekeeper can get away from them. Food, clothing, supplies of all kinds in all of the institutions have doubled in cost today as against the pre-war period.

Salaries and wages of employees all the way from the governor himself down to the woman who cleans the Capitol have been increased to meet new living conditions. The office boy who got three dollars a week before the war now gets twelve. Every grade of help in the state has been advanced in salary in the last ten years. Low salaries in the institutions of the state were producing a type of help which was unable to meet the state's requirements.

Because it applies alike to everybody, I cannot escape the conclusion that the income tax is the fairest form of taxation. A man's ability to support the government is based upon what he is able to earn himself in a given year. Nevertheless, while the federal government is exacting so much for the federal income tax, a state should attempt at the earliest possible moment to get away from a state income tax. In New York it was first imposed in 1919 to meet the deficiency in revenue caused by the adoption of the Eighteenth Amendment to the federal constitution. Liquor-tax certificates were bringing in an income of twenty-six million dollars yearly. One half of this was used for state purposes and the other half was given to the localities to help them. Overnight, the state was suddenly deprived of this enormous income and some form of taxation had to be devised immediately unless this twenty-six million dollars was to be spread upon real property.

At the time that I signed the income-tax bill in 1919 I joined with the Republican leaders in a statement that at the earliest possible moment we would bring relief to the income-tax payers in our state. The increased cost of government, the great growth of the state, the rapid development of her departments have, up to this time, made it impossible to do away with it altogether. We have had temporary reductions several times. In view of the fact that the legislature and the leaders of both parties had consented to a change in our fiscal system requiring appropriations from bonds for permanent improvements instead of cash from tax revenues, the state's financial report, as sent to me by the comptroller in 1924, indicated that our available resources were such as to permit tax reduction, and in January, in my annual message to the legislature, I recommended a reduction of twenty-five per cent to the citizens rendering an income-tax return.

When I made this recommendation, it was publicly received by the Republican leaders with acclaim and privately referred to in unprintable language. It must be borne in mind that 1924 was a presidential year and there was a governor to be elected in the fall. The Republican machine was unwilling to take the responsibility of turning down anything they might later be unable to explain. One of the members of their own party took the leadership for income-tax reduction and fought for the report of the bill and for the political advantage it would give him to put through a tax reduction. The leaders delayed until the last moment and set up every means possible to prevent the adoption of this measure. They finally gave in and a twenty-five per cent reduction to the income-tax payers of the state was made possible.

In 1925 the second passage of the bond issues was assured and finances for progressing public works were in sight through the sale of bonds. In addition, the comptroller's report of 1925 showed available resources sufficiently large to permit me to renew my recommendation

339

for tax reduction for that year also. The election of 1924 being over and the Republican President having been elected for four years and the Republican candidate for governor having been defeated, the legislature changed its tune entirely, and the leaders fought it vigorously.

At an all-night session and in caucus behind closed doors, they prepared a statement of what they declared to be necessary appropriations, which, if put into effect, would make tax reduction impossible for that year. They scurried around the Capitol in an effort to include everything that would add to the total amount of appropriations. Without going into them in detail, it is sufficient for me to say that they suggested an appropriation to meet judgments in the Court of Claims not yet rendered, even to the tune of millions of dollars in the case of some condemnation proceedings, in order to defeat tax reduction, and all in the vain hope that they were making some political capital for their party.

At that time I had little experience in talking through a microphone, but I felt that I must get the story to the people quickly and intelligibly. I asked and obtained from the nearest broadcasting station, at Schenectady, permission to use the radio from my desk in the executive chamber. I prepared a comprehensive statement of the whole financial situation of the state and reduced it to simple, every-day language, so that everyone would know exactly what I was talking about. I spoke over the radio for an hour and a half on Saturday night, April 11, 1925. At the close of my radio speech I suggested to my listeners that they communicate either by mail or telegram with their respective representatives in the senate and assembly, and impress upon them that they forget political considerations, forget political advantage for their party, and do the palpably honest and right thing for the tax payers of the state.

My suggestion met with instantaneous response. Before I left the Executive Chamber on that Saturday night, telephonic communications indicated to me that citizens throughout the state were ready to heed my advice and use the rest of Saturday night and all of Sunday dictating suitable messages to their representatives.

It was interesting to watch the mail bags arriving at the Capitol Monday morning. The telegraph wires were busy and the post office at Albany, antiquated and old as it is, was inundated. Members of the legislature were overwhelmed with communications from home. The radio had done its work. Reluctantly the legislative leaders made their concession. Income-tax reduction was again made possible and ample provision was made for all actual needs of the state.

There has been agitation to free those in the lower-income groups entirely from income tax. In fact New York State has gone far along these lines in exempting those having an income of less than seven thousand dollars a year. Now, I would do it in a different way. I would increase the allowance for dependents. For instance, an unmarried man is earning five thousand dollars a year and a married man with five children receives the same salary. Under my plan the married man would probably get enough of an allowance to free him from paying any income tax at all. Instead of doing it that way the state is doing it so that nobody earning less than seven thousand dollars a year pays income tax. A single man with no dependents getting five thousand dollars should pay an income tax and a married man with five children earning five thousand dollars should get an exemption for his dependents sufficiently large to relieve him from income taxation. That, to my mind, is the fairest and most scientific way of handling an income tax. It is well for everyone to pay some taxes so that he will have some interest in the government. As a matter of fact, everybody is a tax payer.

In the large cities, where only a very small percentage of the population own the houses in which they live, it is always easy to get a popular vote in favor of having the state spend more money. The rent payer, in view of the fact that he never receives a tax bill, does not believe that he is a tax payer. When he votes in favor of a proposition to spend a large amount of money for public improvements he really believes that the landlord is going to pay for it and not he. I have no recollection of any proposal to spend money ever being defeated at the polls. On the contrary, Albany is besieged during the legislative session by organizations of all kinds demanding the expenditure of more money for public works and public improvements.

The size of the appropriation bill is not an indication

of waste or extravagance in the government although the political press-bureaus seek to lead the people to believe that large appropriations of public money are synonymous with waste and extravagance. Sometimes a low appropriation bill may be more wasteful than a high one.

Prior to 1923 the state rented property in various sections for headquarters for the state police, and I discovered in 1923 that the state was paying ten per cent of the actual value of the property every year in rent. That would mean that in ten years the state would pay enough rent to own the property. I recommended that the property be purchased. It cost four hundred thousand dollars. That meant an increase in the appropriation bill that year, but it brought about economy to the state by relieving it of the necessity of paying rent annually.

The federal government today is spending twenty million dollars a year in rent. No such condition should be permitted to go on. All of this property is actually needed for the transaction of the federal business. Why should not the government own it rather than make an enormous outlay of twenty million dollars every year in rent? Similarly much of the federal property is inadequate for the proper transaction of the government's business and results in loss.

It has been, year after year, certified by the Postmaster General of the United States that a large part of the cost of operating our postal service in this country is due to the fact that it is carried on in inadequate structures which in this day of modern devices makes the handling of the mails twice as costly as it otherwise would be. In the city of Albany because of inadequate postal facilities, business is interfered with and business men of the Capitol city have just cause for complaint. The business of the state itself has grown so as to absorb nearly all the postal facilities in the city of Albany. At Christmastime it is not unusual for the mail to be two days late. During the various periods for the payment of taxes the Albany post office, in handling the state's business alone, is burdened to the limit of its capacity not to speak of the ordinary growth of general business in the city.

I have had many arguments and debates during my governorship with the leaders of the Republican party on this question of state finances. They invariably approach it from the political angle. Nothing is more amusing than the attempts, from time to time, of some of our newspaper editors to comment editorially on the state's fiscal condition. You have but to read the editorial to find out immediately that the writer has not himself the slightest understanding of the subject.

During all my administrations I have been able to secure the support of newspapers willing to approach the subject in a non-partisan way, by the publication of detailed reports in simple understandable language and by personal contact.

It is little wonder that the average citizen pays little or no attention to the fiscal operations of the government, and this is not meant in a spirit of criticism. Few members of the legislature have a real understanding of the state's fiscal system. Underlying the whole theory of the executive budget was an attempt to compel the legislature as a whole to pay more attention to the fiscal operations of the state and to make a closer study of the state's method of conducting its financial program. This is no recent condition in the state. It has been going on as far back as anybody can remember.

It became quite apparent to me before I was in the governorship very long that the reports of the comptroller were drawn up by men expert in dealing with the state's finances but couched in such terms and put in such a way that, while readily comprehensible to themselves, nobody else could understand them. I took upon myself the task of making direct report on the state's fiscal operations at the close of the legislative session every year. I must frankly say that I copied my form from an advertisement of a well-known bank appearing in theater programs and journals. It enabled me to set forth the facts in such a way that the financial process was easy to understand.

My own inability to understand figures and fiscal terms thoroughly because of lack of experience or opportunity was a handicap to me in 1911 when I began to study the state's finances. I was compelled to acquire my knowledge of them late in life and at a great sacrifice of time. I sat in the Capitol in 1911 and 1912 night after night and by hard work and constant study I brought myself to the point of understanding them. That effort was very helpful to me in after years when I became governor.

Some years ago, I remember, the legislature included an item in the appropriation bill for the expenses of an investigating committee. Governor Hughes did not believe that the investigation was necessary and he vetoed the item. A month later he picked up the morning paper and read that the committee was about to start on a tour of the West to study conditions. He sent for the deputy comptroller and said, "Who's paying the expenses of this commission?" The deputy commissioner said, "The State." "Why," the governor said, "I vetoed that item." The deputy comptroller said, "You vetoed it only once. It was in the bill twice." In other words, it appeared in two different places in the appropriation bill.

Year after year the same old appropriation bills keep cropping up. As late as 1925 the legislature sent to me, in special bills, items totaling $5,650,000 all of which I vetoed as entirely unnecessary. All these bills came from a Republican legislature and in less than two weeks after I vetoed them the Republican press was speaking of the extravagance of the governor.

The constitution of the state provides that money not expended within two years from the date of appropriation lapses into the general fund and must be re-appropriated. The comptroller automatically certifies to the legislature the amounts about to lapse. It is only by very careful study of re-appropriations that the governor is able to check the great waste of public money.

In my very first year as governor I profited by my experience in the legislature. I placed upon the department heads the duty of certifying to me exactly what was to be done with that portion of the appropriation which was about to lapse. Invariably I found that the work originally contemplated had already been completed, but that if the department had had the use of a little more money it would put in some fancy finishing touches, not at all necessary. One re-appropriation made to the state engineer and surveyor was disapproved of by me because the work had been completed the year before the re-appropriation was made. In one instance, a re-appropriation was made for the water supply and screens for cottages at an institution and was vetoed by me because the institution was not being used.

Notwithstanding my consistent opposition to private and local appropriation bills during my legislative service and all I said about them in the Constitutional Convention, the first year I was in office the legislature sent to me what was probably the largest number in any one year up to that time.

One of my strangest experiences in my first year as governor, was to have in front of me special appropriation bills for local improvements, which I had opposed as leader of the minority while I was in the legislature. I remembered the bills themselves and I had a very distinct recollection of the arguments made by me on the floor of the assembly as to why they should not pass that body. They provided for the dredging of Canadaigua Lake. They provided for the repairing of the abutments of the Cayuga Lake. They provided for the improvement of Mill Creek in Schuyler County. They made appropriation for the clearing of the channel of Craven Creek. They made appropriation for the improvement of the channel of Mud Creek in the town of Cicero. They authorized the improvement of the Oriskany River, provided for a girder bridge and another bridge across the Black River at Hillside and still another one across the Black River at Hill Farm. There was a bill for the improvement of the Shadokin River and the cleaning out of Limestone Creek.

Tad Sweet always enjoyed great popularity in his district because of his ability to secure improvements intended to build up the city of Oswego. Through his efforts several bridges were built by the state across the Oswego River. He was following what was customary in the state at that time although the constitution provides that a vote of "two thirds of the members elected to each branch of the legislature shall be requisite to every bill appropriating public monies appropriated for local purposes."

The constitution was nullified in that respect by some important judicial decisions which held that money, though appropriated for a local purpose, might also be said to have a state-wide benefit. I never entirely agreed to that, notwithstanding the court decision, and endeavored to fix the state policy so that localities should pay for their own improvements. During my governorship I discouraged the custom of saddling the cost of local improvements on the state by vetoing all such bills.

When Tad Sweet was Speaker, I had an opportunity to drive home this point. It is the custom in Albany that the Speaker introduces no bills, but Speaker Sweet had some local bridge bills introduced on his behalf by another member and one day one of them came on the calendar. On behalf of the minority I opposed it. Realizing that the opposition was a mere formality, I sought by ridicule to set the party right and to discourage the entire theory of building all these bridges for localities with public funds that were raised on a state-wide basis. On a motion to strike out the enacting clause I suggested that if the state was to continue building bridges for all the localities it might be well to buy them by the wholesale and store them up in the Adirondack preserve. I suggested that we could get them in different sizes and different weights and even in different colors. After seriously debating it I withdrew the motion and allowed the bill to undergo a roll call. It was was passed by the Republican majority in control of the assembly.

About a week later the Speaker's second bridge bill came on the calendar and I simply arose in my place and said, "Mr. Speaker, on a point of information." He recognized me and I asked, "What color?" He replied, "Green." Whereupon we took a party vote and the second bridge bill was authorized. All of these matters provided material for debate in the Constitutional Convention on the subject of appropriations and the Executive Budget.

Most of the special appropriation bills for local improvements, I am satisfied, are sent to the governor to allow the legislator to make political capital for himself and his party in his home county. All such bills while I was in office were introduced by Republican members from the small Republican counties of the state. The improvement, of course, would be beneficial to property in that particular locality but its cost should have been borne by the locality itself and not by the whole state.

Another kind of bills which, while they make no appropriation of public money, may prove costly to the state, are the special claim bills. They are usually introduced at the request of lawyers or individual constituents of the legislators. To get away from this system the state set up a Court of Claims where people may apply for the liquidation of damages to person or property at the hands of the state. I gave careful attention to claim bills and accepted those that on their face were just, fair and equitable but I vetoed the great majority of them, largely because they were drawn in such a way as to admit by law the liability of the state although prior to the enactment of the claim bill no such liability existed.

A favorite form of claim bill is for damage to land from the overflow of the waters of the canal. That is a legitimate claim but under the law it must be filed within six months. If so filed, the state would be in a position to defend itself, but the claimant usually waits three or four years. The statute of limitations having then run against the claim so far as filing it is concerned, he seeks to have it met later by special act of the legislature.

350

The veto memoranda on some of the claim bills sent to me gave the executive staff in my office considerable amusement. One bill sought to awaken a claim against the state on the part of people who were shot by the state troops in the great railroad strike when Grover Cleveland was governor. There was a bill to make appropriation for salary to a man during the period of his suspension from office dating back to 1913. Another one was for a horse that was alleged to have been killed by some of the building machinery of the state five years before the claim was presented. One claim bill vetoed by me in 1919 was passed again in 1920 for alleged damages by reason of overflow of the Seneca River in the years between 1912 and 1916. When the bill came back a year later three more years were added to it. In 1920 a claim bill alleging the overflow of the Mohawk River during the year 1914 was presented. The very title of that bill declared in so many words that it intended to extend the limits of time for introducing such claims, from six months to four years.

Claim bills are largely personal matters with the introducer. The legislature pays little or no attention to them. There is no record of any debate ever being held upon them. Apparently the introducer is not called upon for an explanation as to why his bill should become a law. It gives some indication of the lack of interest, in that one bill was sent to me twice in one session. It was a just claim and I had accepted it and it had become a chapter of the laws when the identical bill came down a second time. In 1920 claim bills were sent to me that had become law in 1919.

Nothing seems to me nearly as important to the state as careful study by the legislature of all appropriation bills. There is no way that anybody can get a clearer or better idea of the government and what it is doing than by a study of the expenditure of money for the carrying on of its activities. This applies to all legislative bodies not only in the state but in the nation and likewise to the appropriating authorities of all local governments.

Good, sound, modern business principles can be introduced into the state's fiscal system when the rank and file of the people discourage political leaders from attempting to make political capital out of false and misleading statements about the state's fiscal and financial operations. It is a mistake to think that the people approve of reduced appropriations when in the process of reducing them the state or any of its activities are to suffer. What the people want is an honest accounting for every dollar appropriated. They want every dollar of public money to bring a dollar's worth of service to the state. They have no patience with waste and there is a great difference between large appropriations and waste.

It was with this knowledge that I earnestly advocated biennial sessions of the legislature. So far as general law making is concerned we have too many laws now. We should compel, at least every second year, careful and close study of the state's fiscal needs and the method of taxation. In such years we should permit no other legislation to be considered except of an emergency nature and by special message from the governor. This would also prevent confusion in the public mind incident to the conflicting reports put out by the different political press agencies at the close of each legislative session.

It is difficult for public men, no matter how high their station in public life may be, to resist the temptation to seek political advantage from distortion of facts in their relationship to figures. Some of the most important men in the Republican party in the last presidential campaign actually tried to tell the American people that the difference between operating this government on a war basis and a peace basis was the result of rigid economy on the part of the Republican administration which succeeded President Wilson. To show the enormous difference in the cost of government supposedly brought about by the operation of an executive budget and the cheese-paring of minor expenditures here and there throughout the various departments of the federal government, they used the ridiculous figure of two billion dollars.

Economy in government certainly is to be encouraged. I practiced it rigidly. The cost of operating my own department in the state government went down under my administration. But that is one thing. It is an entirely different thing to give misleading figures and misstatements of fact in order to win the approval of the electorate. That should be discouraged if our public affairs are to be intelligently and ably conducted.

CHAPTER XXII

Fifth Campaign and Fourth Term

IN 1926, I was beginning to reap a part of the harvest of the work of preceding years, so far as seeing accomplishment of my undertakings went. At the previous election the constitutional amendment for the reorganization of the state government had been adopted, and there remained only the legislative mechanics of making that amendment effective. After a long and bitter struggle the legislature had for the first time adopted the constitutional amendment establishing the executive budget. The four bond issues recommended by me were beginning to show results. Additional patient beds were added by the construction of a new hospital for the metropolitan district, and the hospital for the mentally disabled veterans of the World War which had been begun in 1923 was nearing completion. Fire-protection methods adopted in state institutions brought the commendation of the National Board of Fire Underwriters. Additions and enlargements to the hospital for crippled children were under way. The program for state parks and parkways was taking shape, and the other improvements made possible by the various bond issues were going forward.

The vehicular tunnel between New York and New Jersey was in the last stages of construction. Parkway extension and road widening in Erie and Nassau Counties were in progress. A decided advance in education was made by the appropriation of an additional eleven million dollars for the support of rural schools. State aid was established for public health work in rural communities and an advanced medical-practice act, to control quack doctors, had been passed.

The workmen's compensation laws and the Labor Department had been strengthened. Agriculture was aided by the passage of the coöperative marketing act. Large tracts of land were added to the forest preserve and a vigorous policy of conservation was instituted.

One thing remained about which nothing of a constructive nature had been done. Water-power development had not kept pace. Republican opposition to all suggestions for state development and control remained in full force and effect. Taking advantage of the general lack of understanding of the whole subject on the part of the people, their opposition to the plan I advocated for state development and control of water-power resources persisted. That seemed to be the last line, from which the reactionary old guard would never be willing to retreat.

I was personally fully convinced that at the close of the session of 1926 I would be relieved that year of any further duties as governor. Having already served three full terms, I looked forward to retirement to private life in 1926. The labor, the worry and the anxiety of the governor's office were beginning to tell upon me, and I was anxious to retire in order that I might see more of my family and that they might have more of my time.

Then an event occurred in Albany on June sixth which brought into my life a great deal of joy and satisfaction. My oldest daughter, Emily, was married to John Adams Warner, superintendent of state police. The wedding was attended by people from all over the state. All my old friends and neighbors from the downtown district of New York City were in Albany, including Louis Fook, the leader of Chinatown.

The day before, and the day after the ceremony, while political leaders from all over the state were gathered in Albany, I began to realize how difficult it would be for me to escape renomination. The argument and persuasion of the party leaders was something with which I had to deal. An army of interested people supplemented the call of the leaders. These were disinterested friends who desired to see a program well begun carried out in full. They entertained the belief and freely expressed it to me that my absence from Albany might lessen interest in the final consummation of the program of state reconstruction.

Men and women in all ranks and all stations of life besieged me to offer myself again to the electorate. Each particular group had something in mind that it desired to see accomplished, and feared the consequences of what might happen if the governorship fell back into reactionary hands. They were stimulated by the general belief that the candidate of the Republican party would be Congressman Ogden L. Mills, who had vigorously opposed practically all of my propositions. He had openly challenged the wisdom of the bond issues and had lost no opportunity, whenever he thought it presented itself, to find fault with my management of the state and to criticize it publicly.

I owe it to Congressman Mills to say that he was of great help to me and to my administration in urging the bond issue for the rehabilitation of the state hospitals. It did not take him very long to discover that I was right about that, and he gave me genuine, whole-hearted and intelligent support. And in view of that I cannot escape the conclusion that his opposition to further bond issues just as urgent and for practically the same purposes, was for political reasons, and that he hoped to be nominated for governor because of it.

Although he may not have been successful in any of his arguments, he had established himself in the minds of the Republican leaders of the state as the foremost figure in the 1926 state convention of the Republican party, and was accordingly nominated for governor.

I have been reliably informed that in the early spring of 1926 Mr. Mills, seeking an issue, caused a thorough and minute investigation to be made of the state accounts through the office of the state comptroller, then in charge of a member of his own party. This was an effort to establish either waste, extravagance, recklessness, or perhaps something worse in the handling of the state finances. It was without success.

I fully appreciate today, and I did at that time, that Congressman Mills found himself in a rather awkward position. Every constructive achievement of my administration had received a certain amount of Republican sanction. Nothing accomplished up to that time would have been possible without the assistance of the Republican legislature. Though it is true consent often was given reluctantly, it nevertheless had to be forthcoming under pressure of the better judgment of the leaders of the Republican party, or these accomplishments could not be recorded as fact. He realized, when he entered the campaign, that all these constructive achievements had the approval and active support of former Gov. Charles E. Hughes, former Attorney General George W. Wickersham, Henry L. Stimson, Adelbert Moot, Addison B. Colvin, Elihu Root, and other Republican leaders of distinction from one end of the state to the other.

With Ogden L. Mills nominated by the Republican party, the people of the state had every reason to believe that the campaign would be waged on a high plane and based upon issues that had to do with the betterment of the government of the state and its relation to our people. Disappointment was expressed on all sides when Congressman Mills, instead of discussing the state issues, accepted the support of the Hearst forces and renewed the ridiculous milk-bugaboo campaign started by Hearst in 1919 in an effort to injure me then.

I remarked, when I heard of it, that Hearst had given him "the kiss of death." By that I meant that Hearst's power, as expressed through his newspapers, was finished in the Eastern part of the country.

Of course the milk issue blew up in the middle of the campaign, when a chemist who had been retained to testify to poisonous impurities in milk sold in New York City recanted and told the truth—that his figures were misrepresented. This left the Republican campaign hard put to find a substitute issue.

There is no doubt in my mind that this disappointment was reflected in thousands of Republican votes that were cast for me. The entire campaign was summarized in a speech I made on the Saturday night before election at the Metropolitan Opera House, the title of which was "Looking for an Issue." I pictured and dramatized the despair of the Republican leaders when they found themselves in difficulty with every argument they wanted to make and had to fall back on the milk issue and Mr. Hearst's support.

Every public man and every candidate for public office is now and then the victim of some stupid advisers. Congressman Mills was surrounded by them. One of his publicity agents invented the slogan: "Al had to work or starve; Mills never had to work." How this was received by the general public is best epitomized in a comment on it in the *New York Times* of November 4, 1926: "We don't know who the publicity man was who opened up this jug of asafetida in Mills' office. Whoever it was, Mills should turn him loose to work at something else or starve."

In that campaign I was victorious by 257,000 votes plurality and with me were elected the state comptroller and lieutenant governor. The only Republican candidate surviving was Albert Ottinger, former state senator from New York City, who was re-elected attorney general.

Robert F. Wagner was elected to the United States Senate that year to succeed James W. Wadsworth. This seemed almost an impossible feat. The overpowering prohibition issue seemed to favor Wadsworth because he had voted and worked against submission of the Eighteenth Amendment, and as United States senator had voted against it. New York, by referendum and in other ways, had shown itself to be a wet state. But Wadsworth was a victim of the duplicity of his own party. The wets firmly believed that he had not gone as far as he should in representing this state known to be wet. They charged, whether rightly or wrongly, that he refrained from acting in an endeavor to hold both sides of the question.

Because of his close friendship with me personally I was often charged by my political enemies, particularly inside of my own party, of secretly favoring Wadsworth and, while seeming to oppose, at the same time deeply desiring his election. Especially among women, many stories of secret understandings between the parties circulated as gossip.

At the opening of the 1926 campaign this gossip was intensified, but the ultimate result dissipated it completely. The nomination of Wagner as the strongest candidate who could be named, having powerful party support and a fine record of achievement in social legislation, was suggested by me, and I gave him full, whole-hearted and vigorous support.

Wadsworth, naturally, had the enmity of the drys, and they set up a third party in an effort to bring about his defeat. It drew just about enough votes to weaken him and to insure Wagner's election.

Immediately following the election of 1926, and before the inauguration, history repeated an episode of 1922 at a similar period. It indicated that private and special interests are continuously on the job. By the provisions of the law construing the reorganization amendment, all state agencies then in control of leasing water-power sites for development were legislated out of office. After January 1, 1927, control of the leasing of water-power sites was to be brought closer to the governor by placing it in a commission, two out of three of whose members were to be appointed by the governor. It was to be further safe-guarded by requiring distinct and specific approval of all leases by the governor himself.

My re-election was taken as a warning to private power interests to keep off the public domain. They attempted to take advantage of the interim between election and January first, when the new order would begin, as they had once before in 1922. They pushed vigorously to se-cure a lease immediately at the hands of the existing Water Power Commission, which had less than six weeks to live. I promptly communicated with the conservation commissioner, who was a member of the Water Power

Commission, expressing my unqualified disapproval of any such action by the very nearly defunct commission.

The threatened action seemed imminent. The commission held a public hearing on the applications and even announced a date when they would give their decision. They made public the form of lease they proposed to grant.

I secured the services of Samuel Untermyer as special counsel to the governor. He expressed a willingness to give his time and ability without compensation to prevent what I still believe was intended to be the alienation of the state power resources by private leasing. Mr. Untermyer hastened to the Executive Mansion on a Sunday and made a close and careful examination of the proposed lease. It revealed that it was nothing more nor less than an option extending over a three-year period, for which the state received only such recompense as might be expended by it for engineering services.

After the entire matter had been publicly aired and discussed throughout the state and over the Eastern part of the country, the nearly defunct Water Power Commission receded from its position and caused the withdrawal of the application by the companies.

On January 1, 1927, when I was inaugurated for the fourth time as governor of the state, I sat in the chair used by Governor George Clinton, the only other four-term governor in the history of the state. During the 1927 session further progress was recorded in making the various bond issues effective, and the reorganized government came into existence on the first of January. I made no changes in the personnel of department heads except to strengthen several of the departments where vacancies had occurred.

For the first time in the history of the state—acting under the reorganization amendment—I formed a cabinet for the governor composed of the heads of the various departments. The theory of a cabinet for the governor worked out very well. It was of great assistance in bringing about co-ordination of effort among department heads. It gave a better understanding generally of all the problems of the state to those concerned with solving them and administering the departments. At the first cabinet meeting I was astonished to learn that some department heads were not even acquainted with the others. Problems of the state, large and small, were frankly discussed around the table. Committees from the cabinet were appointed to work out the details of some of the graver situations.

The election of 1927 was one of the most interesting so-called off-year elections in the history of the state. Only one state-wide office was being filled, and that was a judgeship of the Court of Appeals. By agreement, in 1926, I had induced the Democratic state convention to nominate Judge Henry T. Kellogg, a Republican from Plattsburg, for the vacancy in the court that year, with the promise that in the following year, 1927, the vacancy then to occur would be filled by a Democrat. The retirement of Chief Judge Hiscock because of the age limit provided for in the state constitution, would create a vacancy in the position of Chief Judge of the Court of Appeals. To this vacancy I insisted that Judge Benjamin N. Cardozo be nominated. He was the senior judge of the court, and it is not necessary for me to comment on his ability as a jurist. Many times I have had occasion to discuss legal problems with him, and I have felt deeply complimented when he would call me counsellor and treat me as if I were a member of the bar.

Just before the state convention in 1927 there became apparent among some of the lesser leaders of the Republican party throughout the state a desire to repudiate the agreement. I insisted upon the nomination of my appointee, Judge John F. O'Brien, the son of Dennis O'Brien, who during his lifetime had been a judge in the Court of Appeals. John F. O'Brien was recommended to me by the sitting judges of the Court of Appeals because they were familiar with his ability to present cases on appeal. He had been connected with the office of the corporation counsel in the city of New York for a quarter of a century. The arguments of the wiser minds within the Republican party prevailed and the leaders in search of patronage were defeated in their purposes by the unanimous nomination of Judge O'Brien.

During the legislative session of 1927 the Republican legislative leaders had maintained their steadfast attitude of hostility toward water-power development under state auspices, but chastened by defeat at the polls, they mellowed considerably with respect to some other large problems. This state of mind resulted in the submission to the people, after legislative approval, of nine additional amendments to the constitution. Six were of minor importance and intended only to correct previous amendments. The three outstanding ones were the recommendation of a four-year term for governor, the final adoption of a constitutional executive budget, and extension of the debt limit of cities by exempting them from the computation of certain debts incurred for water supply. This last was intended to aid transit construction in New York City and other public works elsewhere.

Deep interest in amendments to the constitution manifested itself throughout the state. Few people knew anything about the election of the judge of the Court of Appeals, but the history of that campaign indicates that the people carefully studied the amendments to their own constitution. Most remarkable of all in that election was the adoption of all but one of the amendments. The defeated one provided for the four-year term of the governor, election to occur in the year in which the President was being elected. That amendment caused wide debate. It was universally known as No. 6, because it happened to be the sixth amendment on the ballot. Public disfavor was evinced by discussion on all sides. Political leaders, newspaper slogans, billboards everywhere voiced the sentiment: "Vote No on No. 6 and Yes on all the rest." And that is exactly what happened.

It is interesting that the results of the vote on these amendments were known election night. In previous years the secretary of state and the boards of elections in various election districts did not take the trouble to tabulate votes on constitutional amendments, sometimes for many weeks after election was over, on the ground that there was no public interest in them.

I believe that the campaign of 1927 not only improved the constitution of the state of New York and made a contribution to the state's orderly business procedure, but it tended also to awaken interest on the part of the electorate in amendments to their fundamental law.

Immediately following the election of 1926 it was apparent at Albany that a nation-wide interest in me was developing. This was evinced by personal visitors from other states and by the enormous volume of letters, printed circulars and inquiries that poured into Albany. By 1927 correspondence and requests for interviews had grown to such volume that I did not believe that the state employees should be taxed with the care and consideration of them. Accordingly, I permitted the organization of an unofficial volunteer committee of personal friends in New York City to assort and answer as best they could the great volume of correspondence that came in day after day.

The trend of public thought in America began to take shape in May of 1927 when the *Atlantic Monthly* published an open letter from Charles C. Marshall, who to my way of thinking challenged the fundamental declaration contained in the United States constitution guaranteeing the right of citizens of the United States to freedom of religious belief. The appearance in the public prints of the Marshall letter was a warning of what would have to

366

be met later and what would unquestionably become a campaign issue in the event of my nomination for the presidency. My reply printed in the same publication a month later brought a new volume of mail to the Albany post office that taxed it to the utmost of its capacity.

My correspondence indicated to me that the Marshall letter came as something of a shock to thoughtful people throughout the country. Here was the first time in our history that the qualifications of a man for public office were openly challenged because of his adherence to a particular religious belief. During our national existence we have prided ourselves upon our accepted declaration of political faith that no man was to be questioned because of the church he attended in the worship of God. Small-fry politicians may have used such tactics and they undoubtedly did under cover, and conducted "whispering campaigns." But the Marshall letter brought the religious question into the open, printed as it was in one of the most reputable magazines published in this country.

I saw a copy of this letter in galley form before the publication of the magazine, and after consultation with a number of advisers I promptly determined to make open answer to it and to publish my reply in the same magazine. I gave the reply no title, but the publishers of the magazine entitled it "Alfred E. Smith, Catholic and Patriot, Replies."

The Marshall letter raised questions of theology. At no time in my life have I ever pretended any fundamental knowledge of this subject and in the preparation of my reply I was assisted by Father Francis J. Duffy, chaplain of the 69th Regiment and at one time professor of theology. I was also most ably assisted by Justice Joseph M. Proskauer. So far as the fundamental principles contained in the reply had to do with the relationship of the Church and the State I had but my own experience to draw upon and I was reasonably sure that I was on solid ground. Nothing that has happened since has refuted a single line contained in that reply. Nothing in it has ever been successfully challenged and that observation does not come to me from people of my own faith alone. It comes generally from fair-minded, reasonable, liberal and intelligent people. The last section of my reply to Mr. Marshall summarizes the whole contents. It says:

I summarize my creed as an American Catholic. I believe in the worship of God according to the faith and practice of the Roman Catholic Church. I recognize no power in the institutions of my Church to interfere with the operations of the Constitution of the United States or the enforcement of the law of the land. I believe in absolute freedom of conscience for all men and in equality of all churches, all sects, and all beliefs before the law as a matter of right and not as a matter of favor. I believe in the absolute separation of Church and State and in the strict enforcement of the provisions of the Constitution that Congress shall make no law respecting an establishment of religion or prohibiting the free exercise thereof. I believe that no tribunal of any church has any power to make any decree of any force in the law of the land, other than to establish the status of its own communicants within its own church. I believe in the support of the public school as one of the corner-stones of American liberty. I believe in the right of every parent to choose whether his child shall be educated in the public school or in a religious school supported by those of his own faith. I believe in the principle of non-interference by this country in the internal affairs of other nations and that we should stand steadfastly against any such interference by whomsoever it may be urged. And I believe in the common brotherhood of man under the common fatherhood of God.

In this spirit I join with fellow Americans of all creeds in a fervent prayer that never again in this land will any public servant be challenged because of the faith in which he has tried to walk humbly with his God.

The year 1928 bid fair to be historical in my lifetime. I clung steadfastly to my determination not to let any future happening no matter of how much moment interfere with the duties of the position to which I had been elected. I began anew on the first Wednesday of January my last battle for the progressive reforms for which I had worked throughout. When I penned my annual message to the legislature of 1928 I fully realized that it would be the last document of its kind to be signed by me, because whether I was nominated for president or not I had definitely determined to retire from the office of governor.

With this in mind I wrote the longest annual message ever sent to the legislature by a governor. Length alone is no merit. I reviewed the history of the state over a period of ten years, listing accomplishments and laying stress upon the necessary measures for further improvement of the government of the state in its relation to its people.

The session of 1928 was uneventful. The Republican machine adhered to its position on the fundamental questions. They refused to consider any plan for state development of water power. They stood out against the extension of the term of the governor and maintained throughout the session the attitude of men desirous of adjourning at the earliest possible moment.

By this time national politics had found its way into the minds of the Republican legislators and above all other times in my administration they were anxious that nothing happen which might add any prestige to what I was able to claim after eight years of struggle.

The legislature withheld appropriation for the completion of the State Office Building at Buffalo in the hope that it might influence the voters of Erie County against me, although by previous legislation the State had committed itself to build it.

Opposite the Capitol and surrounded by the Education Building and other public structures was the Albany Boys' Academy. The State had purchased all the land surrounding it for a park to beautify the Capitol group of buildings. The trustees of the Boys' Academy offered the building to the State for $300,000. It is of historic architecture and very beautiful. In making my annual address to the State Bar Association in February, I offered to have the State set aside the use of the building as a headquarters and permanent library for them.

The legislature delayed action and on the score of economy said the purchase could wait over for some other year. The trustees of the Academy thought otherwise. They withdrew the offer to sell at $300,000 and increased it to $400,000 because a New York syndicate desirous of building an apartment house on the site had offered that price. One Republican leader to whom I told this simply smiled, and replied to me, "You do get the breaks, don't you." That was his only comment on the loss to the state of $100,000.

Withholding an adequate amount for the completion of the Southern Parkway in Long Island had as its undoubted purpose the delay of the completion of that work beyond my term. Realizing that water power development would be a national issue the legislative leaders sought to square themselves with the people and repeated the proposal I had refused the year before, to appoint a committee to suggest a policy with respect to its development. By the use of names of men high in the public estimation, whom they suggested as members of such a committee, they sought to becloud and befog the real issue between development by the State of its own resources and the leasing of them to private interests over a long period of years.

When the legislature adjourned on the seventeenth of March, 1928, after less than seven full weeks of deliberation, it left me with a mass of bills for consideration. Many were sent to me to embarrass me. Many others had a distinctly political angle. The thirty-day bills disposed of, I turned my attention to the administrative departments of the state government, and by the time the National Convention met I had the state problems fairly well under control.

CHAPTER XXIII

Widening Horizons

USUALLY Albany is a fairly quiet place. One month after the adjournment of the legislature the hum of the winter's business dies down, the excitement of the session has passed away like a storm after which comes calm. But in 1928, thirty days after the adjournment of the legislature, it seemed, at least to me, that Albany was the hub of the universe. People from all over the country, either on business or on vacation, found their way to Albany and immediately came in search of me. Sheriffs, constables and police officials generally representing other states, appearing in the capital for the purpose of having the necessary papers signed to extradite men accused of crime, usually returned home as quickly as possible. Now they remained around the executive chamber until they had a chance either to see me or speak to me. As one sheriff put it, "I don't want to go back home and tell my people that I was in this building and that I did not see you." That apparently was in the mind of every visitor who came within gunshot of the city of Albany during the period between the adjournment of the legislature and the national convention.

My friends who had organized the committee to take care of the pre-convention correspondence continued in charge of the pre-convention campaign. I am indebted

THE PRESIDENTIAL CANDIDATE
1928

MRS. ALFRED E. SMITH
1928

deeply to the loyal friendships of many years' standing which produced the devotion of such men as James J. Hoey, who had been in the legislature with me; George R. Van Namee, who has twice been my secretary; Col., now Lieut.-Col. Herbert H. Lehman, James J. Riordan, John F. Gilchrist, William H. Todd and William F. Kenny. The old neighborhood produced men strong in their friendships and loyal to the last degree in their devotion to one another. The testimony of William F. Kenny and William H. Todd before the senate investigating committee examining into campaign contributions revealed two new characters to the American people. Editorial writers and newspapermen spoke of the devotion of my army of friends, and all made special mention of W. F. Kenny's great desire to promote my welfare. To those who know us both, and who come from the old neighborhood, it is easily understandable. He began, like myself, at the bottom rung of the ladder. His father was a fireman. He started as a truck driver and by hard work and the devotion of his friends he attained his present position in the financial and business circles of our city.

To add to the excitement of this period, my youngest daughter, Catherine, was married to Francis J. Quillinan in the Cathedral of the Immaculate Conception in Albany on June ninth. The newspaper accounts of the impending wedding brought visitors from all the adjoining states, and that particular Saturday saw a tremendous gathering in and around the cathedral. My son, Alfred, Jr., had given us a surprise wedding in 1924. I learned of it while campaigning in Binghamton. Arthur, my second son, followed his brother's example and was quietly and secretly married in 1925. That leaves only Walter, the youngest of the family, at home, so that I often remark to Mrs. Smith that we are almost back again on the honeymoon where we started nearly thirty years ago.

The wedding over, the family started for the Houston convention. Mrs. Smith, my sister and all my children attended the convention as the guests of Mr. William F. Kenny. My eldest daughter, Mrs. Warner, and her husband, remained in Albany with me. My two little grandsons, Arthur Jr. and Walter, sons of Arthur, and my little granddaughter, Mary Adams Warner, also remained with me to keep me company. I was in daily communication with the family in Houston by a direct telephone wire between that city and the Executive Mansion in Albany.

Nation-wide interest in the convention and in the prospect of my nomination had brought representatives of the press from all parts of the country to Albany, and every morning at eleven o'clock and every afternoon at four during the convention days, I was in conference with no less than forty newspaper representatives, usually at the Executive Mansion.

One of the pleasantest experiences of my public life has been my association with newspaper reporters and writers. I have said much to them in my time for publication and much more in confidence. That confidence was never broken from the day I first set foot in Albany up to this writing. I have always had their trust and, in a very marked degree, their friendship.

Many of the Albany correspondents were writing for newspapers during my governorship who had been there ever since I was a member of the legislature. The oldest of them all is George M. Janvrin who was in Albany as a newspaper correspondent before I reached there. He was one of the last men to say good-bye to me last New Year's Day when I was starting for New York. W. Axel Warn, of the *New York Times,* known as the Baron, Charlie Armitage of the Buffalo *News,* Charles S. Hand, now secretary to Mayor Walker, all date back to my days in the legislature. Joseph Cohn, long a political correspondent, had several times taken leave of absence from his own paper to act as publicity man during my campaigns. He became my personal press representative during the national campaign.

Political reporters and writers are keen-minded men and in the pursuit of their calling acquire much valuable information. I found them exceedingly helpful when I was seeking advice. They were always frank and open with me, and whether they were working for newspapers politically hostile to me or not, they were personally friendly and always ready to help me.

Never, except possibly in one instance, did I regard newspaper criticism as being directed against me personally, and for that reason I have never hesitated to talk to the owners and editors of the papers and present my side of a question to them as clearly and as frankly as I could. In my daily conferences with the newspapermen I always permitted them as much latitude as they desired. I never hesitated to speak to them over the telephone at any hour of the day or night, either from the executive chamber or the executive mansion. It is told of a group of them, discussing a question at the Ten Eyck Hotel in Albany, not so long ago, that a bet arose along about midnight. It was decided that my word would be accepted to settle the bet. So they called me on the telephone at the executive mansion and I obliged with the facts in the case.

By visiting their newspaper offices personally I made warm friends among owners and editors of newspapers when I felt that they were not in possession of the facts to permit them to editorialize effectively. It was in that way that I became acquainted with the late Frank Cobb, editorial writer of the New York *World*. In the same way I first met Frank Munsey. I went to his office in the *Sun* Building at 280 Broadway and sent in a card which read "The Governor of the State of New York." I was promptly ushered in. I will never forget the look of surprise on his face when I told him that I had come to correct an editorial in his newspaper which did not set forth the facts.

During the presidential campaign I enjoyed my association in the daily press conferences with the large corps of newspapermen from every part of the country who traveled with me. In fact I treasure among my possessions a letter which they sent me at the end of the campaign with the personal signature of each of them. I always looked forward to press conferences, sure that my confidence would be kept and that I could gain much from the give and take of easy conversation with these observers.

I have a very large collection of the originals of political cartoons sent to me by the cartoonists. I have preserved them all and during my stay in Albany they adorned the walls of the private library of the Executive Mansion and my room at the Capitol. Photographers, motion picture men and now the movietone have had much of my time. I find the exactions of the movietone very difficult because of my inability to speak effectively unless extemporaneously; but I like movies and can be fairly patient with photographers. They must earn a living too.

The pre-convention period as well as the time that the convention was in session were trying times for me. I had often said that victory for the sake of winning was empty, and I took a strong and determined stand that so far as the state of New York was concerned, we could not permit ourselves to be placed in any hypocritical position with respect to certain proposals for the Democratic platform. Merely finding fault with existing conditions would not satisfy me. I insisted upon a definite, understandable and simply expressed proposal for betterment. This applied to agriculture and the tariff, as well as to prohibition. I listened anxiously over the radio for the report of the platform committee and I was in frequent telephone communication by direct wire with Senator Robert F. Wagner, who represented the state of New York on the platform committee.

Unable to have my views and those of the delegates from New York State definitely incorporated in the platform with respect to the Eighteenth Amendment and the Volstead Act, I was unwilling that the convention adjourn without knowing my views and what I proposed to say in the campaign and to do about this much discussed and debated question. Accordingly I insisted that a telegram setting forth my views in unmistakable language, as clear and as definite as I was able to make it, be read to that convention before the hour of adjournment. I told Senator Wagner over the wire that I wanted this done so that the convention might have an opportunity to nominate somebody else if they were unwilling to accept my views. Great as the distinction might be to be called upon to lead the forces of the national Democratic party in a presidential contest, I was unwilling to accept it, if I had to pay as the price the abandonment of any conviction that I entertained or if I had in any way to compromise with the principle involved.

Contrary to the general belief, absolutely nothing was definitely settled before the convention was called to order. That refers not only to the details of the platform but also to the nomination for vice president. Usually that selection is made by the candidate for president. I was unwilling to make the selection and insisted that it be made by the convention itself. It was a great pleasure to me to find that the choice had fallen on Senator Joe T.

Robinson, with whom I had campaigned in New York State eight years before.

I have never taken any stock in the fairly general political belief that territory or place of residence has anything to do with national nominations and I do not believe that the average man or woman pays much attention to where any man comes from if they are satisfied that he stands for that which is right. Residence is largely a matter of accident. I visited the birthplace of Abraham Lincoln and there was no one living there in 1928, and I am certain there could not have been many there when he was born. I was never sure where Andrew Jackson came from until I ran for president.

When the convention opened, newspaper men, members of my cabinet, state officials, as many of the neighbors as would fit into the house, my daughter and her husband, and Dr. and Mrs. Henry Moskowitz, who were stopping with me during the whole convention, gathered into the reception room and listened to the accounts of the convention over the radio.

We lived as quiet and simple a life at the Executive Mansion as the progress of events in those days would permit. The difference in time between New York and Houston meant that we sat up at the Executive Mansion listening to the proceedings until the small hours of the morning, while it was still early evening in Texas. On the eventful night when the balloting for president began, the mansion was crowded to capacity and several thousand people were gathered in the streets around the house, on the lawn and on the porch of the house.

When the radio announced that the chairman of the convention directed the call of the roll there was a deadly silence, and as each state was called and the result announced, those inside the mansion gave vent to their feelings. Those on the outside were unable to understand what was going on until Senator Pomerene of Ohio rose in his place in the convention hall and asked that the Ohio delegation be recorded in favor of me, whereupon my daughter Emily, sitting beside me, jumped up and threw her arms around my neck. That was taken from the outside as a notice that the nomination had been made, and bedlam immediately broke loose. The people on the lawn stormed into the Executive Mansion and were on all floors of it.

The moving-picture operators stationed men in the trees on the mansion grounds with flare lights and the entire scene took on the appearance of a great Fourth of July rally, the flare lights taking the place of the fireworks. It was then three o'clock in the morning and the assembled crowd had been around the mansion since eight o'clock the night before. By the time I made a speech to them, greeted them, shook hands with as many as I could, it was five o'clock in the morning. I was of the opinion at the time that were it not for the efficient handling of the crowd by the state and city police, they would probably have remained there for the rest of the day.

There followed days of excitement, with congratulatory letters and telegrams literally flowing in from all over the world. One man whom I hardly knew insisted upon telephoning to me from Copenhagen.

The convention over, naturally I was eager for the return of Mrs. Smith and the children in order to get their observations and impressions of the convention. They arrived in Albany at five o'clock the following Sunday and brought with them as a souvenir a live burro named Sam Houston. Notwithstanding the event and the central figures therein, Sam took his place in the front line and for quite a while was the center of attraction. He was very young and I saw no need of housing him, so I granted him the freedom of the executive grounds, where he chewed Albany grass to his heart's content and frolicked with the dogs and other animals on the Mansion property. In the fall, the chilly northern winds were too much for him and he contracted pneumonia and died, much to the grief of all the household.

My family and the friends who accompanied them back from the convention, I came to New York City on the third of July, and on Independence Day addressed the annual patriotic gathering of the Tammany Society in the morning. In the evening I spoke from the City Hall steps to our newly naturalized citizens.

Every candidate for public office must always be prepared to listen to those who speak what they call "words of caution." "Be careful what you say about this." "Don't do something else." "Above all other things do not attend any unnecessary functions, gatherings or meetings."

Had I accepted the advice of the coterie that preached caution I would not have spoken in Tammany Hall on the Fourth of July just one week after my nomination for the presidency. But, strange to say, I had my strongest inclination to speak in Tammany Hall at just that very time. I had been identified with Tammany Hall for a quarter of a century. I always had its full and loyal support. Not a single senator or assemblyman from Tammany Hall ever offered the slightest resistance to any part of the program that I had sponsored for the state of New York. I felt that in my hour of great success my place was among my friends. I disregarded the advice of the apostles of caution and appeared in Tammany Hall and paid to that ancient and historic organization the compliment I felt was due them at their annual meeting to celebrate the signing of the Declaration of Independence.

Immediately following the convention there arose the all-important question of selecting a national chairman. This is by custom a responsibility resting on the candidate himself. I suggested John J. Raskob as an eminently successful business man with a clear mind, a broad view and a knowledge of men. He was born in the city of Lockport in my own state. Aside from my knowledge of and confidence in his ability, I believed it to be wise political strategy to let the businessmen of this country know that one of the great industrial leaders of modern times had confidence and faith in the Democratic party and in its platform. While it is true that Mr. Raskob had no previous political experience, he certainly had a knowledge of the problems pressing the country and was in sympathy with the Democratic proposals for solution of them.

We were in accord on the four leading issues—government ownership of water power sites, government relief for agriculture, scientific and business-like treatment of the tariff, and sane, sensible amendment to the constitution and the Volstead Act to produce real temperance as against the prevailing conditions so much complained of by leading men and women of every political faith.

At my suggestion the Democratic National Committee met in New York right after the convention and after acting on Mr. Raskob's selection as chairman, chose Mrs. Nellie Tayloe Ross, former Governor of Wyoming, as vice chairman. I had met Mrs. Ross on several occasions, once as my guest at the Executive Mansion in Albany. All who had the pleasure of her personal acquaintance knew the real influence she had with women generally and respected her ability and knowledge of political affairs.

I met, formally and informally, with the National Committee in New York, and conferred with Senator Reed, Senator Pittman, Senator Gerry, Senator Robinson and others on the conduct of the campaign. Then I returned to Albany to prepare my speech of acceptance and to arrange other conferences for the discussion of details of the campaign issues.

CHAPTER XXIV

Campaigning for the Presidency

JULY and August of 1928 were probably the busiest months in my life. Many of the national issues were new to me. I had made no detailed study of them and was without knowledge of the party's attitude. That required that I confer with Democratic members of the national legislature to acquaint myself with the details and to get their viewpoint on what should be stressed in the campaign and where. Senator Pittman of Nevada spent five days in Albany with me and gave me much valuable assistance. He had been chairman of the platform committee of the national convention and was, moreover, well versed in the basic tenets of the party's policies and performances in congress. Congressman Byrns of Tennessee, Senators Carter Glass and Claude G. Swanson of Virginia, and Governor Byrd of that state, Senator George of Georgia and Josephus Daniels of North Carolina, all visited with me on different occasions at the Executive Mansion and each discussed the problems with which he was most conversant.

Everyone was eager and willing to help to such an extent that it became almost confusing and rather difficult to steer a steady course through the stream of well-meant advice, suggestion and information that was offered. Everybody thought, too, that unless the particular advice they had to offer could be told to me in person, the campaign would be sure to fail. So I met with farmers, tariff reformers, people with prohibition panaceas, publicists and committees of all kinds, in addition to those whose counsel I myself had sought.

One of the most difficult tasks that confronts a candidate for office is the preparation of a speech of acceptance. All during my public career, while campaigning, I have made it a point to devote an entire evening to a given subject, and to exhaust it so far as that evening is concerned, giving my audience enough of the details to let them have a pretty thorough understanding of just what I am aiming at. Many of our political orators lose much of their force and effect because at the outset they assume that all their listeners understand the technical terms they so often use.

One of the chief dangers in speeches of acceptance lies in the possibility that if you say too little on a given subject there is the fear that you are minimizing the importance of the topic. Other issues, as for instance water power, when treated in a speech of acceptance must be treated at full length so that the people who listen to or read the speech may really understand the subject. You are either going to say a little about a lot of things or say so much about a few things that the speech is out of proportion, impossible of delivery in a reasonable time and may tire your audience and your readers. So many people listen in on the delivery of a speech today because of the widespread use of the radio that they too must receive consideration.

With all of this experience and all of these facts in mind I worked hard to prepare it, and my speech of acceptance was the only speech I read during the whole campaign. I was never able to deliver a set speech; never able to write it, and never able to read it. In all of my debates and speeches, I used only a single envelope or two with just the headings jotted down, and such exhibits as I might wish to show or read to the audience inside of the envelope.

I adopted the same policy during my legislative career and during all of my campaigns for the governorship and in the recent presidential campaign. I spoke in the city of Milwaukee during the last campaign for an hour and twenty minutes, and recently I picked up the envelopes I had used. Prohibition was the subject and I used ten envelopes upon which was written nothing that I said but only memoranda designed to keep the speech running in order.

The memoranda run as follows:

> Plain speech.
> Eighteenth amendment and Volstead Act.
> Failure officials to talk frankly to people.
> Pre-conceived notions.
> Prohibition party during the war.
> Anti-Saloon League drive.
> Support of people used to restriction of their personal liberty during the war.
> Ratified 1919.
> Volstead law enacted over veto of the president.
> What's best for the country.

Campaigning for the Presidency

We never had prohibition.
Reference in speech of acceptance.
Evidence to sustain it.
New York, New England, Pennsylvania and the West.
Leading thought.
Ida Tarbell.
President Butler.
Institute for social and religious research.
Andrews' report.
Collier's Weekly.
Chester P. Mills.
Only 5 per cent of the smugglers caught.
1,720,000 stills operating.
Ostrich.
Police records.
Deaths.
Quote Harding.
What's Republican answer.
Hoover speech.
Referendum popular states.
Constructive recommendation.

These envelopes are always in my own hand-writing and abbreviated. That is useful in two respects. I am developing the thought while writing the memo, and then I seem to be better able to recollect and formulate the thought looking at my own handwriting than looking at typewriting.

Of course this method of speaking requires a considerable amount of practice and I had it for twelve long years in the assembly, afterwards in the constitutional convention and during all of my campaigns. I became so accustomed to this way of making a speech that six months after I have made a speech I can take the same envelopes and make it all over again. I have saved all these envelopes through the years and while I may make different speeches upon a single subject the envelopes are frequently useful in the preparation of a new envelope. By looking them over I can tell where and in what particular campaign a speech was made.

As far back as I can remember I have always had my own system of keeping track of public events. I started first with a home-made scrap book using a receipt book of the Wells-Fargo Express Company. In that I have all the items of interest to me, politically and socially, that occurred up to about my twenty-fifth year. Among other things in the Wells-Fargo Express book are all the programs of the school commencements, school happenings and afterwards the press comment on our amateur theatrical productions along with the programs of them. Pasted in the scrap book is Bryan's famous Chicago "crown of thorns and cross of gold" address and many of the public utterances of Bourke Cockran, State Senator Grady and Senator Elihu Root, whose style I greatly admired.

Later I filed the information I wanted to keep, under subjects, filing the original newspaper clipping in an envelope. I found these clippings of very great use in later years as a readier reference than I would be able to get from books or publications. They were accurate as to date because I had the original copy; they were written in a way that was readily understandable; and

NOTES FOR A PRESIDENTIAL CAMPAIGN SPEECH
Written in Governor Smith's own hand on the backs of envelopes.

THE PRESIDENTIAL "BALLYHOO"

The candidate runs the gauntlet for the cameras.

the very fact that they were in my possession indicated that originally I had some interest in them. It was this habit, acquired years ago, that led me to the use of envelopes in preparing topic headings for speeches.

My speech of acceptance of the presidential nomination had to deal with so many issues and had to be given to the press so far in advance, that I departed from my custom and read it.

I decided to have the Committee notify me of my nomination on the steps of the State Capitol at Albany, as that had been my high school and college and it was there that I had found out all that I knew about government. The date once fixed, the city of Albany became crowded with visitors. The hotels were taxed to capacity, the Chamber of Commerce, representing the business men, decorated the city and prepared for a gala day. A platform was erected on the Capitol steps and loud-speaking apparatus was provided throughout the Capitol Park. In the early morning of the day on which the speech was to be delivered a rain-storm came up and it poured incessantly throughout the day. Although we were in possession of information from the United States Weather Bureau that the storm had a radius of only thirty miles right around Albany, it did us no good. It gave the wag a chance to spin his pun and the newspaper boys referred to it as appropriate weather for a wet candidate.

It was evident by five o'clock in the afternoon that the rain was to be continuous throughout the night and sudden arrangements were made for the transfer of the radio apparatus to the Assembly Chamber. In that historic room where my voice had been heard for so many years and where I had four times been inaugurated governor, I delivered my speech of acceptance of the Democratic nomination for the presidency, setting forth the principles for which I proposed to battle.

My picture was taken so often during July and August that I began to think there was nothing more to a national campaign than talking to newspaper reporters and having your picture taken. But I had a rude awakening when my advisers in the Democratic National Committee laid my itinerary before me. Requests for my appearance poured in on the National Committee from all over the United States. I sat in the headquarters one day and looked them all over and came to the conclusion that had the Committee consented to even one per cent of what was asked, the campaign would have run up to New Year's day.

In company with those of my advisers who were familiar with my method of campaigning in the state, given subjects were selected for different parts of the country. Making allowances for time to gather material, get the proper rest, cover the necessary number of miles to get from one place to another, we agreed that I could deliver three speeches a week.

The march of progress in every human endeavor has not overlooked methods of conducting political campaigns. I have spoken of the old-time methods that are within my personal recollection. The improvement, however, was not a sudden development but was a gradual growth.

In my first campaign for the governorship I was compelled to rely almost entirely on newspaper accounts of my speeches and the word that would be passed along by the comparatively few citizens who would have an opportunity to hear me personally.

In my third campaign for governor, in 1922, my campaign committee rather gingerly used amplifiers in some very large halls and for overflow audiences in the street. In the 1924 campaign the radio came into play but in a very restricted way. Campaign speakers were annoyed by the presence of what I called the "pie plate." I referred to it at the ratification meeting for John W. Davis in Madison Square Garden in October of that year. Amplifiers in the halls gave a metallic, tinny sound to the voice which also was disconcerting to those speaking, particularly extemporaneously.

Growth and development of the use of the radio was such that in 1928 it played probably the most important rôle in the national campaign. As an indication of the value of the radio, let us assume that a candidate for public office made a speech every night for thirty nights. In New York State he could not address more than an average of a thousand people a night. That would mean thirty thousand people or less than one per cent of the electorate, the other ninety-nine and a fraction per cent being dependent upon what they heard or read in the newspapers.

Back in the old days of campaigning comparatively few people in the country heard the voice of the candidate or got the slightest idea of his personality or the force and effectiveness of his spoken word. In the recent campaign millions of people listened to both candidates every time they spoke and acquired a familiarity with their characteristics and mannerisms of speech as well as with their voices. While at Palm Beach this winter a friend introduced me to her young daughter. As soon as I spoke the little girl turned to her mother and said, "Oh, Mama, he has the same voice that he had on the radio."

Radio replaces the antiquated method of attempting to circularize the electorate by the mailing of speeches of acceptance and of debates. A large part of these documents was always wasted. Nothing makes such an impression on a person as the spoken word. Oratory and the power of speech will always be effective.

Throughout the campaign I traveled on a special train on which were 60 to 75 newspaper men, stenographers, mimeograph operators and members of my personal party, consisting of Mrs. Smith, my daughter Emily, my daughter Catherine, Mr. William F. Kenny, my nephew John Glynn, and at various times, Mrs. Charles Dana Gibson, Mrs. Caroline O'Day, General Charles W. Berry, Major General William N. Haskell, my son Alfred, Norman H. Davis of New York, Bruce Kremer of Montana, Congressman Byrns of Tennessee, Judge Bernard L. Shientag of the City Court, companion of many previous campaign trips, and Justice Joseph M. Proskauer. We were joined by many other friends for short trips between points.

We left Albany on a Sunday night and even my little grandsons aged two and three years came to the train to say good-bye and wish me luck, as did all the grown-up children and a host of friends.

My first speech of the campaign dealt with farm relief, and was delivered at Omaha, Nebraska. I was conscious that this speech was awaited with eagerness throughout the country because it was the opening one in the active campaign and dealt with one of the live issues. To prepare it I gave much careful thought and study, much as I would have done if I were to carry a bill in the legislature on a new subject. I read much of the literature available and especially the bills which had failed in congress or by the President's veto. A group of agricultural leaders, men and women, came to Albany from the middle west and even before my speech of acceptance threshed out with me what I had determined on as my position. I understood and sympathized with their situation and in my Omaha speech determined to state in my own way what I believed to be their difficulty and the remedy I would propose.

I found the city excited because of an advertisement inserted in the local papers asking me a number of questions. I made frank and clear answers to these and turned the embarrassment intended for me on the local Republican committee. Answering questions from reliable sources always results in the biter being bit. The subject matter of this speech had been nearly all prepared before I left Albany and the trip to Omaha being a reasonably unbroken run, I was ready for the platform when the time came and it was easy to add the answers to the questions.

After leaving Omaha countless hundreds of people came aboard the special train to ride along with us between stations for the purpose of shaking hands with me and advising me what to talk about. All kinds of people sent letters and telegrams to be delivered to the train at the various stops. I had an active office force working with me all through the trip to sift these communications and get the important ones to me. With all the stops and the handshaking my personal preparation of material for speeches could be made only between midnight and two or three o'clock in the morning.

From Omaha to get into Oklahoma the train traveled by day through Kansas. Along the route there are what are called "operating stops." These are known to the people of the different towns and villages. The news was spread ahead of time that our train was to come through and just as I would get comfortably seated in my room smoking a cigar and reading over the Republican platform to compare it with the Democratic platform, the train would suddenly come to a stop and I would find thousands of people waiting at the rear of it. After this had happened four or five times within an hour or so, I sent for the operating manager aboard the train and asked him what it was all about. He said frankly to me, "You are accustomed to traveling on the New York Central Railroad that goes 150 miles without stopping. We haven't the facilities in this part of the country that they have. Our first stop was for water, the next for ice, the next for coal, and so on. It is not possible in our part of the country to assemble all the necessities at one place."

In order to have a little idea of campaigning, ask yourself the question, "How would you like to get to bed at three o'clock in the morning after working over books and papers for four hours, only to find yourself in a station at seven in the morning with the village orator perched on the platform and shouting 'Come out here Al, and give us a look at you.'"

The women members of the party who retired early would rise early and attempt to take my place on the platform, but it did not prove to be satisfactory until I made my appearance. I might just as well have gone out myself in the first place because I could not sleep anyway with the local brass band playing "East Side, West Side, all around the town."

I was met at Oklahoma City by an enormous crowd and it was quite apparent to me that the foremost issue so far as that part of the country was concerned was religion. I therefore determined to make my speech that night on the subject of religious tolerance.

There was considerable opposition to my making that type of speech at any time during the campaign and particularly in Oklahoma. I listened to both sides of the argument and concluded that inasmuch as I had personal knowledge of the underhand attacks and the undercurrent of the whispering campaign that was being conducted against me and my family and as I personally had knowledge of the scurrilous, blasphemous literature being circulated throughout the country against me and my people, I felt deep in my heart that I would be a coward and probably unfit to be president if I were to permit it to go further unchallenged. Without any thought of the consequences I went into it with all the vigor I could command. I referred to the Klan by name, to the Women's Christian Temperance Union, Mabel Walker Willebrandt's attempts to rouse religious hate, and to all of the other forces that appeared to be taking any part in any such un-American and undemocratic campaign as that.

The auditorium at Oklahoma City was the largest place in which I have ever spoken. My recollection is that it holds close to 30,000 people. My friends in the east and for that matter in other parts of the country had a tense evening while I was speaking at Oklahoma. I thought nothing of it at the time but I afterwards learned of the fears that they entertained of a possible attack upon me. Listeners in on the radio were particularly disturbed because of the noises in the hall which were believed to be disorder. The fact is that a large part of the noise was created by an individual about half way down in the hall who continuously shouted: "Pour it on 'em, Al, pour it on 'em."

One thing I noticed about Oklahoma was that the people who were for me were very strongly for me and by the same token those opposed to me were most bitter in their hostility. That many friends there expected trouble was shown by the fact that they borrowed a large number of soldiers' uniforms and called for young men to volunteer as a personal bodyguard for me while in the city.

Mrs. Smith and I rode in an automobile between the hotel and the meeting hall. A tall, square-jawed man apparently of the Indian type was chosen as a personal bodyguard. His extreme reticence caused me to question him. I asked him if he did not expect some trouble at that hall that night and he replied, "The Democratic Committee has appointed sergeants at arms for the speedy removal of anybody who attempts any disorder or interrupts or interferes with the speaker."

It indicates how tense was the feeling in New York and how strong was the apprehension of possible danger to me that immediately upon my arrival at the hotel after the speech, I called Mrs. Moskowitz on the telephone, and she said: "Where are you?" "Back at the hotel," I replied. "Thank God for that," she answered.

Finishing in Oklahoma I went on to Denver, Colorado, where on Saturday night I spoke on the question of water-power development, our water-power resources and their potential value to the people. Having attended mass on

Sunday morning in Denver and with the prospect of the long ride into Wyoming ahead of me, I desired to get some fresh air before going to the train. I walked from the church to the depot. I had gone but a short distance when I was recognized and the crowd began to accumulate. When I reached the depot it had assumed the proportions of a full-sized parade.

All day Sunday was spent riding between Colorado and Cheyenne, Wyoming. This part of the country was all new to me and I was impressed by the great waste and barren condition of the land. We had been riding at the rate of about fifty miles an hour for a solid hour. I saw not the slightest sign of civilization—not a house nor a barn—when suddenly my eyes lit upon a horse. I looked around to see where he belonged. I said to the man in charge of the train, "We must be coming near to civilization." He said, "You will ride for another hour before you come to a house." "But we are going fifty miles an hour. How does that horse get home?" I asked. "He is at home now," replied my friend. "In the only home he has. He is a wild horse."

We arrived in Cheyenne about four o'clock on Sunday afternoon. I received a rousing reception and was taken from the train and paraded through the streets in an automobile. We continued on, reaching Helena, Montana, the next morning.

Here I attended the County Fair and was initiated into the tribe of the Blackfeet Indians. With great solemnity the Indian chiefs went through the complete ritual and observed all their tribal customs. I was brought to the platform and one Indian put paint marks on my face, another put the helmet with all its feathers on my head, and I was christened "Big Chief Leading Star."

From Helena we paid a visit to Butte, arriving at midday. The mayor declared a half holiday for the school children and I would be willing to make a good-sized wager that every child in Butte came down to the depot to meet me as well as some from other places. I never saw so many children gathered together in any one place in my life.

At Minneapolis and St. Paul we were greeted by a large outpouring of people. I finished the week's work in Milwaukee on Saturday night. I came directly from Milwaukee to the city of Rochester, New York, where the Democratic state convention was scheduled for the following Monday. For the time being I was compelled to brush the national situation out of my mind and delve again into the politics of New York State; to assist the leaders in nominating my successor.

With very little time for resting up, all of the newspapermen still with me, letters and telegrams of suggestion pouring in, some absolutely necessary state business in connection with the budget to be transacted by me, I started out again after a few days on a southern tour which was finally to terminate in Chicago.

On the way south I stopped over in Richmond and the whole party visited Governor Byrd at the Capitol and the Executive Mansion. I opened the speech-making of that week at Nashville, Tennessee, where I reviewed the issues generally up to that period in the campaign.

From Nashville, I went to Louisville, Kentucky. My whole speech there was devoted to a discussion of the tariff. In this city I was received by United States Senator Barkley and Mr. Bingham, the owner of the *Louisville Courier*. The city of Louisville was in the hands of a Republican administration and under its charter the police force is political. It changes with each administration, there being no civil service requirements. A new guardian of public safety if he is a Democrat appoints Democratic policemen; if a Republican, he appoints Republican policemen. The very forces which should have made for order in the great gathering at Louisville displayed a hostility to my party and to me that was so apparent that the two New York City detectives who were with me asked that the Louisville policemen be removed from the floor on which I was living in the hotel.

They went to ridiculous lengths to cause me discomfort. When I spoke that evening in Louisville, the heat in the meeting hall was noticeable to everyone. We afterwards learned that somebody had deliberately turned on the steam heat. When I left to go to the train, a number of local newspapermen accompanied me and an hour after I went aboard they asked to see me. I had a conference with them and was unable to understand why they had come down to the train after having left me at the hotel. One outspoken newspaperman revealed that a member of the local police department notified the newspapermen that I was intoxicated, although I had been seen by thousands of people only a half hour before that coming out of the hotel with Mrs. Smith and my party and walking to the train.

The attitude of the police became known to the citizens of Louisville generally and scathing denunciation of their conduct to me and my party appeared in the *Louisville Courier*. I was asked by some people in Louisville who did not believe that things happened as stated, to correct by a public statement what they thought was an erroneous impression. I was compelled to reply to them and say that I could not deny the written matter because it was the truth.

While at Louisville I visited the birthplace of Abraham Lincoln and saw for the first time, preserved inside of a stone structure, the original log cabin in which the Great Emancipator was born. I wish every boy in the United States could see that cabin. There could be no more forceful lesson in American democracy.

From Louisville we went to Sedalia, a small town in Missouri, mid-way between St. Louis and Kansas City. Here I discussed the financial aspects of the federal administration. Sedalia is a Democratic section of the state of Missouri while both Kansas City and St. Louis are Republican. The situation in the state of Missouri presented some interesting political phenomena. The Democrat running for senator on the ticket with me was a pronounced dry and he carried Sedalia and the country sections of Missouri which have always been Democratic but lost the city of St. Louis and Kansas City. On the other hand, I carried St. Louis and very materially reduced the Republican majority in Kansas City but was overwhelmingly defeated in all of the Democratic sections of Missouri. No other reason in the world could be advanced except religion and my views on prohibition.

I saw little evidence of practical prohibition in Sedalia. Next door to the hotel where I was stopping a party was in progress until the small hours of the morning and I am satisfied that the hilarity was not produced by grape juice of the non-alcoholic variety. Norman H. Davis and Mrs. Charles Dana Gibson were in my party. Mrs. Gibson asked Mr. Davis to take care of her money for her and he put it with his own in a wallet in his hip pocket. At some time during the evening, whether in the meeting hall or in the crowds outside of it somebody relieved Mr. Davis of the purse. It furnished much amusement to the people on the train. They said he went all the way from Broadway to Sedalia to have his pocket picked.

Leaving Missouri after a brief visit and parade in St. Louis, we went to Chicago. Here a tremendous reception awaited us at the Union Depot. So great were the crowds that my daughter, Mrs. Warner, and General Berry, became separated from the party and were lost in the crowd. General Berry approached a policeman and said to him "This is Governor Smith's daughter." The policeman said, "Forget it." They had to take their chances with the mob in the depot and did not arrive at the hotel until two hours after we did. The street parade in Chicago indicated that it was a holiday in that city.

I visited the University of Chicago and the Northwestern University. At the Chicago University I was presented with a scroll signed by the professors and members of the faculty who were supporting my candidacy. The character of support I received in Chicago, with George Getz, a Republican, leading a group of Republicans and independents and the enthusiastic local Democratic organization working together, reminded me of the kind of support I received in my own state when running for governor.

On the way back from Chicago to Albany, I stopped at Indianapolis long enough to pay a visit to the veteran democratic leader of Indiana, Senator Thomas Taggart, who was then in the hospital and who has since passed away.

In Albany I straightened out some matters in connection with the state budget, held some meetings of the cabinet and official committees, and then went to Boston. Here I received the greatest ovation of the entire campaign. So intense was the feeling, so large was the throng, that at times I feared for the safety of Mrs. Smith riding with me in the open automobile. I was greeted and cheered by a tremendous audience at Mechanics Hall, where Mrs. Francis B. Sayre, daughter of Woodrow Wilson, presided. The value of the radio for campaigning was further demonstrated in Boston when two halls other than the one where I spoke in person were hooked up on the radio and crowded to the doors.

While in Boston I also had my attention directed to the statement made and signed by a group of professors at Harvard University. After saying that one of the reasons for their support was my record as governor, they said:

In voting for such a man we are glad to express our adherence to the frequently ignored provision of the United States Constitution which made religious toleration a fundamental part of our government: "No religious test shall ever be required as a qualification to any office or public trust under the United States."

Some of us favor national prohibition and some oppose it. We think that differences of opinion on this question should not be allowed to overshadow other important matters, such as the establishment of friendly relations with other countries including Latin America; the protection of national water-power; and the relief of agricultural depression, as to which Governor Smith's desire for action contrasts sharply with the eight years' inactivity of the administration to which his opponent has belonged.

Government is something greater than an efficiently administered business corporation with a multitude of inactive shareholders. We support Governor Smith, above all, because of his power to reverse the present trend toward political apathy and arouse in the citizens of the United States an active intelligent interest and participation in their government.

Only recently I met this group of professors at dinner in Boston and discussed with them some of the social, political and economic problems of government.

THE DAILY PRESS CONFERENCE ON THE 1928 CAMPAIGN TRIP

Joseph L. Cohn, the candidate's press agent, stands behind him. All the others are reporters.

SMITH CROWDS IN LOUISVILLE AND CHICAGO — 1928

Campaigning for the Presidency

From Boston I came through the Blackstone Valley into Providence and down to Hartford, riding through Connecticut with innumerable stops and arriving in New York in the late evening.

Beginning next to the last week of the campaign I addressed a large audience in Newark and received a tremendous welcome in Philadelphia. In point of enthusiasm and crowds Philadelphia was second only to Boston.

After speaking in Philadelphia on Saturday night I spent the week-end at the residence of Mr. Raskob at his home in Delaware, outside of the city of Wilmington. On Monday night I spoke in Baltimore.

On the Friday night before election day I spoke at the Academy of Music in Brooklyn and confined myself to state issues, the state government and the state ticket.

At an enormous rally in Madison Square Garden on Saturday night the campaign ended as far as speaking to great audiences was concerned. In that speech I attempted to sum up the issues of the entire campaign and on Monday night made my final and last appeal to the American jury over the radio.

CHAPTER XXV

Election Day and Some of the Issues

TUESDAY, Election Day, November sixth, was Mrs. Smith's birthday. I arranged for a birthday cake the night before and determined that election or no election the birthday could not be overlooked and we'd have the birthday party anyway.

The usual crowd of people was at the voting booth in the morning when I went to cast my own ballot in company with Mrs. Smith. To me the day was uneventful as I was attempting to relax after the strain. After dinner in the evening I went to the Sixty-Ninth Regiment Armory where the members of the Tammany Society were receiving the returns. Quite early in the evening it was apparent to me that my opponent was victorious and that I must meet defeat. I went back to the Biltmore Hotel and called my wife and sister and all my children into a room and prepared them for what I knew would be very unwelcome news to them. It did not take much persuasion on my part to reconcile them to the inevitable. They received it like good soldiers, Mrs. Smith's only remark being: "It's all for the best. It's God's will. Some of the threats against you might be carried out. Aside from all that, we will see more of you."

I returned to Albany on Friday after election and plunged into the business of the state over the week end, returning to New York on the following Tuesday when the Democratic National Committee had arranged for a national hook-up on the radio. There was much ill feeling and such apparent dissatisfaction with the result that I felt that the great army of people who had followed me should have a word of cheer from me directly. When all is said and done the American people must live together in peace and harmony no matter who is president. The bitterness and the rancor injected into the hearts of so many not only by the campaign but by the character of it had to be wiped away and I felt that that duty devolved upon me.

The success of our party form of government requires that the cornerstone of a political party rest on a sound foundation. Dishonest arguments and dishonest issues are just as much to be detested when resorted to by political parties as dishonesty would be condemned in the argument or conduct of an individual. There will always be certain classes or groups of people, probably outside of the control of a political party, who will make false and misleading statements either about a party or its candidates or will make an appeal to passion or prejudice; but I think I am safely within the truth when I state that some appeals of that nature and some of the false and misleading statements in the last campaign were at least condoned by the Republican party if they did not have their origin within it.

The Republican party, for thirty-five years, in each succeeding presidential year has resorted to the false and misleading issue of prosperity. The surprising thing about it is the number of independent American citizens who are willing to believe that the Republican party as a political organization or because of the policies of its platform automatically produces prosperity. The fact of the matter is, if prosperity is to be judged from the high wage scale, that was adopted during a Democratic administration and because of the exigencies of war.

Nevertheless the Republican party resorted to its old tactics and once more brought down from the garret the old full dinner pail, polished it up and pressed it into service. No sensible person believes that the success of the Democratic ticket in the last presidential election would have had any effect upon the prosperity of the country. I do not personally believe that the leaders of the Republican party believe their own issues or have faith in them as far as prosperity goes. But it is a good catchword. It appeals to millions of unthinking people. Certainly the Republican leaders are responsible for some of the advertising intended to impress certain classes of our people. One Republican advertisement in every newspaper in the eastern part of this country last fall was, to my way of thinking, an insult to the intelligence of the American working man. It said in effect that he ought to be entirely satisfied with the government of his country as long as he has enough to eat. It really advised that he should not be concerned about any foreign policy, that he should have no interest in the development of the water power resources on our navigable inland streams and waterways, and that the question of official dishonesty is not a matter of concern to him. In the language of the advertisement, he has an automobile in the backyard, a chicken in every pot and he is wearing silk socks. And that result is supposed to have been produced for him by the beneficent Republican party in control of the government at Washington. They proceed upon the theory that that is sufficient for him to know about the government. That advertisement pre-supposed that he has no other interest. I have faith that American working men and women have at least as much interest in their government as in their own individual material well-being.

Just as the prosperity issue was misrepresented, the platform plank and my public declarations with respect to the amendment of our immigration laws were likewise misrepresented. Restriction of immigration first took place under a Democratic administration and it was one of the policies calculated to maintain the high standard of American wages. There was no difference between the Democratic platform and the Republican platform on that issue. In my speech of acceptance I found fault with the mechanics of bringing about the desired result and so did President Hoover. It is an indication that he was not satisfied with the laws making it effective that in the present session of Congress he has been unsuccessful in securing the change he suggested in the national origins section of the Immigration Law. My attitude was misrepresented, although the president, after his election, expressed his dissatisfaction with the law making the principle of immigration effective, just exactly as I did in the campaign.

Of course the hypocritical attitude of the Republican party on the question of prohibition is known to every man, woman and child in the country. In control of the government for eight solid years during which prohibition is supposed to have been effective, they were themselves compelled to deplore the conditions incident to an attempt at its enforcement. The Republican party has used the prohibition issue to soft-soap the drys and to exercise a kind of political blackmail against the wets. In the last campaign, if you follow the speeches of their leading orators, you will find that they started out to capture the West by being dry and struggled to hold the East by being wet. That was best illustrated by a little story in the *Evening World*. Willie said to his papa, "Why does Senator Borah say that 'prohibition is a leading question' while Governor Hughes says, 'prohibition is a sham battle?'" To which Willie's papa answered, "Senator Borah was talking in a dry place and Governor Hughes was talking in a wet place."

The Republican party in New York State and for that matter in the nation led the drys to believe that everybody else opposed whispering against the candidate personally; and yet I was probably the outstanding victim of the last half century of a whispering campaign. Suddenly, as though by a pre-concerted arrangement a story started to circulate about me, and came from various parts of the country with the same general purport. A woman in Syracuse wrote to a woman in West Virginia that I was intoxicated at the New York State Fair on Governor's Day and to such a degree that it required two men to hold me up while I was delivering an address from the grandstand. A Republican state senator who acted as escort to me that day by appointment from the State Department of Agriculture, flatly denied that any such thing happened. Photographs and motion pictures had been taken of me from the minute I entered the fair grounds until I stepped aboard the New York Central train to go home. These showed plainly that the story had absolutely no foundation in fact. When the lie was nailed the woman in West Virginia refused to produce the letter and the woman in Syracuse denied that she had written it.

Shortly after that a Protestant minister from Albany in the course of a speech delivered at a Chautauqua in Indiana made the statement that I was so intoxicated while talking over the radio on the Sunday my family returned from Texas that it required two men to hold me up. When I sent for him he denied that he had ever made any such statement, although the Democratic National Committee was in possession of six different affidavits from six reputable people stating that they had heard him say it.

The whispering campaign along these lines evidently had its origin in some one place because half a dozen different stories were carried back to me and each time my supposed degree of intoxication was so great that it required two men to hold me up.

It was apparent to the newspapermen, than whom there are no keener observers, that the story of two men holding me up was invented by somebody and passed along to unscrupulous people for repetition. Whenever I went anywhere I was always accompanied by two people and generally one on each side of me. One was my bodyguard and the other person someone supposed to escort me to the place where I was going to speak. I seldom walked alone. It was this that enabled them to get away with the story that two people had to hold me up.

Other equally vicious stories with many variations were spread and with such similarity in detail that one was forced to the conclusion that they emanated from some well-organized central source. It is not difficult to spread this kind of propaganda. There are so many thousands of people who like to have people believe that they know something personal about a candidate. It seems to be a human frailty to which a great many people are prone. This of course was a despicable method of campaigning, and should have had the outspoken condemnation of the leaders of all political parties.

The most un-American and undemocratic issue that could be raised against any man was raised with startling effect against me in the last campaign and that was the question of my religion. It started with the Marshall letter in the *Atlantic Monthly* in March, 1927, in which Mr. Marshall raised the question on a high plane. My answer should have ended the matter but the Republican leaders, it seems, could not resist the temptation to try to gather in the fruits of such a campaign for their party.

It would be interesting to know how it was financed. The woman chairman of the Democratic county committee of North Carolina told me that that state was flooded from one end to another with all kinds of anti-Catholic literature and anti-Catholic propaganda containing lying and scurrilous statements about the Catholic church and about me. She ventured the suggestion, borne of her experience in campaigning, that it could not have been sent through the state to such an extent as it was, for less than half a million dollars.

The distressing thing about any degree of success in a campaign of that kind is the exhibition of so much ignorance in a country which has expended so many billions of dollars in the cost of public education. The very people who are asking us to adhere to our constitution on the liquor question seem to be the first to disagree publicly with that part of the constitution which says: "No religious test shall ever be required as a qualification to any office or public trust under the United States."

It is amazing in this day and age that such countless thousands of people are so stupid as to believe the absolutely false and senseless propaganda that was whispered around during the last campaign. It has its humorous side. I was talking to a prominent citizen of Georgia who told me that in certain churches in that state they had pictures of me attending the ceremonies incident to the opening of the Holland Tunnel under the Hudson River between New York and New Jersey, and he expressed himself as

413

surprised to think that opponents of mine were able to convince large numbers of people that that tunnel was actually to be constructed not to New Jersey but into the basement of the Vatican in Rome in the event of my election. The Holland Tunnel is approximately two miles long and cost forty-eight million dollars, or nearly twenty-five million dollars a mile. It is not difficult to figure the cost to build one to the Vatican, which is about thirty-five hundred miles from the foot of Canal Street, New York City.

One of the most important problems in connection with the Holland Tunnel, although only two miles long, was its ventilation; and here we have voting citizens of a sovereign state actually believing that the Atlantic Ocean could be tunnelled under and that it would be possible for people to travel under the Atlantic Ocean between Rome and New York. One man made the deliberate statement over the radio that a convent in New Jersey was purchased by the Catholic Church as the American residence of the Pope in the event of my election.

In the city of Savannah two Democratic women, one a supporter of mine and the other an opponent, were arguing about my election. The woman who had opposed me stated that she had done so because of my religion. When her friend reminded her that she had supported a Catholic for Mayor of Savannah she replied, "That's different. He is an Irish Catholic. Smith is a Roman Catholic."

Recently published documents make the conclusion inevitable, that certain Republican leaders in this country promoted the religious issue, and that the Republican National Committee approved it. Certainly United States Senator George H. Moses of New Hampshire, vice chairman of the Eastern Republican National Advisory Committee knew something about it. In the last days of the campaign there came into the possession of the publicity department of the National Democratic Committee a letter admittedly written by him to an editor of a newspaper in a small town in North Carolina. The letter was mistakenly addressed to Kentucky.

ZEB VANCE WALSER, LEXINGTON, KENTUCKY.
Dear Zeb Vance: I am sending you an article for newspaper publication which is written by a native of South Carolina, who is now engaged in editorial work in New York City. It is red hot stuff and I wish you could get it put into some North Carolina papers.

Will you not do so and if you can do so, will you not send me some copies?

Yours, ever,

(*Signed*) GEORGE H. MOSES

The article to which Senator Moses referred contained an attack upon me full of religious bigotry and personal vilification.

Senator Moses has just been appointed Chairman of the Republican Committee on Senatorial Elections in 1930.

The farmer is inherently a Republican. I never made any impression on any considerable number of them in New York state. As far as the tariff is concerned, in my

Louisville speech I enunciated a new Democratic doctrine with respect thereto. It was a complete change from the Democratic position on that subject during the last third of a century and I am satisfied that it had the full support of the Democratic leaders in the rank and file of the party.

To my way of thinking, neither the tariff nor, for that matter, the farm problem were important factors in the determination of the election. In its broad aspect the campaign appeared to me to be one of Smith or anti-Smith. Very little was said about Mr. Hoover. But that is no new thing in American politics. There have been as many elections determined negatively as there have been affirmatively. A great many people predicate their vote on something that they are against rather than something that they are for. The campaign proved that the one thing which has not yet been overcome in the conduct of campaigns, is the ability of organized groups to mislead large masses of the electorate by false propaganda.

The national campaign was a great experience for me. While I naturally would have liked to be elected president of the United States, I can truthfully say that I did not take the result, even considering the kind of a campaign, with bitter disappointment. I honestly felt that I did something for the country when I laid the issues before the people in a clear way. I was strengthened in that belief when after the election I was asked by a professor of Harvard University if I did not believe that there was a weakness some place in our form of government when a man who receives fifteen million votes but not enough to be elected, automatically retires to private life and leaves the fifteen million unrepresented except insofar as their senators or their congressmen are concerned. He asked me the point-blank question if it was possible to remedy that and I answered him by saying we can amend our constitution to provide that the candidate for the presidency who receives the second highest number of popular votes should be entitled to a seat in the United States Senate as a senator-at-large during the term of his successful opponent. He would be in a position to introduce into the Senate of the .United States bills carrying out his platform promises and pledges and defend them before the whole country. He would naturally become the leader of the minority party and a good, forceful, vigorous minority is the people's own check upon the possible tyranny of a majority.

The very apparent breakdown of party lines as seen in the last election introduces a new element for consideration so far as the rank and file of the people themselves are concerned. While it is true that I lost several southern states that have been in the Democratic column since the Civil War, many hundreds of thousands of Republicans and Independents supported me and voted for me. The Republican chairman of the Senate Committee on Judiciary, Senator George W. Norris of Nebraska, advocated my election, as did Senator Blaine of Wisconsin, also a Republican, to say nothing about the thousands of people who usually voted the Republican ticket. My theory of the senator-at-large is to have everybody who voted for him for whatever reason, represented by his voice in the halls of the national legislature. There are millions of people in this country who belong to no party. They like parts of the Republican platform and they like parts of the Democratic platform and when they finally make their decision they are choosing the man who comes the nearest to their general ideas of what is best for the country. It cannot be said that they are represented in Congress by any party.

CHAPTER XXVI

Up to Now

WHEN the stress and strain of the campaign were over, it was natural to seek a place of rest and relaxation. In company with Mr. Raskob, Mr. Kenny and a number of my friends I went for a short vacation to Biloxi in the state of Mississippi. When the newspapers flashed the news that I was to leave for Biloxi, United States Senator Pat Harrison from Mississippi was calling on President Coolidge on a matter of federal business. The President said to him, "Senator, I understand Al Smith is going down to Mississippi on his vacation." Whereupon the Senator replied, "Yes, and I am going with him." President Coolidge immediately remarked, "Tell him not to overlook Massachusetts."

I had never heard of Biloxi before. In fact from its spelling I had difficulty in pronouncing it. Mr. Kenny called up the weather bureau on the telephone and asked what part of the country had the mildest climate on that particular day and the reply was "Biloxi," where it was 78° in the shade. That is how I happened to go to Biloxi.

The trip was made in Mr. Kenny's private car, and naturally was heralded in the press. It resembled a second campaign trip. At every stop of the train the crowds poured around the station to remind me of the pre-election days.

I will never forget the reception that was given to me when I returned to Albany after the national election was over. I could not have been received with wilder acclaim had I been elected President of the United States. The entire police reserve of Albany was stationed along the line between the Union Depot and the Executive Mansion. I marched with the paraders all of that distance. Women seemed even more enthusiastic than men.

One of the great satisfactions of my governorship as I look back over it was the love and affection of the people of Albany. They never neglected an opportunity to display it. Probably no governor in the history of the state knew personally as many of the residents of the capital city as I did. Due largely to the twelve years of residence during the winter time and the long period of time I spent in the Executive Mansion, I came to know the prominent men of Albany and their families as well. I became acquainted with almost all the neighbors living around the Executive Mansion.

There was no political significance whatever in the friendships that I formed in Albany. As a matter of fact, before I reached that city as governor the section around the Mansion was strongly Republican. Many of my closest Albany friends were and are today Republicans. The Chamber of Commerce of which I was an honorary member was made up largely of Republicans. Among my personal golfing companions, Chief William Humphreys, former Chief of Police of the New York Central Railroad, was an active Republican in Albany. Charles

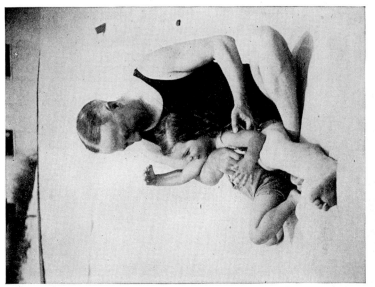

THE GOVERNOR AND HIS GRANDDAUGHTER
On the Long Island sands.

THE TWO SMITH GRANDSONS
Arthur Jr. and Walter in the Albany sand pile.

THE LAST CHRISTMAS AT ALBANY

All three generations of the Smith family are assembled.

M. Winchester, president of the J. B. Lyon Company, ran for Congress on the Republican ticket while I was governor. I spent much of my leisure time in Albany with these two friends and they traveled with me to French Lick Springs and Absecon, New Jersey, whenever I went on vacations to play golf. I think so much of Chief Humphreys that I hesitate to say that he was my golf professor for fear that it may interfere with his own reputation as a golfer. It is only fair to the Chief to say that I never played golf for the sake of the game. It was the opportunity to get away from telephones, conversation, and the stuffy, ill-ventilated rooms of the Capitol, and the opportunity for three or four hours of fresh air and sunshine that constituted the great attraction of the game for me. That is true even today.

It was always a pleasure for me to visit the farms of my friends Parker and Edwin Corning in Albany. Ed Corning was lieutenant governor during my last term and was exceedingly helpful to me. Parker Corning was second to nobody in his enthusiasm for my election in the last campaign. When I left Albany all the dogs I was unable to take away with me were taken over by Parker Corning to be cared for on his farm. The Great Dane, Jeff, my personal dog, lives in the house with him.

It was gratifying to me during my whole administration to have the pronounced approval of my policies which was evidenced by Republicans holding state office. In all matters that had to do with the Department of Education I always had the support and approval of

Frank Pierrepont Graves, Commissioner of Education, for whose ability I have great admiration. The same could be said of Adelbert Moot of Buffalo, a strong Republican and a regent of the University of the State of New York. Addison B. Colvin of Glens Falls was elected treasurer of the state of New York on the Republican state ticket before I was old enough to vote and during his lifetime was a consistent Republican. He vigorously supported every statewide measure advocated by me during my governorship. He was appointed by me to the Reconstruction Commission and afterwards was president of the New York State Association. He instituted in the city of Glens Falls what came to be known as Governor's Day where every August I addressed the assemblage from a platform in the public square. It gave me an opportunity to speak from the central part of the state not only to the immediate audience but to the whole state. I made report to them there on the progress of improvements in the state government sought by me.

When I returned to Albany after my short rest in the South, I took up in real earnest the difficult job of preparing the estimates for the appropriation bill and the executive budget, and the report of the fiscal condition of the state. This I attended to personally.

In due course we prepared for the last Christmas Day in the Executive Mansion. There was a full gathering of the family including my son Arthur's two boys and my daughter Emily's little girl. They were just at an age when they had some understanding of how Santa Claus

422

really performs. The spacious open fireplaces and big chimneys of the Executive Mansion gave me a good opportunity to explain to them that miniature automobiles, small horse wagons and baby carriages and dolls were brought down through the chimney by Santa Claus from the sleigh on the roof the night before Christmas.

Finally at midnight on December thirty-first I laid down the reins of government after six long and trying years and found myself out of employment for the first time in forty years. I had been in the service of the state or some of its civil divisions for thirty-four years and under the state retirement law, being a member of the Employees Retirement Bureau, I found myself entitled to a pension of about six thousand dollars a year for the rest of my life.

On New Year's Day at the formal inauguration I handed the government over to Franklin D. Roosevelt. After the ceremonies I shook hands with as many of my old friends as I could and started back to New York City. Arriving at the Grand Central Station, I found to my surprise and delight, the Sixty-Ninth Regiment and their band, who had brought me to Albany in 1919 and now brought me back again to my home.

I heaved a deep sigh of relief and felt that I was coming into a new freedom it had not been my pleasure to enjoy for a long while. Never having been out of the city of New York in the winter time in my life, I journeyed to the south where my favorite recreation of open air swimming was at my command. I visited Palm

Beach, Sarasota and Miami Beach. At Miami, I paid a friendly visit to Mr. Hoover and we told each other stories of the lighter side of campaigning for the presidency.

At Sarasota I was the guest of John Ringling, the owner of the Barnum and Bailey and Ringling Brothers' circus and spent two full days with the animals in their winter quarters. I had been such a frequent visitor to the circus that I took great delight in playing with the animal actors in their cages.

In February I made a trip from Miami to Havana, Cuba, and when I stepped from the deck of the steamer I had put my foot on foreign soil for the first time in my life. Havana was the first place I ever was in that did not fly the American flag and I was quite thrilled with the city. Foreign customs, foreign language, difference in the advertisements on the billboards, the street-cars and busses, and the generally old-fashioned character particularly of that part of Havana which borders on the harbor, were all exceedingly interesting to me.

Vacation over I returned to New York and found a novel task awaiting me, the writing of what you have herein read. I very earnestly and sincerely hope that it has entertained and interested my readers. I have tried to make it a plain story of a plain ordinary man who received during his lifetime, to the fullest possible extent, the benefit of the free institutions of his country. It is written from memory and is a recital of fact and experience from as far back as that memory goes, up to now.

Index

Index

Index

Index

Index

Hays, Nicholas J., 60
Health Instruction, 189
Hearst, William Randolph, 195, 196, 229, 232, 233, 239, 332, 358, 359
Hecksher, August, 328
Hedges, Job E., 123
Herald, New York, 240, 242
Herrick, D-Cady, 78, 174
Herring, Fanny, 48
Higgins, Frank W., 78, 79
Highways, Department of, 242
Hillquit, Morris, 156, 202
Hiscock, Frank J., 363
Hoey, James J., 111, 373
Hoffman House, 35
Holland Tunnel, *see* Vehicular Tunnel
Home Rule Amendment, *see* Home Rule for Cities
Home Rule for Cities, 142, 146
Homeward Bound, 250
Hoover, Herbert, 387, 409, 416, 424
Hoover's Law Inquiry Committee, 226
Hospitals, Rehabilitation of, 220, 237, 323, 324, 354, 357
Hotel Biltmore, 162, 164, 167, 178, 239, 245, 248, 292, 327
Hotel Bossert, 14
Housing, Bureau of, 266, 267, 271, 272, 274, 276
Housing Conditions, 130, 186, 188, 190, 220, 269, 270, 271, 274, 275
Housing, State Bank of, 274, 275
Hughes, Charles Evans, 80, 81, 82, 86, 127, 184, 190, 202, 224, 243, 256, 325, 346, 358
Hughes Committee, 256, 258
Humphreys, William, 208, 420
Hylan, John F., 155, 229, 233, 332

Income Tax, 116, 335, 338, 339, 341, 342
Income Tax Reduction, 339, 340, 341
Indian Tribes, *see* National Board of Indian Commissioners
Ingersoll, Raymond V., 203, 256, 292
Ireland, Recognition of, 197, 215

Jackson, Andrew, 379
Jackson, Edward D., 92
Janvrin, George M., 375
Jefferson, Thomas, 200, 213
Jenkins, Mrs. Helen Hartley, 91
Jenks, Edmund B., 260
Johnson, Alfred J., 166
Jury Service, 194

Kaminsky, Paul M., 67
Kean, Monsignor John, 40
Keating, Johnny, 9
Kellogg, Henry T., 363
Kelly, William F., 159
Kenny, W. F., 12, 373, 374, 392, 419
Kingsbury, John, 91
Kiralfy Brothers, 47
Ku-Klux Klan, 164, 284, 285, 287, 396
Kremer, Bruce, 392

Labor, Department of, 93, 178, 237, 355
Lace, Jenny, 43
Lackawanna Works, *see* U. S. Steel Corporation
Land Board, 328, 329
Larkin, James J., 315, 316
Leader, 9
League of Nations, 216, 220
Legislative Bludgeon, 144
Lehman, Herbert H., 275, 373
Lewisohn, Adolph, 321
Liberty Bonds, 153, 159
Life Insurance, Committee on, 75, 80, 113
Limited Dividend Corporations, 274, 275
Lincoln, Abraham, 213, 379, 400
Liquor Traffic, *see* Prohibition
Literacy test, 141, 142
Littleton, Martin, 121
Lockwood, Charles C., 270
Loeb, Sophie Irene, 127, 130
Long Island Park Commission, 327
Long Island Railroad, 19
Louisville *Courier*, 400
Low, Seth, 142
Lowman, Seymour, 237, 238, 239, 260, 295

430

Index

Index

Index

Index

Walker, James J., 43, 59, 60, 166, 332, 375

Wallace, Ambassador, 289

Walsh, Blanche, 46

Walters, Henry M., 184, 185

Ward, "Boss," 242

Waring, Colonel, 34

Warn, W. Axel, 375

Warner, Mary Adams, 374

Warner, John A., 181, 182, 356

Warner, Mrs. John A., *see* Smith, Emily

Water Power Control, 127, 134, 237, 246, 247, 248, 355, 361, 362, 364, 370, 371, 385

Welfare Legislation, 253

Wende, Gottfried H., 111

Wet and Dry Issue, *see* Prohibition

Wheeler, Wayne, 286

Whitman, Charles S., 86, 133, 167, 180, 258, 259

Wickersham, George W., 137, 139, 144, 149, 226, 243, 358

Widowed Mothers' Pension, 127, 130, 139

Wild, Johnnie, 47

Willebrandt, Mabel Walker, 396

Williams, Alec, 26

Winchester, Charles M., 421

Wilson, Woodrow, 110, 155, 163, 175, 197, 207, 208, 213, 215, 224, 225, 289, 353, 403

Women in Industry, Bureau of, 237

Women's Christian Temperance Union, 396

Women's City Club, 218, 260

Women's Suffrage, 56, 57, 125, 126, 162, 164, 191, 192, 193, 194, 269

Woodruff, Timothy L., 37

Workmen's Compensation Act, 122, 126, 134, 135, 139, 237, 269, 355

World, New York, 239, 283

YOUNG Democratic Club, 163